The Politics of Indians' English

The Politics of Indians' English

Linguistic Colonialism and the Expanding English Empire

N. Krishnaswamy
and
Archana S. Burde

OXFORD
UNIVERSITY PRESS

YMCA Library Building, Jai Singh Road, New Delhi 110 001

Oxford University Press is a department of the University of Oxford. It furthers the University's objective of excellence in research, scholarship, and education by publishing worldwide in

Oxford   New York

Auckland   Cape Town   Dar es Salaam   Hong Kong   Karachi   Kuala Lumpur
Madrid   Melbourne   Mexico City   Nairobi   New Delhi   Shanghai   Taipei   Toronto

With offices in

Argentina   Austria   Brazil   Chile   Czech Republic   France   Greece   Guatemala
Hungary   Italy   Japan   Poland   Portugal   Singapore   South Korea   Switzerland
Thailand   Turkey   Ukraine   Vietnam

Oxford is a registered trademark of Oxford University Press
in the UK and in certain other countries

Published in India
by Oxford University Press, New Delhi

© Oxford University Press 1998

The moral rights of the author have been asserted
Database right Oxford University Press (maker)

First published 1998
Oxford India Paperbacks 2004
Second impression 2010

All rights reserved. No part of this publication may be reproduced,
or transmitted in any form or by any means, electronic or mechanical,
including photocopying, recording or by any information storage and
retrieval system, without permission in writing from Oxford University Press.
Enquiries concerning reproduction outside the scope of the above should be
sent to the Rights Department, Oxford University Press, at the address above

You must not circulate this book in any other binding or cover
and you must impose this same condition on any acquirer

ISBN-13: 978-019-566979-4
ISBN-10: 0-19-566979-7

Printed in India at Anvi Composers, New Delhi 1100063
Published by Oxford University Press
YMCA Library Building, Jai Singh Road, New Delhi 110001

Preface

The story of English in India, though an interesting one, has not been properly told because the narrators wear (or sometimes the same narrator wears) several masks while telling the story. Print-capitalism and book-trade, money and power, media and the pop-culture, nationalistic sentiments, western linguistic notions like 'native' and 'non-native' varieties, and many other factors have made the narration of the story very complex. As a result, current research in this area is marked by an ambivalence. At one extreme, guided by nationalistic sentiments, some narrators have taken up the extreme position that English in India has been 'Indianized' and that it has become 'Indian English' (though the idea 'nation-India' is fundamentally insecure). Some have projected English as the 'Auntie' tongue of India, a medium of expression that is not 'a member belonging to any direct line of descent' like Sanskrit.

The problematics of English in India has also become part of the politics of the ever expanding English Empire (an Empire 'on which the sun never sets'), the struggle of the subaltern new varieties of English (the plotting linguistic colonies of the English Empire), the launching of several new brands like 'South Asian Englishes', 'Indian English', 'Pakistani English', 'Sri Lankan English', etc., and the attempts to build up a myth of English as *the* international language and the language of science and technology. Such concepts have raised several issues like the status and meaning of the 'non-native' varieties of English, the reality behind the myth of the 'native speaker of English', nature and form of linguistic and cultural imperialism etc. Some of these aspects have been taken up in recent studies like Tomlinson's *Cultural Imperialism* (1991), Philipson's *Linguistic Imperialism* (1992), Parakrama's *De-Hegemonizing Language Standards* (1995), but a lot remains to be studied, especially in the case of English in India. Without belittling the importance of other research studies in this area, this book presents a data-based socio-linguistic perspective on the role of English in India.

A comprehensive and critical review of the research that has been done so far in the area of English in India is presented in order to demonstrate the lack of wholesome perspectives due to which these studies appear disjointed and fractional. It is also pointed out that studies on English in India/'Indian English' suffer from a disorganized state of thinking ('Indian English' is neither used by those who talk and write about it nor claimed as the mother tongue!) that often results in overgeneralized claims of 'Indian/Indianized' English, taking for granted that 'India' and 'Indianness' are pre-defined monolithic entities. The other outcome of the confusion is the dichotomy between acceptance of 'spoken' Indian English as a distinct variety (though English spoken in India is writing oriented) and the adherence of the written variety to the standard one — typically British or American.

The present study argues that this disjointedness is the outcome of a lack of an integrated approach that takes into account an understanding of the history of English in India based on well documented data. That is why this work is based on chronologically documented specimens of English written by Indians from 1600 to 1900 — specimens collected from a variety of archival sources — as the potential means of developing an integrated perspective on the role of English in India.

After examining the Western hegemonic dominance that divides the world into the West and the rest, the technology of power, print-capitalism and other related issues, the study examines the tactics and manipulations adopted by the weak as a part of their survival. Michel Certeau's *The Practice of Everyday Life* (1984) is used to reinforce the arguments about how the subcontinent 'absorbed' languages like Sanskrit, Persian and Arabic and gave birth to new codes like Urdu and how it contained several cultural invasions.

The study demonstrates, through an integrated interpretation of the data, that the basic structure of English in India continues to be the same but it is used in a different manner. The readers are invited to 'judge', on the basis of their reading of the six passages given, whether there is a case for 'Indian English'. The domain-restricted use of English and its 'creative' function in certain areas are explained at the end.

The data was collected by Archana S. Burde for two dissertations submitted for the M. Litt and Ph.D. Degrees of the Central

Institute of English and Foreign Languages, Hyderabad (India). The inspiration for the two projects came from N. Krishnaswamy's article 'The Growth of "INGLISH" in India' (1985). The interpretation of the data has undergone several modifications in the light of various critical studies in the area of colonialism and imperialism and various publications in the recent past.

What is presented in the form of a book is a disturbing experience and the resulting agony of some colonials who have 'humbly' tried to laugh off their agony in English; we hope it is reflected in the style of the book.

A justification for a fairly large number of quotations in the book: this work, being a response to the arguments of other researchers and scholars, relies on the earlier works in the area, and the authors have quoted from them either to support or refute their arguments. Secondly, many of the works cited are not readily available for reference to the readers, particularly in India, and it was felt that mere references will not help. More importantly, the writers from the 'colonies', popularly known as 'quotation bags', have to rely on 'authorities' to establish their claims or points of view; otherwise, they have no credibility. Only a writer from the West can say that his/her book 'relies upon no authority but its own and it comes into the world naked of any scholarly apparatus' (Turner 1995). We want to acknowledge with thanks all the authors whose works are quoted and we thank them for the permission granted to quote from previously published works.

We are deeply grateful to Prof R.K. Agnihotri, Delhi University, Prof T. Sriraman, C.I.E.F.L., Prof C.T. Indira, Madras University, for commenting on the manuscript and generously offering advice and detailed comments that have vastly improved the final version. We owe thanks to Revathi and Kumar of San José State University, who shared their views as Indians who teach English to native-users of English. A final thank you to Lalitha who proofread the book and helped us to keep our cool during the frustrating journey across the labyrinth of data, drafts, and problems of existence.

Contents

1. ENGLISH IN INDIA: PROBLEMATICS OF PERCEPTION   1
   - 1.1 English in India: Between the Cow and the Crown   1
   - 1.2 The English Empire and the Politics of World Englishes   5
   - 1.3 A Few Facts about English in India   11
   - 1.4 Reverence/Abhorrence: Intertwined Attitudes   13
   - 1.5 English in Pakistan   16
   - 1.6 Need for Reading Myths and Redefining Concepts   19

2. INDIAN ENGLISH: COMPLEXITIES APLENTY   25
   - 2.1 Research on Indian English   25
   - 2.2 The Alien Insiders   26
   - 2.3 'Our English'   27
   - 2.4 The Doublespeak   28
   - 2.5 Only the Written Variety   29
   - 2.6 The Kachru Catch   30
   - 2.7 Data-Based Attempts   36
   - 2.8 'Indian English' as Interlanguage — An Ethnocentric View   36
   - 2.9 English as India's Auntie Tongue   38
   - 2.10 The Degree-Yielding Variety   43
   - 2.11 Miscellany-Notions-Conglomerate and the 'Rashomon Effect'   44
   - 2.12 Prator's Prejudice   46
   - 2.13 De-prejudicing the Outlook   47

3. THE TECHNOLOGY OF 'POWER' AND THE POWER OF THE WEAK   49
   - 3.1 The Technology of 'Power'   49

	3.2	The 'West' and the 'Rest': Some Contemplations	52
	3.3	The Power of the Weak	58
	3.4	The Masks of Nationalism	60
	3.5	Print-Capitalism in the Indian Context	64
	3.6	The Native-Speaker Myth	74
	3.7	One for Transaction and One for Contemplation	77
4.	INDIANS' ENGLISH: A SOCIOLINGUISTIC CONTEMPLATION		79
	4.1	Five Phases of the History of English in India	79
	4.2	An Investigation of the Written Mode	80
	4.3	Summary: Restricted Domains and 'English Sustained' Features	136
5.	INDIANS' ENGLISH: A MODULECT		145
	5.1	Is there a Case for Indian English?	145
	5.2	English as a 'Module' in India	152
	5.3	Nomenclature: Indians' English and Inglish	155

Appendix   158

Bibliography   195

Index   202

Chapter One

English in India: Problematics of Perception

> The aspiration of us colonials had been to speak English like Englishmen.
>
> — Ved Mehta, *The Stolen Light*

1.1 English in India: Between the Cow and the Crown

'The English language in India,' wrote a distinguished scholar in 1978, 'shares at least two characteristics of its existence with the cow in India.' Both the cow and the English language are held in reverence and worshipped, though for different reasons and with different expectations of a reward. Cow-worship is enjoined on Indians by their ancient scriptures and is believed to bring them, in the distant future, the infinite riches of the *paraloka*, the unseen other world, while the 'worship' of English is expected to bring the devotee the wealth of this world in the *ihaloka*, the here and now — a promising career, a prosperous bride(groom), a coveted greencard and a Non-Resident Indian status with all its 'perks'.

So much for the first point of similarity between English in India and the cow. The second is even more interesting and pertinent. Indians worship the cow, but do not think it necessary to look after it; neither will they let it die in peace. The English language in India likewise has been steadily declining for a long while but Indians are resolved to let it neither die nor flourish (Nagarajan 1978). This was written some years ago and the charge — with regard to the cow as well as to English — was perhaps not entirely valid even then. It is to be noted that the White Revolution that has taken place in many parts of India is some indication of the care being taken of the cow. What about the English language?

The Story of English (McCrum et al. 1986), a popular television series and the book that goes with it, tells with masterly comprehensiveness, remarkable clarity, and entertaining readability, 'the extraordinary tale of the language that came from nowhere to conquer the world', of course, from the Western point of view. It provides a wealth of information about the historical aspects of English and its present use around the world. English in India finds a place in the chapter titled 'The New Englishes' and comprises fourteen pages (322–35). It begins with the statement that English in India 'is the representation of the English language by the Indian people' (op. cit. 324). Then follows the heading 'The Jewel in the Crown', the oft-used metaphor for India that has now become a part of the 'Raj nostalgia', under which there is a description of Indian loan words in English like *brahmin, calico, curry, coolie, juggernaut, jungle, pundit,* and so on. Some works in the area of loan words like *Hobson–Jobson: A Glossary of Anglo-Indian Words* are also discussed in this section. The authors comment that 'the imperialists' fascination with India — its people, its culture, and its landscape — was expressed in a substantial adoption of Indian words and phrases' (op. cit. 325) and that 'throughout the nineteenth century the English administrators added more and more local words to their basic vocabularies' (op. cit. 326). The attitudinal implication underlying the words 'fascination' and 'adoption' is that of approval, appreciation and acceptance. The expressions 'English administrators' and 'added to their basic vocabulary' point out the fact that the adoption was done by Englishmen and that Englishmen's vocabulary was basic.

By contrast, the next section titled 'The Indianization of English' shows a different kind of attitude. Here the authors point out the peculiarities of Indian English: the use of pompous and archaic words and literal translation of idioms, and these are said to constitute the 'idiosyncratic' Indian English. They describe an Indian academician studying the 'unique character of Indian English' as a great collector of mistakes and add that 'he is at odds with those who believe that Indian English should take pride in and develop its native idiosyncracies'. The authors go on to point out that English has come to be used for intranational communication by the Indians, and that Indian English literature has its own identity, and 'has gained such a flourishing international reputation that it is now being recognized as one of the *Indian* literatures' (op. cit. 332). At the same time, they quote another Indian academician of the Centre for Linguistics and English at the Jawaharlal Nehru University, New Delhi, who believes that in their school they have developed what they like to call 'a non-aligned variety of English' but they make a point of 'exposing their students to the native pronunciation of British English, through the BBC tapes and some of the BBC films' (op. cit. 335). The authors cite Professor P. Lal, who runs a Writers' Workshop and makes this prediction:

> You'll always find Indians who speak very good and correct English. But in fifteen or twenty years we might have evolved a language which is so truly and richly and uniquely and indigenously our own, that you will have to carry a tourist guide, with footnotes, as to what these words mean. This will be a language written for Indians by Indians. And with no other outside audience in mind. . . . We will create another indigenous language, like Urdu, like Sanskrit and Hindi. . . . English is not my mother's tongue, but it is my mother tongue. And that's the way it is with many Indians — we have no choice of it (op. cit. 332).

This prediction of Mr Lal poses a question: whether Indian English will become a creole?

The answer, in a way, is provided by the authors of *The Story of English* in a different section on Jamaican creole, which is in some ways similar to the state of English in India:

> A British or American visitor to Jamaica would probably conclude that there are two basic levels of language usage. In a newspaper like the *Gleaner*, the editorials and the news reporting are done in Standard English. Engaged in conversation, the journalists in the *Gleaner* will use a spoken version of Standard English, mildly influenced by Jamaican English. This will be fully comprehensible to the visitor, but it might have a number of words, *nyam* (eat) or *tacko* (ugly), and perhaps a few constructions not found in Standard English. Certainly, it would not *sound* like Standard English. Extending in a speech continuum, the second level — Jamaican English — is virtually unintelligible to the outsider (op. cit. 309). The appeal of Standard English lies in its association with money and success. The outside world — the world of the dollar and of international trade — speaks Standard English, and the Caribbean, dependent on the goodwill of the United States and, to a lesser extent, Britain, needs to get on in that world. Lawyers, doctors, businessmen, scholars and economists have little incentive to promote the strongest forms of Jamaican (or other Caribbean) English.

There is only lukewarm enthusiasm among the professional and educated elements in Jamaican society for a separate 'Jamaican' language, and the reality of Third World poverty means that for the mass of the population the idea of a nation language is a rarefied concept confined to the seminar rooms of the University of West Indies. For the majority of the people, the realities are the price of food and fuel (op. cit. 317).

The situation, though not identical, is equally puzzling in India. Ambivalence, confusion, and contradictions in the proposed 'theories' of separate language evolution in areas where 'New Englishes' are emerging are quite obvious in the chapter on 'The New Englishes'.

The Story of English has been quoted in detail here because it highlights the problems related to the perception of English in India, and the fact that English remains encaged in 'the Crown' though its existence is acknowledged. In spite of some research, writing and thinking in the area of 'Indian English', there is no comprehensive perspective or clarity on the status and meaning of English in the wonder that is India. As in many other areas, in the land of contradictions there are only questions awaiting answers; a few representative ones are listed below:

Is English in India 'Indian' because it is identified with the nation called 'India'?

Is it the nationalistic sentiment of the English-using Indian that projects 'Indian English' as a distinct variety though the vast majority of people in India do not use English?

Is it 'Indian' because the users of this variety are of Indian nationality?

Is it 'Indian' because it has been in India for a long time?

Is it the language of the metropolitan English-educated Indians?

Is it the language of the indigenous elite, sustained by the elite for furthering their own interests?

Can it be said that 'Indian English' is the language taught in the educational institutions in India?

Is English in India a dialect of English or a non-native variety or an Indian variant of English or a pidgin/creole or an Interlanguage?

Does the spoken mode alone constitute 'Indian English'? Does the written mode reflect/follow the variations manifested in the spoken mode?

Is English in India one entity (Indian English) or are there many Indian Englishes?

Many more questions can be asked but they do not have any clear-cut answers. At the same time, the problem of the status and meaning of English in India and the vacillation between 'English in India' and 'Indian English' raise a number of interesting issues that are relevant to areas such as English in the global context, neocolonialism, cultural studies, sociolinguistics, dialectology, cross-cultural communication, non-native varieties, linguistic and cultural imperialism, the power and politics of languages, etc.

1.2 The English Empire and the Politics of World Englishes

According to some 'guesstimates', there are about two billion users of English all over the world — more than those who speak Chinese. Kachru (1995: 235) says:

> The Inner Circle represents the traditional bases of English, dominated by the 'mother tongue' varieties of the language. In the Outer Circle, English has been institutionalized as an additional language. The estimated population of the countries represented in this circle is over 1,303 million. Out of this population, if only ten per cent use English, it adds up to 130 million. And this is a very conservative estimate indeed. The Expanding Circle includes the rest of the world where English is used as the primary foreign language, and the users of English are unpredictably increasing, for example, as in the erstwhile Soviet Union, China, and Eastern Europe. Note that countries such as South Africa (population 29,628,000) and Jamaica (population 2,407,000) are not placed within the above concentric circles, since their sociolinguistic situation is rather complex, particularly with reference to the English-using populations and the functions of English.

It is worth recalling at this point that all these developments have taken place after the two World Wars in a very short span of time indeed. It is almost as if God said, 'Let there be language', and there was English.

The statistical support comes from *U.S. News & World Report* in its special report entitled 'English Out to Conquer the World' (Feb. 18, 1985). It says that English is spoken here, there and everywhere:

> What the French call *la langue du Coca-Cola* now dominates the globe in a way that no other tongue has since ancient Latin reached

civilization's farthest shores. . . . It began as a rude tongue spoken by obscure Germanic tribes who invaded England in oared warships at the onset of the Dark Ages. Today, 1500 years later, the English language encompasses the globe. . . . English has become to the modern world what Latin was to the ancients, dominating the planet as the medium of exchange in science, technology, commerce, tourism, diplomacy and pop culture. Indeed so wide is its sweep that 345 million people use English as their first language and an additional 400 million as their second. . . . Initially, the language spread with the British Empire. After the World War II, English with a twist — American jargon — circled the globe, boosted by U.S. economic and political power. Finally, the language captured the lead in the knowledge explosion: English is the medium for 80 per cent of the information stored in computers around the world . . . 1 of every 7 people in the world claim some knowledge of English. . . . English is the native language of 12 countries and an official or semi-official tongue in 33 others where it is used to conduct at least some government business. Further, it is either a required subject or one widely studied in the schools of at least 56 additional countries. . . . Japanese high-school graduates, after six years of required English, often enroll, in professional English-language schools to qualify for better jobs. . . . So popular is English that France has 150 professional language schools that teach it. . . . In Italy, English is a must for many technical jobs. . . .

In brief, in terms of the market potential, it is a gold rush and teaching English has become a multi-million dollar business. It is estimated that the BBC English-teaching telecast 'Follow Me' is seen by 100 million viewers in China alone, and the programme's textbooks sold a million copies in Germany and Spain within the first three months of their publication. The worldwide market for teaching English, according to the Economic Intelligence Unit, is about 6.5 billion a year. This has created thousands of jobs for native speakers of English ('native' here refers to only the white native speakers), as Tom McArthur comments in response to the editorial in the *EFL Gazette* of August 1992.

> Beyond their own countries they remain a step behind the native speaking import, lacking some 'magic ingredient' associated with a 'good' accent, a firsthand knowledge of Anglophone culture, or up-to-date EFL methodology. Local teachers might tolerate the expatriate natives among them, but are less keen on competition

Where is English spoken?

English as a Native Language

North America
  Canada, except Quebec
  United States

South America
  Guyana

Caribbean
  Bahamas   Jamaica
  Barbados   Trinidad and
  Grenada   Tobago

Europe
  Ireland   United Kingdom

Pacific
  Australia New Zealand

English as an Official or Semiofficial Language

Africa
  Botswana   Namibia
  Cameroon   Nigeria
  Ethiopia   Sierra Leone
  Gambia   South Africa
  Ghana   Sudan
  Kenya   Swaziland
  Lesotho   Tanzania
  Liberia   Uganda
  Malawi   Zambia
  Mauritius   Zimbabwe

Asia, Pacific
  Bangladesh   Phillipines
  Burma   Singapore
  Fiji   Sri Lanka
  India   Tonga
  Malaysia   Western
  Pakistan   Samoa

Mideast, Mediterranean
  Israel   Malta

Countries in which English is Widely Studied

North America
  Mexico

Central America, Caribbean
  Costa Rica   Dominican Republic
  Cuba   Honduras

South America
  Brazil   Venezuela
  Colombia

Europe
  Austria   Luxembourg
  Belgium   Netherlands
  Denmark   Norway
  East Germany Portugal
  Finland   Romania
  France   Soviet Union
  Greece   Sweden
  Iceland   Switzerland
  Italy   West Germany

Africa
  Algeria   Ivory Coast
  Angola   Libya
  Burkina Faso Madagascar
  Burundi   Morocco
  Central African Niger
    Republic
  Chad   Senegal
  Gabon   Togo
  Guinea   Zaire

Mideast
  Egypt   Saudi Arabia
  Jordan   Syria
  North Yemen   Turkey

Asia
  Afghanistan   Japan
  China   Nepal
  Hong Kong   South Korea
  Indonesia   Thailand

Source: Information taken from US News & World Report, 18 February 1985.

from non-natives. What have they got, they ask, that we haven't? (*English Today*, October 1992).

The market for the teaching of English, the book trade, the ever expanding media-market, and the new markets that have been created by computers and the multi-media have made English the only language of communication in the world today — from politics to pornography, from medicine to management.

It is well known that the bullet was only a means of physical subjugation but language was a means of spiritual subjugation (Thiong'o 1986). Language has always played a major role in establishing and sustaining empires. Be it Greek, Latin, Sanskrit, French, or Arabic, empires have led to linguistic imposition. English too was imposed on the colonies during the colonial period. In India, the earliest English education was through the Christian missionaries, and therefore it was equated with Christianity. Subsequently, English came to be taught officially to Indians to help create an administrative cadre needed to run the British Empire and that 'incentive' brought about a substantial change in the role assigned to the English language in India. But in recent times, we witness a new phenomenon: language imperialism and its promotion through covert means. There are some useful studies on the power and politics of English; the language teaching aspect of it has been studied by Robert Philipson in *Linguistic Imperialism* (1992) and the cultural aspect by John Tomlinson in *Cultural Imperialism* (1991). (Those interested may see Kachru (1995) and Baumgardner (1993) for detailed bibliographies on various aspects of World Englishes.) These studies are excellent but they represent 'only a very small fragment of the sum of the statements about cultural imperialism' (Tomlinson: 11). There are several other aspects to the problem which are worth studying. The many faces of English language hegemony in terms of its underlying and superficial structures will have to be studied from various angles, political, economic, cultural, neocolonial, post-modern, etc., by those who are experiencing it since this is a new phenomenon that has emerged in this century and will stride into the next century. What is needed is a new kind of integrated, inter-disciplinary approach to the study of the pop-cultural invasion that is taking place through English: how the language of Shakespeare is used by the media to build up new 'colonies'. English has now become the language of *Santa Barbara*, *Star Trek*, and MTV; and McDonalds, Donald Duck, and the Disney empire have emerged as part of the culture-language mix.

It is this 'natural' expansion of the English Empire which makes a British scholar like Randolph Quirk come out with a declaration that smacks of the old-style imperialism. He declares that English is '*the* language on which the sun does not set, whose users never sleep' (Quirk and Widdowson 1985: 1, emphasis original). It has been pointed out by many that imperialism is a multi-faceted phenomenon which has economic, political, military, cultural, social and communications-related dimensions (Kachru 1986; Galtung 1980). Vested interests have brought in many political and ideological issues in the use of the English language because it has become a commodity like oil or the micro-chip. Occasionally, a worried note is struck like the one by David Crystal:

> The question is not so much — *do* people use English internationally, but in what state of mind, with what attitude, do they use it? Are they proud of it, or ashamed of it? . . . should not the quantitative view of English in the world be supplemented by a rigorous qualitative view — a pragmatic or ergonomic view — in which we recognize levels of acceptance, acquiescence and antipathy amongst those who have come to use the language and in the end is not this view of far greater importance for those involved in world English teaching and research than a simple awareness of the unity and spread of the standard language? (quoted in Rajeswari Sunder Rajan 1993: 148).

But the consent manufacturing processes will not allow such reflections.

Even the non-native 'users' of the 'God-given Chosen Tongue' (Tripathi 1992) have rushed to claim it as their own because it has become the language of money and power. There is certainly some warrant for the metaphor of 'industry' when we consider the number, money and power involved in the enterprise. Statistical claims and projections leave certain questions unanswered, for example, how the global census of the users of English is arrived at, and what is the *quality* and *quantity* of the language that is constructed as English. It is common knowledge that in many countries that are included in the list only a small number of the urban-elite use English, and that too for a limited range of functions. What Appadurai says of 'Number in the Colonial Imagination' is true of the statistical projection regarding the use of English all over the world:

> Thus, though early colonial policies of quantification were utilitarian in design, I would suggest that numbers gradually became more importantly part of the illusion of bureaucratic control and a key to a colonial imaginaire in which countable abstractions, both of people and of resources, at every imaginable level and for every conceivable purpose, created the sense of a controllable indigenous reality. Numbers were part of the recent historical experience of literacy for the colonial elite (Money 1989; Thomas 1987), who had thus come to believe that quantification was socially useful. There is ample evidence that the significance of these numbers was either non-existent or self-fulfilling, rather than principally referential to a complex reality external to the activities of the colonial state (1993: 317).

The number of Englishes that have been floated is rather large — Indian English, Pakistani English, Bangladeshi English, Sri Lankan English, Nepali English, Malaysian English, Singaporean English, Nigerian English, Ghanaian English, Filipino English, Fiji English, etc. Don't these look like the airlines of various countries — Air India, Pakistan International, Singapore Airlines etc. with the planes that are manufactured by one or two companies in the First World like the Boeing or the Lockheed and bought by these developing countries after getting the interior decoration done to reflect the local 'culture'? There are middlemen to do the lobbying and promote the sales and, more often than not, the agents are the non-resident natives of the countries that buy these products. These non-native lobbyists are encouraged and exhibited as show-pieces and 'tokens' of the native tolerance but every time a 'new brand' is floated there are more benefits and advantages to the country that exports the product. Some sort of nationalistic sentiment makes these consumer-countries use their own labels, and the business interests of the manufacturing companies and First World countries encourage the use of different brand-names for the same product! The present 'language trade' is the result of a similar 'nationalistic fervour' of the English-speaking elites of ex-colonies, and 'tokenism' on the part of the English-using First World. The latter encourages the non-native users of English who promote the interests of English as tokens. Promoting the different varieties of English of the Third World with their respective 'national' labels is a major strategy used in the 'language trade'. The English-using citizens of the nations where English is a second language, and the non-resident elites of these nations together are championing their 'national' varieties of English in the name of New Englishes, and the politics of English continues in one form or the other.

The politics of 'World Englishes' is closely linked with what has been termed as 'cultural colonialism', 'linguistic imperialism', and the building up of new 'empires' in the technological age, using mass media as its major weapon. Modern technology, media, and money power have become inseparable from English as an international language. What Joseph and Taylor say of scientific language is true of English since it is projected as the language of science and technology: 'Any enterprise which claims to be non-ideological and value-neutral, but in fact remains covertly ideological and value-laden, is the more dangerous for this deceptive subtlety' (1990: 2). In our meditations on Third World Englishes we must remember what Tollefson (1991) in his discussion on language in the Philippines points out. He shows that the English taught to lower-class students is both qualitatively and quantitatively insufficient for those who might want to apply for higher-level jobs. One is tempted to ask whether the same is true of Third World Englishes! As Gramsci says 'the starting point of critical elaboration is the consciousness of what one really is, and it is "knowing thyself" as a product of the historical process to date, which has deposited you in an infinity of traces, without leaving an inventory' (cited in Said 1978: 25).

1.3 A Few Facts about English in India

Treating English in India as a case study (since English teaching in India is the world's largest democratic enterprise of its kind), let us look at some approximate figures for 1990–91. They will give us some idea of the potential market for English teaching.

> The student enrolment at the primary level (about 99 million) is approximately twice the total population of the United Kingdom.
> The total number of learners at the upper primary/middle level (about 33 million) is more than the total population of Canada.

The student population at the secondary level (about 20 lion) is more than the total population of Australia.

The learners at the college and university level alone repre double the total population of Singapore.

The student enrolment at all levels taken together equals the total population of the USA, and the teacher population (stitutes the total population of Hong Kong.

The above information regarding educational statistic: India is only the approximate 'official' estimate. Like the par: economy in India, there are parallel educational enterprises go by different names — parallel colleges and schools, pri schools, coaching classes, tutorial institutes, open schools universities, etc. — for which no figures are available. parallel enterprise must be a huge one, judging from 'the str corner English Medium Schools' that have been started in ev town in the country by any enterprising person who can in some money. Even assuming that only about half the stuc population is learning some kind of English, the total num of learners of the language will be more than the total populat of many countries in Europe. The market potential for Eng can also be judged from the popularity of the English press : print media in the country. According to an estimate in 19 one third of all the published books in India, and one fifth the periodicals are in English. According to the 1981 cen: the *literacy* rate in India is 32.23 per cent, and the Eng *literacy* rate may be about 6.5 per cent; this will roughly m about 25 to 30 million users of English in the country. some other estimates, there are now more speakers of Eng in India than in Britain, and their sounds range from the m 'pucca' Oxbridge accent to the bazaar variety. The 'users' English in India outnumber the speakers of some Indian l guages like

Assamese (12.6 million: about 1.7% of the total population),
Gujarati (36 million: about 4.7%),
Kannada (30 million: about 3.9%),
Kashmiri (3.4 million: about 5%),
Malayalam (30.5 million: about 4%),
Oriya (27.5 million: about 3.62%),
Punjabi (23.4 million: about 3.1%),
Sindhi (2.2 million: about .28%),

Urdu (37.0 million: about 4.8%).
(*Source: India — A Country Study*, 1985).

But there is a basic difference — the Indian languages are the mother-tongues of their respective speakers, used at the grass-root level. English is used only by a few, typically in the urban areas of each region, and that too only in certain domains, and hardly ever as the language of intimacy.

1.4 Reverence/Abhorrence: Intertwined Attitudes

There are those who, like the late C. Rajagopalachari, have looked upon the English language as 'goddess Saraswati's gift to India', as a blessing which Indians were somehow privileged to receive. Henry Kissinger, in an interview (*India Today*, 28 Feb. 1985), pointed out: 'India, precisely because it speaks English, is a democracy, and all of us know Indians, we like and have easy relations with them'. In other words, there are some who think that the colonial rule gave Indians a language with which to talk to one another, and to others in the world. May be, if it failed to give them a song, it at least gave them a tongue for singing! Indians got a tongue without a song. It must be clearly stated that Indian nationalism and the renaissance of the arts and sciences in India are the unexpected reversals of the aims of British education or, at the most, the by-products of English education that provided the roots for questioning colonial authority and, eventually, subverted it though that was not the intention of the rulers. Obviously, it cannot be stated that the tools of enlightenment were put into the hands of the subjects by the benevolent masters at the risk of endangering their own position! There is always a difference between what message is intended and how it is received and used, and the gap quite often helps subversive forces. It has been pointed out that India became a nation not because of the British rule. At the most, one can say that it brought about two nations — India and Pakistan, though it is the claim of some historians that Britain bestowed nationhood on India through conquest and administration. Aijaz Ahmad rightly says:

> The fact, however, is that, to the extent that India is a nation at all, it became so not through the British administration but in the course of the anti-colonial movement, which was internally far

more democratic than the colonial state and which mobilized some 20 million peasant households in the struggle against colonialism; the main British contribution to this process was that, at the beginning of the second World War, and in response to the Quit India Movement, Britain made an irrevocable commitment to Jinnah and thereby contributed to the subsequent partition of the country. The 'historically adequate referent' for Indian nationhood exists in India in the shape of the history of the national movement itself (Ahmad 1995: 4).

There is also the question of the attitude of non-native users of English towards non-native varieties; what Kachru says is worth thinking about: 'The non-native speakers themselves have not been able to accept what may be termed the "ecological validity" of their native or local Englishes. One would have expected such acceptance, given the acculturation and linguistic nativization of the new varieties' (1992: 60). On the other hand, the native models of English such as British or General American are also not accepted without reservations. He adds: 'There is thus a case of linguistic schizophrenia, the underlying causes of which have yet to be studied' (1982, 1992: 60). He further points out that 67.60 per cent of Indian graduate students, and 66.66 per cent of the faculty prefer only British English though 55.64 per cent of graduate students label their own variety of English as 'Indian English', and another 29.11 per cent think they speak what according to them is 'British English' (1982, 1992: 60–1). There seems to be an attitudinal minefield which should be turned into a research area.

There are others who regard English (and education in and through English) as the symbol of our 'eternal slavery' and degradation, and the cause of our loss of national and cultural identity: the root cause, that is, of 'all our woe' as Milton said, speaking of the mortal taste of the forbidden fruit. They cite Macaulay, who introduced institutionalized English Education in India, to create, in his famous words, 'a class of persons Indian in blood and colour, but English in taste, in morals and in intellect' — a nation of clerks and petty officials. The critics of English, English education, and colonialism make use of Macaulay's arrogant remarks regarding Indian literary heritage such as,

> a single shelf of a good European library was worth the whole native literature of India and Arabia, all the historical information which

has been collected from all the books written in the Sanskrit language is less valuable than what may be found in the most paltry abridgments used at preparatory schools in England, I doubt whether the Sanskrit literature will be as valuable as that of our Saxon and Norman progenitors. . . . But to encourage the study of a literature admitted to be of small intrinsic value, only because that literature includes the most serious errors on the most important subjects, is a course hardly reconcilable with reason, with morality. . . . We are to teach false history, false astronomy, false medicine, because we find them in company with a false religion . . . .

So, they say that we must throw the baby out with the bath water. But it is known that 'angrezi hatao' is more a political slogan, and it has had no effect on the enrollment in English medium schools, nor on the number of students going abroad for higher studies. There are also intellectuals and writers in India who are so loyal to Indian languages that they criticize Indian writing in English but their criticism is voiced in English, and they themselves write in English because of the market potential.

In between, there are those who pragmatically view English as a 'window on the world', and English education as providing to Indians the intellectual and conceptual ability with which to evaluate all experiences, including colonial and neo-colonial experiences in the modern world. In a way, the roots of this attitude can be traced to Raja Rammohan Roy whose approach towards English education is rather complex. Reena Chatterji (1983) has argued that Rammohan wanted a 'more liberal and enlightened system of instruction, embracing mathematics, natural philosophy, chemistry and anatomy with other useful sciences' without any reference to the medium of instruction or to the inclusion of Western literature, philosophy, history and religion in the curriculum. This was very different from what Macaulay formulated. Rammohan, a liberal and enlightened intellectual, and a scholar well versed in Sanskrit, Arabic and Persian, in a way, was used by the rulers in Anglicizing urban India as part of the colonial politics.

After independence, in spite of the ambivalence and politics that goes with the teaching of English, the people of India (as against politicians and indeologues) seem to have assigned clear roles to English vis-à-vis Indian languages. In modern India, Indian languages and English have come to play complementary/supplementary roles in the socio-political-economic context. Consider, for example, the following facts. English, which is not the language of agriculture in India, is the medium of instruction in the agricultural universities because all modern knowledge on agriculture is available in English. English, which is not the language of day-to-day business in the market place, is the language of business management courses in the universities in India because it is the language of international business. English, which is not the language of daily transactions in a factory or workshop, is the medium of instruction in the Indian Institutes of Technology and other engineering colleges because it is the language of science and technology. The complementary role of English and Indian languages has been properly understood by the society in general but it has not been well formulated by the theorizers.

It is the absence of any kind of language planning and political will in implementation, and lack of co-ordination among various agencies — the Central government, State governments, universities, etc. — along with confusing and contradictory statements by various Commissions, politicians and intellectuals that has left the field open for all kinds of vested interests to operate according to their own convenience. For example, the University Education Commission (1950) says that English has 'become so much a part of our national habit'. But, in the same breath it points out that the use of English 'divides the people into two nations, the few who govern and the many who are governed, the one unable to talk the language of the other, and mutually uncomprehending, which is a negation of democracy' (1950: 316). It is generally said that at the secondary school stage a student has to learn at least three languages, one of which is English, but everyone knows that the so-called 'three-language formula' has been interpreted to mean a 'two-language formula' in a State like Tamil Nadu, and a 'one-language formula' in States like Uttar Pradesh and Madhya Pradesh. It is only on paper that English exists in these States.

1.5 English in Pakistan

The situation in the other 'nations' of the Indian sub-continent is not very different. For example, Anjum Riyazul Haque points out in 'The Position and Status of English in Pakistan' (Baumgardner 1993: 16–17).

It is evident that the position of English in Pakistan continues to be both vitally important and highly controversial. There are those who would remove it at one stroke from all walks of life; there are others who would retain it everywhere through argument, rationalization, and subterfuge. Sentimentalism on the part of one group and a hard-line approach on the part of both (though with differing degrees of subtlety) has at times served to obfuscate the issues. It would perhaps be fair to concede that heavy, and partly unnecessary, reliance continues to be placed on English. That English is the language of the elite has also not helped, though deterioration in the quality of English in the country has been stupendous and progressive, and has accelerated since some of the motivation for knowing it well is now secondary. Urdu has been declared the national language of the country. Its use in government documents, particularly those for public consumption, has increased substantially. Government correspondence is divided between English and Urdu. Public functions and speeches are now invariably in the national language. Court proceedings at all levels are permitted in Urdu. Students at all levels in the arts, humanities, and social sciences can take the examinations in Urdu. In science subjects the change has been slower and more limited. But children joining Class I in 1979 started out with Urdu as their only medium of instruction: a fundamental change, the effects of which will work out in time. . . . English has become the language of knowledge; it is the language with the biggest reservoir of information, knowledge, and literature known in history. Advances in science and technology, the paraphernalia of planning and development, and developments in the humanities and the arts are mostly expressed through English. . . . Thus, it may not be possible to alter the position of the English language in the national set-up radically, or to reduce its role across the board by fiat. It has permeated far too deeply and far too long for that. . . . The best course is to accept the inevitable and try to demarcate the territory of English again, to carve out for it the specific role it can play. The future of English in this country has to be clearly identified, albeit limited or compartmentalized, as the language of technology and the language of international communication.

It is also reported that Imran Khan, the former international cricketer and a graduate of Oxford University has attacked the English language schools in Pakistan for turning out 'blind imitators of Englishmen', and has plans for the construction of a university in Islamabad founded on Islamic principles 'instead of

Shakespeare and other Western thinkers'. It must also be mentioned that Urdu, the official language of Pakistan, is 'not indigenous to the area and is the native tongue only of perhaps . . . 10 per cent of the population' (Nyrop 1984: 81 cited in Baumgardner 1993: 86). The 'incongruities, inconsistencies, and ambivalence' are examined in *The Power of English in Pakistan* (Shameem Abbas 1993), and it is pointed out that 'despite massive input into the teaching of English, the national results are abysmally poor. At the college levels, the pass rate is barely 18 to 20 per cent. Since English is a compulsory subject, failure in English means a failure in the entire examination. At the secondary level the ratios are almost the same . . . first, the teaching of English is not necessary for the entire population; second, the pedagogy and materials design are seriously flawed' (op. cit.: 155). If English is not taught to the entire population, elitism is perpetuated; and if it is, colonialism of another kind is perpetuated! The dilemma is well articulated by Ahmed Ali, the author of *Twilight in Delhi* and a well known writer in Urdu and English, in his *English in South Asia: A Historical Perspective* (Baumgardner 1993: 10):

> Whether the British had succeeded in making us Englishmen or not, the social order we had set out to reform had proved us to be Satans and West-stricken devils! . . . The face of the mirror had turned our own visage. In the process of transformation from Indian to brown Englishmen, I found I had lost not only my freedom but culture and identity as well, and had become an exile in my own country, though a rebel too. I have been engaged ever since in the search of my self, my identity. Where between the heart and the mind had it been waylaid? . . . This cause deserved special treatment. It could not be presented in Urdu, for then it would not serve a purpose beyond the regional and parochial, and its echoes would die down within a narrow space covering at best a limited area of North-western India. And it was a subject demanding the widest audience. British Indian history had many instances to show that injustices done by the British in India were dismissed as local matters of no consequence. On the other hand, if a case was brought to London, the British Government became involved, and the home Government depended on public good faith and was answerable to the King. . . . My decision to write *Twilight in Delhi* (Ali 1940) in English turned out to be right, with critics saying in their reviews of the novel: 'It may well be that we shall not understand India until it is explained to us by Indian novelists of the first

ability, as it was that we understood nothing of Russia before we read Tolstoy, Turgenev and the others. Ahmed Ali may be the vanguard of such a literary movement' (Collins 1940). The substance of this judgement was later echoed by *The Oxford History of India* (Smith 1967: 838), which wrote with reference to R.K. Narayan, Mulk Raj Anand, and myself: 'it can be said that they have taken over from E.M. Foster and Edward Thompson the task of interpreting modern India to itself and to the modern world . . . .'

The story is more or less the same in most of the colonies where English is used as a second language.

1.6 Need for Reading Myths and Redefining Concepts

The picture that has been painted so far about the role of English in India is quite confusing because we have attempted, as far as possible, to present the facts as they are. Kachru in *English in South Asia* rightly concludes,

> The case study of South Asian English discussed in this chapter clearly demonstrates the complexity of describing an institutionalized (non-native) variety of English. There are several dimensions to South Asian English: historical, linguistic, sociolinguistic, attitudinal, ideological, educational and cultural. It is only recently that these issues are being raised, and the limitations of the earlier 'paradigm trap' are being discussed. However, in terms of the research potential — historical, linguistic and sociolinguistic — what we have seen so far is merely the proverbial 'tip of the iceberg' (1994: 552). Therefore, certain concepts that are used in the analyses of languages are to be studied carefully with a view to understanding them in the neo-colonial context. It is true that English is used in many parts of the world and that it has become the language of modern technology but there is also a lot of myth making that is taking place.

Joseph Campbell in his *The Power of Myth* recommends the reading of myths: 'They teach you that you can turn inward, and you begin to get the message of the symbols' (1988: 6). We should be more interested in the sociological function of myths — the ones that support and sustain a certain social order (Campbell 1988: 31). The Myth of English as an international language, and its sociological functions offer some interesting and challenging areas of research that may enable us to get the message in symbols such as nationalism, internationalism, and the power of language. Not only the 'Masks of the Empire' but also other masks such as the 'Masks of Nationalism' and the 'Masks of Patriotism', the 'Masks of Regionalism' and the 'Masks of Fundamentalism' are to be studied carefully. The role of the 'First World of the Third World', the subversive forces within and outside the power of English, and the way power gets dismantled also need to be examined. A careful reading of the history of language empires that were built in the past and how they disintegrated might also help us to understand some aspects of this complex problem. At the same time, it is good to remember that we are studying a 'new' phenomenon in a modern technological age, the tools which were not available to the earlier power structures.

The need for a fresh approach arises because much of the writing on linguistics and the power of language has been dominated by the colonial school of thinking, even though some of the writers have been Indians. What Bipin Chandra says of colonialism and nationalism is also true of the history of English in India: 'The social character of the movement, its origins and stages of development, the nature of social support and popular participation, the tactics and strategies evolved or used, and even its real intellectual history were not properly studied' (1979: v–vi).

The origins and stages of development and the social character of what has been glorified as Indian English, Indo-Pakistani English, or Pakistani English, must be properly studied in order to understand the non-native varieties of English and the 'power and politics of English'. The story of English keeps shifting, on the one hand between the English-using indigenous elite, who represent and re-present the 'First World of the Third World' and keep suppressing the subaltern, who, in turn, keeps subverting whatever is being done to suppress the subaltern, and, on the other hand, between the empire-building native-speakers of English and their allies, the non-native users of English. The events in the story are to be read in relation to each other, its historical position in various situations, and the values and politics that are rooted in them. As Pennycook says: '(All) knowledge is produced within a particular configuration of social, cultural, economic, political and historical circumstances and therefore always both reflects and helps to (re)produce those conditions. Furthermore, since all claims to knowledge represent the interests of certain individuals or groups, we must always see knowledge as interested' (1989: 595). In this context, it is necessary to examine the notion of the 'knowledge of English', and how it bestows power, and sustains the dominance of those in power.

A study of some of the parallel systems like Urdu, Islam or Christianity in the subcontinent can be helpful. From one point of view, Christian practices in India can be seen as Indianized. For example, Arogyamatha (the mother of health) is worshipped by the Christian converts in some parts of Tamil Nadu as though Mother Mary is a Hindu goddess, by breaking coconuts, lighting camphor and burning incense. The Christians in Tamil Nadu not only follow the customs and traditions of the Hindus (like wearing the 'mangalsutra' and 'kumkum') but also claim the privileges of the caste to which they belonged before conversion, which has constitutional sanctions too in some parts of the country. Christians of different castes rarely intermarry. It can also be read as the 'subversion' of Christianity from another point of view because the absorption of Christianity in the local culture has arrested the spread of 'true' Christianity, the Christianity of Europe. The position of Indian Christianity in terms of its position and meaning, is very similar to the position of English in India. In one sense it has undergone 'Indianization', and in another sense it's absorption may also be considered a process of subversion.

Similarly, the distinctions between Hindus and Muslims, particularly at the village level, are negligible, and Hindus who got converted retain many Hindu customs and beliefs. Although they acknowledge one god in prayers, many Muslim villages of lower economic status also worship and placate gods and godlings, who they believe affect and control their immediate destinies. Sociologists have pointed out that when an epidemic strikes, they go to the shrine of Sitala, the smallpox goddess, with their offerings and pray at the tomb of the village saint when a son is desired. All Muslims proscribe the eating of pork and enforce the law of circumcision, but in other beliefs, practices, and rules of morality they offer slight contrast to their Hindu neighbours. Most Muslims use as their mother tongue, the language of the community in which they live. Likewise, the process of 'Sanskritization' of India offers some useful insights regarding the processes of 'absorption'. A brief survey of the process is worth recalling at this point.

An analysis of the evolution of Sanskrit provides the key to the distribution of contemporary languages in North India. As Aryan-speaking invaders drifted to the Indo-Gangetic Plain, their languages experienced constant change and development. By about 500 BC Prakrits, or 'common' forms of speech, were widespread throughout the north. By about the same time the 'sacred,' 'polished,' or 'pure' tongue used in religious rites, the so-called Sanskrit, had also developed along independent lines. In common with many ritual languages, however, Sanskrit proved an evolutionary dead end. Its use in ritual settings encouraged the retention of archaic forms; that it was above all a sacred tongue, fostered a high level of interest in its purity and correctness of expression. Similar concerns gave rise to an elaborate science of grammar and phonetics, and an alphabet believed by some scholars to be superior to the Roman. By the fourth century BC these trends had culminated in the grammar written by Panini, which set the form of Sanskrit for subsequent generations.

The Prakrits continued to evolve through everyday use. One of these dialects was Pali, spoken in the western portion of the Peninsula. Pali became the language of the religious reform movement of Buddhism; eventually, like Sanskrit, it too came to be identified exclusively with religious contexts. By about the middle of the first millennium AD, the Prakrits had changed further into *apabhramsas*, or the 'decayed' speech; it is from these dialects that the contemporary Indo-Aryan languages of the subcontinent developed. The rudiments of modern vernaculars were in place by about AD 1000 to 1300.

Throughout their lengthy evolution, the languages of the major families continuously influenced one another. Sanskrit had without a doubt the single greatest influence on both Indo-Aryan and Dravidian languages. Among the Dravidian languages, Tamil, in which the earliest writings date from the first century AD, shows a demonstrable Sanskrit influence that increased over the centuries. Kannada and Telugu, which emerged as literary languages in the sixth and twelfth centuries AD, were centered closer to Indo-Aryan settlements and experienced concomitantly greater Sanskrit influence. The Sanskrit influence is seen mainly in vocabulary, giving rise to a large number of cognates in the assorted tongues and facilitating, to some extent, language learning. Dravidian languages had a notable impact on the evolution of Indo-Aryan languages, including Sanskrit.

Modern Indo-Aryan languages are divided into inner and outer sub-branches. The outer suburbanite includes Western Punjabi, Sindhi, Bengali, Assamese, Bihari, and Marathi. The inner sub-branch comprises Eastern Hindi and Western Hindi, Punjabi, Pahari, Rajasthani, and Gujarati. Most share a common ancestor, Nagara, an *apabhramsa*. Hindi, the language of most speakers, developed from the Khariboli dialect that spread from what is now western Uttar Pradesh. Hindi predominates in Uttar Pradesh, Bihar, Madhya Pradesh, Rajasthan, Haryana, Himachal Pradesh, and Delhi, and its environs.

The development of Hindi and Urdu gives a glimpse of the processes at work in language evolution on the subcontinent. Urdu developed as a lingua franca in North India under the Mughal rulers. As conquerors, the Mughals had learned and adopted the regional dialect in use to the north and northeast of Delhi. In time, the language spread even into Dravidian areas because it served as a lingua franca for trade, administration, and military purposes. Urdu appropriated a significant number of words from Persian, the official language of the Mughal Empire. By the late 1600s to early 1700s, Urdu had developed into a highly stylized form written in a Persian-Arabic script and was far removed from any spoken language. In the nineteenth century Urdu began to serve as the language of administration in the lower courts in the north. Hindi developed at roughly the same time under the leadership of Hindu reformers. In essence, Hindi was Urdu using a Sanskrit-based script, Devanagiri; efforts were made to purge the language of its Persian borrowings. Contemporary tongues and dialects, as they figure in the lives of most Indians, are a far cry from the stylized literary forms of Indo-Aryan or Dravidian languages. (*India: A Country Study* 1985: 186–90).

With the politics of partition and the creation of Pakistan, the impetus behind Hindustani, the Persian-tainted, spoken variety of a Sanskrit-based Hindi and Urdu, was considerably weakened. The so-called 'camp language' of Urdu, the graceful daughter of the marriage between Persian and Hindi, was associated with Muslims, Islam, and Pakistan, and is becoming more and more marginalized in the Indian context because of the politics of Hindi-Hindustani-Urdu. But most people, particularly in the rural areas, neither speak Hindi nor Urdu; they use a local variety. For example, the Muslims in Tamil Nadu use Tamil with a few words from Urdu and they describe the language they speak as Urdu!

What has been said so far may also be true of English. If English has been Prakritized resulting in 'Indian English', will it go the Pali way and become a 'decayed speech'? Or will it remain like Urdu in the subcontinent? In the present-day context, English has the added advantage of the media and modern technology in addition to money, power and status, and the mobility and opportunities that Sanskrit or Hindi or Urdu do not offer. As in the case of Sanskrit or Hindi or Urdu, English has also helped only a very small section of the total population, particularly in the urban areas, and the vast majority of people use neither English nor Indian English but their own local language mixed with a few English words, and they think they speak English. A careful analysis of the way English is being absorbed in India and an understanding of the complex problems in a multilingual, multicultural, multireligious area like the Indian subcontinent with a long literary tradition, linguistic pride, and 'experience' in handling language-imperialism of various hues will, we feel, have great theoretical importance in addition to practical implications.

Chapter Two

Indian English: Complexities Aplenty

> It is when we consider Indian history as a factor determining the Indianness of Indians that we really get to the root of the matter.
> — V.K. Gokak, *The Concept of Indianness*

2.1 Research on Indian English

The term 'Indian English' has gained acceptance as a label to describe the use of English in India but, very often, researchers and scholars do not differentiate between 'English in India' and 'Indian English'. Some have acknowledged the need to differentiate between the two terms but very few address themselves to the task. It has become customary to talk about 'Indianness' and 'Indianization of English', and the Indian social context is said to have Indianized English, thereby justifying the label 'Indian English'. It is quite obvious that the socio-cultural, psychological, historical, linguistic and other components of what constitutes the Indian context are to be studied before we talk about 'Indianness' and 'Indianization of English' but even a cursory survey of the work that has been done so far shows that there is no comprehensive and integrated view of 'Indian English'. *Indian English: A Bibliographical Guide to Resources* (1988), a comprehensive bibliography compiled at the Central Institute of English and Foreign Languages, Hyderabad (India), lists the works done on 'Indian English' under ten sections:

1. Bibliographies
2. Generalia
3. Linguistic Aspects
4. Lexicons
5. Lexis and Vocabulary

6. Borrowings, Loans and Influences (English–Indian languages–English)
7. Phonetics and Phonology
8. Grammatical Aspects
9. Errors and Remedies
10. Stylistics

In a bibliography of 1015 titles, there are a few studies which seem to address themselves to the problem of 'Indian English'; there are studies on 'Malayalam-English', 'Hindi-English', 'Tamil Speakers' English', and so on. There are a number of studies on the teaching and learning of English in India, and on Indian Writing in English. An ambivalent attitude (hesitancy on the one hand and acceptance on the other), anxiety about the deteriorating standards, acceptance of the fact that 'Indian English' is neither adequately described nor properly defined, and acceptance of the complexities involved in the description of 'Indian English' mark the various studies in this field. Some researchers assume that 'Indian English' is a well-defined entity and concentrate on the 'Indianness' of 'Indian English' though quite a few recognize the problem of defining or describing 'Indian English'. There are others, like Kachru, who adopt a nationalistic position and try to establish the identity of 'Indian English' and other varieties of South Asian English. But there are no studies based on a comprehensive analysis of the historical aspects of English in India, the dynamics of the power and politics of the English empire, and that too based on any given data.

2.2 The Alien Insiders

P. Lal of the Writers Workshop in Calcutta is one of the early crusaders for Indian Writing in English. In his book *The Alien Insiders*, Lal argues that Indians can use English effectively for serious literature, and that 'we write in English because we feel we are "doin' what just comes natcherly"' (1951/1987: 17) — a quote from a song in the then current film *Annie Get Your Gun*. Indian Writing in English has its own market and, of late, a very flourishing one though Dasgupta says 'the general Indian public does not seem inclined to read (and nobody produces or publishes) translations of the supposed classics of Indian English poetry and fiction; this indicates that the public does not believe — having no self-serving reasons for doing so — that there are any true classics in that body of work' (Dasgupta 1993: 112). But Lal continues to run his Workshop and there are many more Indians like Lal who write in English. Maybe, 'true classics' are just emerging in Indian Writing in English but the fact is that there is a potential world-wide market for Indian Writing in English, and where there is a demand there will be supply. Lal knows, we are sure, like anyone else in the field, that Indian Writing in English is only one aspect of the use of English by Indians, and that the creative writers represent only a minority within a minority.

2.3 'Our English'

In the book *The World of Words* (Dustoor 1968) there is a chapter titled 'Indian English' (pp. 99–127), and Dustoor uses the term 'Indian English' only once — that too to say that it is not very distinctively Indian. He says: 'seen in perspective then, Indian English is as yet not very different from Standard English — at least not in its written form' (p. 124). After taking note of the history of English in India, he proceeds to discuss the peculiarities of 'our English'. Throughout the chapter, Dustoor uses the term 'our English' to refer to the English used by Indians, and says it is different from the native variety because Indians learn it in educational institutions through books. According to him, bad teaching leads to wrong usage, and the lack of exposure to the living language makes 'our English' unidiomatic, too formal and too polite. He concedes that the gravitational pull of the social and cultural factors in India necessitates the use of new words and phrases, and he calls them 'Indianisms'. The examples he cites are from creative writing and journalism, viz., *waist-thread, lathi-charge, freedom-movement,* etc. Dustoor claims that 'there will always be a more or less indigenous flavour about our English. In our imagery, in our choice of words, in the nuances of meaning we put into our words, we must be expected to be different from Englishmen and Americans alike' (p. 126). He compares the Indian variety of English to a garden that is somewhat exotic, and feels that the exotic plants add charm to the garden but the weeds which spring up whenever ignorance, carelessness or pretentiousness infects the air need to be pulled out by the roots. At the same time, he says quite emphatically that English should not be consciously Indianized, and that an

Indian variety of English should not be taught. Kachru dedicates his 1983 book to Dustoor but Dasgupta predicts that unlike agriculture this garden will die 'if the cultural sun continuing the mystique of the British empire truly sets' (1993: 123).

2.4 The Doublespeak

The authors of *Indian and British English: A Handbook of Usage and Pronunciation* (Nihalani et al. 1979), the first dictionary of its kind, point out:

> Since no comprehensive description of this so called Indian English has ever been made, this group of scholars consider that the term is imprecise and misleading and that it should not be used . . . we prefer to avoid the use of the somewhat controversial term 'Indian English'. Instead, we employ the set of initials IVE, which stand for 'Indian Variant(s) of English' . . . . (p. 3)

Having said this, the authors declare that they do not wish to use the term 'Indian English' as prevalent among scholars and academicians, and state the aim of their book as follows:

> The aim of this lexicon is to provide teachers and learners of English in India with information about the way in which certain forms and patterns of English used in India differ from the contemporary version of the native speaker model to which Indian English is closest, namely British Standard English (p. 4).

It is to be noted that the authors, in the same sentence, have used both the labels, 'English used in India' as well as 'Indian English', and the way these labels are used reflect the identity crisis of English in India.

The authors emphasize that they intend no more than to describe English used in India. 'When comprehensive descriptions of the English used in India come to be written, as they will, questions of a prescribed standard will also have to be evolved. Until then, we have hesitated to do more than describe' (p. 7). But in the second part of the book entitled 'Part II: Dictionary of Pronunciation' they do not hesitate to advocate an indigenous model for Indians; they argue that British Received Pronunciation is unrealistic as a model for Indians, and that Educated Indian English may be used as the basis for developing an Indian model for spoken English. This reflects a 'double standard' adopted by many — one for the spoken mode and one for the written mode. The concept of 'standard' or 'norm' for the written mode is not available to them, and the difference from Standard British English is *the* criterion for their descriptive study but the same difference is used to justify and accept an indigenous model for the spoken mode. This attitude is typical of the dilemma of those who use and write about English, and it is this very ambivalence that negates the possibility of describing or defining it.

2.5 Only the Written Variety

A Study of Some Written Varieties of Indian English (Rubdy 1981), a doctoral dissertation, makes the same point: 'While there is no doubt that IE (Indian English) exists, it has not been easy to define it in precise linguistic terms' (p. 16). Rubdy says that the complexity of the Indian situation makes an accurate description of Indian English very difficult, and rightly points out that 'the answer will require extensive sociological and anthropological research as well as linguistic research' (p. 18). Using some articles from six issues of *The Illustrated Weekly of India* (a weekly magazine which was popular among middle and upper class Indians until it went out of publication in the early 1990s), and 600 samples of readers' correspondence from the daily newspapers published in India, she attempts to describe what seems 'to have been known as the educated variety of Indian English' (p. 20). She lists the deviations and Indianisms found in her data, works out their frequency, the reasons why they occur, and so on. She does not treat the deviations and Indianisms as errors; according to her, these deviations reflect an ongoing process of change, and some of these deviations will determine the norms of acceptability in the Indian context if Indian English continues to develop in the direction indicated by the deviations. This study does not help to define 'Indian English' because, as she herself points out, 'various studies have concentrated only on one or other aspect of IE (Indian English), the full complexity of this variety does not become evident. Extensive research is required in order to determine scientifically what really constitutes IE . . .' (p. 17). However, there is no attempt to capture the 'directions' indicated by the 'deviations'.

2.6 The Kachru Catch

Kachru, an important player in the game of 'World Englishes', has written a number of books and articles on 'Indian English' and English across cultures. If Quirk represents the imperialistic attitude, Kachru represents not only a nationalistic point of view but also, what might be called, the voice of a non-resident native who talks about 'Indian English' in some sort of native English. In his 'Liberation Linguistics and the Quirk Concern' (*ET* 25, Jan. 1991), Kachru criticizes Quirk for his conservatism and asks challengingly whether international codification can be 'applied to a language which has over 700 million users across the globe'. As Gerry Abbot points out in 'English Across Cultures: The Kachru Catch' (*English Today* 7 (4), Oct. 1991: 55).

> With regard to the international use of English, Braj Kachru is quite right in drawing our attention to the fact that things have changed linguistically and demographically since imperial days. What was the British Empire is now the English Empire — or would be if a standard English grammar, lexis and phonology were enforceable as a moral code, which is patently not the case.

It is obvious that slogans like 'World Englishes' and 'Commonwealth of Englishes' have a lot of sentimental appeal, and they have their own functions in the scheme of things but it is also true that not only Quirk but all scholars 'have other roles and functions than those required by the dispassionate pursuit of knowledge' (Tripathi 1992: 5).

Kachru has coined a number of terms to explain his point of view and built up a lobby, and one has to sift through the jargon to understand what he means. In *The Indianization of English: The English Language in India* (1983), Kachru brought together his important contributions that were 'written over almost two decades' and Archana Burde (unpublished Ph.D. thesis 1992: 54–78) has given the following painstaking analysis of Kachru's book. She takes the following statements from the 'Introduction (pp. 1–14) to his book and tries to sift through them to arrive at the circularity of Kachru's conceptualization:

    i.   The Indianness in Indian English is the result of the acculturation of English in the linguistically and culturally pluralistic context (of India).

ii. Acculturation is language change and language adaptation determined by the parameters of Indian culture.
iii. Indian English is the result of the institutionalization of an interference variety of English.
iv. Interference is indicative of linguistic changes caused by pluralistic language contact situations.
v. Indianisms are deviations.
vi. Indianisms in Indian English are linguistic manifestations of pragmatic needs for appropriate language use in a new linguistic and cultural context.
vii. Deviations refer to the linguistic and cultural nativization of a variety of English.
viii. Nativization is the result of the new 'unEnglish' linguistic and cultural setting in which English is used as a tool of communication.

She demonstrates that (if we manage to go beyond the jungle of jargon) we get the following picture:

Indianness is — result of acculturation.
Acculturation is — adaptation of a language to the cultural needs.
Indian English is — result of institutionalization of interference variety.
Interference is — linguistic changes caused by culturally and linguistically pluralistic context.

Therefore, Indian English (the result of institutionalization of interference variety) = Indianness (result of acculturation) = Indianisms (linguistic manifestations of pragmatic needs of new linguistic and cultural contexts) = Deviations (linguistic and cultural nativization of a variety of English) = Nativization (result of 'unEnglish' linguistic and cultural contexts in which English is used).

Thus, we arrive at the following formula:

Acculturation = Interference = Indianisms = Deviations = Nativization = Indianness = Indian English.

The sign '=' is used here to show how these terms become interchangeable in the statements made and how processes, outcomes of processes, and actions and names form a merry-go-round; it is like Winnie the Pooh chasing his own footsteps. [Dasgupta too points out a similar circularity in Kachru's argument: 'Kachru finds no basis for the mistake/deviation distinction, no correlate, no cause, no concomitant. All he offers is the observation that there are clear cases of mistakes and clear cases of productive or systemic deviations, and a catalogue of facts organized around this observation' (1993: 125).]

Burde's analysis demonstrates that 'Kachru's terminology is circular and results in obfuscation'. She goes beyond the terminological merry-go-round and looks at the chapter 'Indian English: A Sociolinguistic Profile' (pp. 66–95). She says that in this chapter

> Kachru does not talk about Indianization as such. The sociolinguistic profile done by Kachru in this chapter consists of various aspects of English in India, viz. how English came to India, the spread of English in India, Indian English literature, English and language planning in India and so on. Kachru also gives a brief description of English used by educated Indians; that is, he lists certain features in the sound system, grammar, lexis and semantics.

She further points out that Kachru equates daily life with literary and intellectual activity. In the chapters titled 'Contextualization' (pp. 99–127) and 'The Indianness' (pp. 128–44), Kachru gives a number of examples of Indianisms. Not only are the examples cited in both the chapters more or less the same (with a few additions and deletions), all of them are mostly taken from creative writing. Such Indianisms should be considered a part of the creative strategies employed by Indian authors writing in English to create an Indian milieu in their writing, keeping the audience in mind. But Kachru treats them as examples of the axiomatic 'Indian' English, and also summons Raja Rao's phrase for support. Kachru says, for example, 'In India the English language has blended itself with the cultural and social complex of the country and has become, as Raja Rao says, the language of the "intellectual make-up" of Indians' (p. 139). It is true that English has become indispensable for the Indian intelligentsia, and that a creative writer like Raja Rao, writing in English, has to convey 'the spirit that is one's own in a language that is not one's own'. But the question is: Is it true of the vast majority of people in India? Does it mean that the English-using intelligentsia alone constitute India? It is a pity that this has to be stated but it must be: the Taj Mahal is in India but the Taj Mahal alone is not India!

A similar criticism was voiced by Meenakshi Mukherjee: 'One cannot postulate "Indian English" based on examples from Indo-Anglian writers. The Indo-Anglian writer should be allowed the freedom to experiment with the language for his own artistic needs rather than be heaved into a system of linguistics in search of that elusive medium — a standard Indian English' (1971: 214). Kachru in his reply says that 'one is confronting a confusion between language use and prescriptivism.' He adds: 'Standard Indian English is no more "elusive" than is standard American English or standard West African English. An individual author experiments with the style repertoire which a speech community uses, whether for "artistic" or practical needs. In the description of language use, "artistic needs" for creative use of language are as much a part of the total range of language use as is purely functional use (e.g., in ordering one's meal)' (1983: 77). The crucial point is how many people order their meal in 'Indian English'; in India most people are worried about their meal and not about 'Indian English'! Dasgupta (1993: 116–46) gives a detailed analysis of 'Kachru's Context' and points out that 'the main problem with Kachru's account, as most readers must have noticed by now, is the fact that it is not grounded in any systematic characterization, but proceeds anecdotally from item to item.'

Another point of view is expressed by Rajendra Singh in his 'Indian English: Some Conceptual Issues' (Agnihotri and Khanna 1994: 369–81); Singh says: 'The basic problem with B. Kachru's work is that although he pays lip service to non-standard varieties and multilingualism, he generally equates nativeness with standardness and monolinguality' (p. 375). He critically examines the arguments of Kachru and similar arguments by Yamuna Kachru in the same volume (pp. 289–304) about alleged peculiarities of 'Indian English' and wonders 'if Y. Kachru has ever asked identificational questions regarding her own writing'. He adds,

> My own informal tests suggest that (i) speakers of American English (AE) have no difficulty in processing 'IE' academic discourses and generally do not suggest any modification or restructuring of these discourses and (ii) written discourses by American ethnographers writing about India, for example, are sometimes judged to be 'akward' by native speakers of AE.

In addition, Yamuna Kachru, a non-native judge, first looks at the name of the writer and then locates the peculiarities in discourse strategies (She invokes the 'native spirit' only in the footnote!). It is as prejudicial as judging the qualities of a person by the colour of the skin.

Unmindful of all the criticisms, Kachru keeps repeating his position. He points out only 'the two faces of English':

> The contact and convergence of English with other languages and cultures has resulted in two processes, *nativization* and *Englishization* (Kachru 1989).
>
> These two processes have developed, as it were, two faces of English, one showing what the contact has formally done to various varieties of English, and the second showing what impact the English language and literature have had on other languages of the world. This process of 'give and take' has, again, been unprecedented, and has contributed to the development of new English-mixed codes in various parts of the world. Englishization is not restricted to phonology, grammar and lexis, but has had deep impact on discourse, registers, styles and literary genres (Kachru 1983a: 196–7).

This should make any Englishman or American feel very happy, indeed. But are these two faces that of a Janus or are they face to face with the likelihood of interaction, Kachru does not say.

Though Kachru talks about 'cultural context' and 'pragmatic needs', he does not go into the makings of the Indian cultural context. Perhaps, as Burde points out, the historical processes that shape the cultural contexts of India should be studied, so that 'the scope and nature of the interaction between the English language and the Indian cultural context will then show us the kind of pragmatic needs that arise out of this interaction'. To illustrate her point, Burde cites an example:

> Let us suppose that we find English is being used in the domain of Indian dances. Then we must investigate the degree of interaction between the English language and Indian dances. We might find new dance forms and new principles of aesthetics forged out of this interaction being expressed in a language which is the blending of English and Indian languages. It is also possible that English does not interact with the Indian dance forms but it is used by Indian dancers and performers to present their dances to non-Indian audiences. In that case, there will be a lot of loan words and borrowings in the English used. Yet the English

language will remain English with a supplementary Indian lexicon for a specific purpose (p. 77).

In addition, a study of similar processes like the Sanskritization of Indian languages, the 'birth' and spread of Urdu in India, or even processes like attempted Christianization of India and 'Indianization' of Christianity etc. can help us to understand 'Englishization' and 'nativization'. But Kachru does not attempt an in-depth study of these historical processes; he is driven more by nationalistic sentiments and what is called 'revenge history' (Bhalla 1993: 11). As we see it, the fundamental difference between Quirk and Kachru is 'ideological'. Quirk is like the missionaries who wanted to Christianize India but succeeded in converting a part of it, and Kachru represents the forces that 'Indianized' Christianity to a large extent. A small percentage of Indian Christians who were converted got the benefit of it but the vast majority of Indian Christians continue to be in the same state as they were in before conversion — without any change in the quality of their lives, call them Christians, Indians, Tamilians, Bengalis, or by any other name that you prefer. A similar story of one section reaping the benefits is true of English in India and Indian English. Only a section of the users of English in India has blended English with their day-to-day life, and that minority community does not represent the entire Indian population.

To sum up, Kachru's work on 'Indian English' has the following limitations: (a) He does not present any systematic data to substantiate his claims, (b) he does not go into the historical processes that produce social contexts and pragmatic needs, (c) he mixes up literary writing in English with the use of English in everyday life, and makes creative writers representative of the entire Indian population, (d) he treats the influence of English in certain areas as symbolic of Indianization of English, (e) he is caught up in his paradigm trap of native and non-native varieties and models of linguistic perceptions developed in the monolingual West, and (f) he oversimplifies a very complex process, the result being overgeneralization.

Undoubtedly, there is a lot of nationalistic appeal in Kachru's arguments but such projections and proclamations of victory can do very little to arrest the manifestations of the old-style colonialism or 'erase our own involvement throughout the age of colonialism in those events which disfigured, violated, penetrated and marked our world' (Bhalla 1993: 5).

(For a detailed list of Kachru's writings see Kachru's 'World Englishes' in Douglas Brown: *Readings on Second Language Acquisition* (1995); as expected, he does not list the publications of his critics).

2.7 Data-Based Attempts

Most of the research done on 'Indian English' is not based on any comprehensive corpus, says Shastri in his article, 'Towards a Definition of Indian English' (1983). According to Shastri too, Kachru focuses only on one aspect of English in India — the imaginative use of the language by Indian creative writers. In the first part of his article, Shastri enunciates the need for a large data base of both the written and the spoken language so as to investigate the Indian features of 'Indian English'. In the second part of the article, he proposes a detailed study of the lexis of 'Indian English' because, according to him, the Indianness of English is located in the lexis. In the third part of his article, he describes very briefly how he is building a corpus of 'Indian English' — a project of building a million-word-computer corpus of written English that consists of 500 texts of approximately 2000 words each; the texts are drawn from published edited material in the calendar year 1978, representing fifteen different types of prose.

2.8 'Indian English' as Interlanguage — An Ethnocentric View

If 'Indian English' does not fit into the 'language/dialect/variety' paradigm, is it possible to look at it from any other point of view? Tirumalesh offers an alternative in his article 'Indian English' (1990).

In this article he uses Larry Selinker's theory of interlanguage (1972). Selinker views all second language varieties at best only as interlanguages with characteristic features at the levels of phonology, syntax and lexicon. According to Tirumalesh, English is a language that is learnt formally in the class-room through textbooks, and the influence of the mother tongue on the acquisition of English is inevitable. So, as learners of English, Indians can never approximate the native variety. At the same time, it is not likely to become a pidgin (and later, a creole) because it is learnt in a formal set-up with textbooks, grammar books and dictionaries that have the native variety as the model. Tirumalesh argues that English in India is an interlanguage, and only such an acceptance will help Indians to evolve the norms that are essential for teaching English in India. In another article, 'In a Manner of Speaking' (1990), Tirumalesh discusses 'Indian English' with reference to the spoken mode. He says that there are Indians who speak good English; there are Indians whose English is bad and yet others whose English is ugly. He puts the good, the bad, and the ugly on a vertical axis and the regional variations like Tamil English, Bengali English, Punjabi English, etc. on the horizontal axis. In his view, the vertical axis is related to the upward mobility that becomes an indicator of social identity and the upward mobility, in turn, will create alienation from the lower classes. Thus, if Indians speak good English with proper stress and intonation, it sounds un-Indian, unnatural, and put on; if they do not speak good English, it creates the problem of intelligibility and affects the upward mobility. Indians using English are in a state of dilemma. Tirumalesh concludes his article with the statement that 'a second language should be spoken like a second language' but he does not spell out what he means by 'spoken like a second language'.

It must be pointed out here that Selinker's interlanguage (IL) theory is basically an ethnocentric theory. According to Selinker, 'fossilization' is the 'regular reappearance or re-emergence in IL productive performance of linguistic structures which were thought to be eradicated' (1974: 36), and 'fossilizable phenomena' are 'linguistic items, rules, and subsystems which speakers of a particular NL will tend to keep in their IL relative to a particular TL' (p. 36). He further notes that 'many of these phenomena reappear in IL performance when the learner's attention is focused upon new and difficult intellectual subject matter or when he is in a state of anxiety or other excitement, and strangely enough, sometimes when he is in a state of relaxation' (ibid.) and cites 'Indian English' as an IL with respect to English. Selinker considers only the native varieties as the 'norm' and all non-native varieties as interlanguage, and treats interlanguages as inferior languages. In addition, as Sridhar and Sridhar point out, in the case of most non-native learners the acquisitional target is 'not the native norm but an indigenized one' (Agnihotri and Khanna 1994: 50). Whether the concept of 'interlanguages and fossilization' does violence to indigenized varieties of English or not, it certainly is another version of the old view that the white man is the norm and all others are deviant/deficient versions of the norm; deficient versions may have their own 'grammar' but they belong to the intermediate area and can never reach the summit. This, by implication, will always put second language learners in a disadvantaged/handicapped position and an L2 learner can never succeed in learning English and achieve full target language competence; the L2 learner gets fossilized in the interlanguage area, linguistic as well as cognitive! This is what every ruler wants and this was what Macaulay wanted, as Horace Wilson says 'by rendering a whole people dependent upon a remote and unknown country for all their ideas and for the very words to clothe them, we should degrade their character, depress their energies and render them incapable of aspiring to any intellectual distinction' (*Asiatic Journal* 1836, 29: 14). It is well known that people have learnt foreign and second languages very successfully, maybe in limited domains, and the evidence is available in the form of written discourses in various languages. So, accepting 'Indian English' as an interlanguage will have serious theoretical and ideological implications.

2.9 English as India's Auntie Tongue

Dasgupta has argued that:

> English in India signifies technique and technology and technicality. It is not primarily a human language here. Its presence here is a rider carried by the technical planning apparatus to which this country, especially since independence, has entrusted its social and economic development.... Notice that the vehicle of this planning, throughout, has been English as a language of technical expertise.... Vehicle is the key word in our formulation. It points in two directions at the same time. First of all, it expresses the role of English in the non-metropolitan (or non-'First-World', if you prefer) areas where it is used as a second language; the word Vehicle reminds us that English is an auxiliary, an instrument, or an adjunct in the communication network of such regions.

Second, the word draws our attention to the fact that a language is not a neutral range of possibilities of saying what anybody likes, but is a going business of some people having said certain sorts of things and other people stepping into the flow of discourse in order to renew or modify some of the themes. . . . We have seen that the presence of English in India is built around its essential technical-legal-scientific registers. The machinery enabling some Indians to use 'native like' English to speak to each other is also an intricate social technology of resistance to the corrupting Indian influences and an inter-cultural technology of continual pumping of contemporary Anglo-American idiom and mores into the Indian elite. Thus, the presence of the language in this country is a matter of keeping a standing army of English words in a state of constant readiness, wearing combat gear. When you are in combat gear, you cannot relax, and the arts of relaxation, including a creativity that is in touch with your community's cultural consciousness, are denied to you. Thus the enthusiastic academic community of Indian English authors has been unable to experience the inwardness of genuine creative writing and therefore has produced no reflections on the predicament of such creators in the modern world, no contributions to the theory of literary analysis stemming from such an inwardness. However, this community has done very well in the domain of translating from Indian languages into English, which includes the enterprise of independent renarration in English of fictional or analytical narratives from this culture. The community has also produced a rich body of insightful commentary on the successful experience of such translation and renarration. This is in keeping with our hypothesis, for translation and retelling are technical jobs and perfectly compatible with being in combat uniform (Dasgupta 1993: 214–18).

Dasgupta argues that 'Indian English' has no reality of presence comparable to Sanskrit in ancient India. He says: 'One difference between English in post-modern India and Sanskrit in the Gupta empire lies in the sphere of the creative expression of the cultural reality of India. Classical India's Sanskrit exhibited independent, substantial creativity; our India's English is anaphoric to the creativity of metropolitan English and quite devoid of independent creativity' (1993: 110). As he himself points out, this is similar to the point of view expressed by A.K. Ramanujan in his paper 'Is there an Indian way of thinking?' (1990) in which he suggests that 'the use of English by educated Indians may be compared to the way in which the educated class in classical India used Sanskrit' (op. cit.: 71).

It is true that both Sanskrit in ancient times and English today play an artificial 'high' role, and that Sanskrit was very creative in classical times. It is true that even the minority metropolitan variety called 'Indian English' lacks that kind of creative vitality. But it has a different kind of vitality that is visible in the writing of Indians in English. It is true that Sanskrit literature has been translated and adapted in other Indian languages because of its creative vitality in spite of its high role, and that Indian Writing in English has not been adopted by Indian languages. But it is too early to predict that these works are not going to be accepted by other languages in India. It is true that there are not many plays in Indian Writing in English because 'Indian English' has not taken roots in India; it is true that there are no films made in 'Indian English' and this variety is used only in films like 'Gandhi', 'Passage to India', 'Mississippi Masala', etc. to portray the colonial period, or the life of the immigrant population outside India, or the English-using urban-Indians; it is also true that the majority of Indians cannot enjoy English pop music because they don't know the language. But as the second medium of the bilingual creative activity (as in the case of the works of Dilip Chitre, for instance), English also serves as the co-language of expression.

However, English is mainly a language of technical expertise. Dasgupta very rightly points out that 'even for the sake of tokenism, one would have expected at least a semblance of new thinking to appear, and official grammars and metacritical theories to be produced' but 'even this has not happened'; he adds that 'the rhetorical stances taken by the top theoreticians have amounted to a lukewarm Mukherji/Kachru debate over the very existence of Indian English as a language possessing a speech community shows clearly how little energy Indian English has in its sails, or what a tepid level of creativity has been powering its engines' (op. cit.: 140).

There is a footnote to all these indisputable observations, that is, we (Dasgupta as well as the present authors and many others) have to present these arguments only in English! It is a pity that even our anger and frustration has to be expressed in English, the Auntie Tongue, as Dasgupta calls it. In his conclusion, Dasgupta says: 'We would like to think of the Auntie Tongue image as a compressed presentation of the upshot of the analysis. English the teacher is adopted by the Indian cultural family, but not as a member belonging to any direct line of descent. The family gives English the Auntie role that politeness sets up for guests and acquaintances who are not regarded as true relations' (op. cit.: 218).

It is not clear why Dasgupta has not thought of the label "The Uncle Tongue', an expression that clearly indicates the power and authority of the male in a patriarchal society, which, in a way, indicates the power and position of English. Maybe, it is a convention to talk about only the mother tongue (even in the case of English or German) and not about the father tongue — a point that should please the feminists. Secondly, the word 'Auntie' has more of class connotations in the Indian context than of family relationships. In a way, it indicates the class status of English but not any 'line of descent', as indicated by Dasgupta. Thirdly, the 'aunties' do belong to India and they are very much a part of Indian life. It is surprising that in these days of intercaste, even interreligious marriages, and an emerging cosmopolitan culture we are still talking about the 'true line of descent'! What is the true line of descent for children born out of intercaste marriages? These creations are also children and are living in India, and their number is on the increase in urban India.

Though one can agree with Dasgupta's critique of earlier works on English in India or 'Indian English', it is difficult to accept his own line of thought. It is commonly believed that English is the language of technology in India. But it must also be stated that unfortunately English is not even the language of technical expertise in India. The technology that has been brought about by the English educational system is only borrowed technology; a borrowed language has produced a set of technologists (more precisely 'techno-coolies') who can only borrow and imitate. Technology in India means only what has been called 'screw-driver technology' that gives us finished products. It has not become a part of the developmental process, and is not integrated with the mode of life in the country as a whole. If the vast majority of people live in the rural areas and technology has not reached those areas, we cannot say that English has brought about a technological change. It cannot even be said that English is centred around technical-legal-scientific registers. On the other hand, English is now on the MTV and STAR TV network and is increasingly becoming the carrier of pop-culture.

It is quite obvious that the world now is very different from what it was during the classical period, and the instruments that were not available to Sanskrit are now available to the builders of the English Empire. Sanskrit had only spiritual, religious, and literary motivations but English offers material incentives in addition to the pleasures of pop-culture. The influence of people like Michael Jackson on modern Indian dance forms can be seen in all the films now made in Indian languages, be it Hindi or Tamil, and English (H/Foreign, according to Dasgupta) has become 'a threat to the very identity of a Third World speech community' (p. 73) because of 'its spill over into the sphere of what we may call L/Authentic' (ibid.), the language of the community.

It must be said that Dasgupta's insightful meditations raise a number of interesting questions about the future of English in India but his study is not based on any systematic corpus of data, and he does not go into the historical processes of absorption in the subcontinent; as he himself confesses, he has not taken into account the Dravidian areas of Bharat-India. He is silent about the Islamic layer and the Urdu-part of the story. Robert Phillipson in his review of Dasgupta's book rightly points out:

> English is not the first language that was imposed by incoming overlords in India, and it is hard to see what theoretical justification there could be for Persian/Arabic being welcomed into the family with full procreative rights, while English is an irredeemable maiden aunt. English has presumably been the medium through which Indians have become familiar with all sorts of values, paradigms, and traditions in many domains, political, intellectual, literary, and technological. That the use made of these importations may have served the interests of the few rather than the many raises serious ethical and political questions. Dasgupta is right to raise them, though his prolix style will have restricted his audience. Those Indians who read him are presumably the ones who most readily identify with English. There is certainly a need for more analysis of the sociology of English and its place in — or out of — the family of Indian languages' (*Applied Linguistics*, vol. 16, no. 2, Oct. 1995).

In *After Amnesia* (1992), Devy has argued that Indian criticism is torn between 'Westernization' and 'Sanskritization'; what Devy says about Indian criticism is true of the approach of some Indians. Sanskrit fixation, if it may be so labelled, is not unique to Dasgupta's approach to English in India. Douglas Haynes and Gyan Prakash (1991: 6) have also argued that 'this tradition insisted that the essence of India existed in a number of key Hindu classical scriptures such as the Vedas, the Codes of Manu and the Shastras, texts that did prescribe hierarchical ideals . . . and that the way to study India is through certain core texts rather than through the experienced social life of its peoples . . . .' Such fixations, perhaps, result in Dasgupta not accepting English or 'Indian English' as an authentic Indian language. It is not known what is meant by 'authentic' and 'real life of India'; all that we know is that real life for the vast majority in the country means poverty, filth and dirt, absence of proper sanitation, lack of drinking water, struggle for a square meal a day, continuous exploitation, etc. If that is what is meant by real life, then neither Sanskrit nor English represents it. Maybe, the concept of 'real life' is one of the 'necessary illusions'; in the land of illusions and contradictions called Bharat-India, the real is unreal and the unreal real.

2.10 The Degree-Yielding Variety

There are other studies that take up only certain aspects of English in India like Bansal's *Intelligibility of Indian English* (1969), *Some Aspects of the Phonology of Indian English* (1982), Choudhary's doctoral thesis, and *Tense in Indian English* (1988) by Agnihotri and others. 'Indian English' seems to be a 'degree-yielding cow' since there are varieties within varieties and each of these can be a topic of research — *A Phonological Analysis of Rajasthani English* (Dhamija 1976), *A Study of Intonation Patterns in Marathi and Marathi English* (Gokhale 1978), *The Vowels of Malayalee English* (Premalatha 1978), *Butler English: Form and Function* (Hosali 1982), etc., to cite a few dissertations done at the Central Institute of English and Foreign Languages, Hyderabad (India). Some of them take it for granted that there is something called 'Indian English' and start researching some aspect of that variety. Quite often the orientation is pedagogic. Sometimes it is pointed out that 'Indian English' is not yet adequately described or defined. Sometimes 'Indian English' and 'English in India' are taken to be the same. Maybe, the area is too vast and too difficult to investigate and, as a result, we end up blaming the 'dominant minority'/'elite minority' though everyone would like to become a member of that very 'minority'.

The problem is that when we say that something is Indian we do not know what it is that makes it 'Indian'! Even the Government of India started an institution called the Central Institute of Indian Languages (of which English is not a part because it is not an Indian language), and a Central Institute of English and Foreign Languages (it is not a part of 'Other Foreign Languages' because English is not a foreign language). In short, the 'intellectuals' do not know how to classify English though it is a part of their everyday life. Some insist that English is not an integral part of Indian life and its culture, and hence does not symbolize the land and its people. The others use only some section of the population or some aspect of English to justify their stand on 'Indian' English. The story of the blind men (and women) trying to describe the elephant is well known in India.

2.11 Miscellany-Notions-Conglomerate and the 'Rashomon Effect'

Second Language Acquisition: Socio-cultural and Linguistic Aspects of English in India (1994) edited by Agnihotri and Khanna is a good example of the wide spectrum of views, often contradictory, on the problematics of English in India/'Indian English'. In the first article in the volume Kachru goes round, by now well known, 'concentric circles' and repeats his arguments regarding the native and 'institutionalized non-native varieties of English' (INNV). In the last article, Rajender Singh reviews the native/non-native distinction and says that such distinctions are 'based on the naive assumption that 'Nativeness' can be so predicted' and that pleas for the recognition of 'Indian English' 'including the by now classic pieces by Kachru, display their Orwellian colours almost immediately: *indigenized, deviant, awkward* are not much more opaque than wrong, incorrect and substandard' (pp. 370–1). Parasher in his article 'Indian English', based on a sample survey, concludes that 'educated IndE conforms to the major syntactic rules of the language and has peripheral differences in syntax and marked differences in lexis and style as compared with native educated varieties' (op. cit.: 163). But Jean Aitchison and Agnihotri observe that 'Indian English syntax often appears odd to British speakers. These oddities could perhaps be summarized by the statement: "It's probably all right, but I wouldn't say it like that myself". This suggests that we are dealing with similar syntactic rules, but dissimilar preferences when it comes to choosing between the possible options in cases where more than one construction is permitted' (op. cit.: 166).

Yamuna Kachru suggests: 'Whereas in native varieties, "beating around the bush" is not desirable in business negotiations, such a strategy is highly appropriate in a non-native variety in which "coming to the point directly" is perceived as uncivilized' (op. cit.: 300) and, like Kachru, feels that native and non-native notions of competence vary. But Rajendra Singh says:

> The Kachrus, for example, seem content to identify what they find in 'IE' as a feature of 'IE', to designate it as a 'non-native' feature, and to plead for the recognition of 'IE' as a 'non-native' outer-circle variety. They are like the anthropologist who proudly notes the fact that each member of the tribe he has been studying has long hair and proceeds to plead for their recognition as somewhat less equal, outer-circle homo sapiens, forgetting that those who will grant the plea may have amongst them at least some people with long hair. The time for such discoveries and pleas is, hopefully, over (p. 375).

He pleads for an empirical demonstration of the uniqueness and alleged 'non-nativeness' of 'IE' and concludes by saying;

> I want to know precisely where its uniqueness lies; it may well be non-native, but I want to know precisely what formal properties make it so; it may in fact not even be there, but then people do talk about English in India (cf. Dasgupta 1993) and not about 'IE'. In other words, I see the counterpoint presented above not as an exercise in closing doors but as one in opening the doors which 'the Standard' — based enterprise seems to have closed (p. 380).

Patnaik and Geetha observe: 'Probably IE is what it is because it reflects the characteristics of the Indian languages' (1995: 229). If that is so, there can only be Bengali English, Telugu English, Rajasthani English, and so on but there can be no Indian English.

Here then is a book that exemplifies the story of the blind men and the elephant — twenty-three articles about 'Indian' English, as miscellaneous as the nationalities of executives of a multi-national company staffing its regional office for South Asia. Considering that the non-resident Indian academic is more articulate in the assertion of the non-nativeness of English, the business of 'Indian English' indeed resembles a multi-national conglomerate. A conglomerate is not just a large business firm, it refers to a firm that controls production of goods of very different kinds. Little wonder then that we have miscellaneous views, angles of vision, and notions on 'Indian' English with no consensus on how to define English in India! One is left with what is called the 'Rashomon effect'! (In Akira Kurosawa's film *Rashomon*, a murder takes place and those who witness it give totally different versions of what happened.)

2.12 Prator's Prejudice

Another angle of vision that is not very palatable is presented by Clifford Prator in an article titled 'The British Heresy in TESL'. He says:

> The doctrine of establishing local models for TESL, thus appears to be a natural outgrowth of the much deplored colonial mentality. It is met with sporadically almost everywhere in formerly colonial countries but is particularly prevalent, for reasons that I shall attempt to explain later, in formerly British possessions such as India, Pakistan, Ceylon, Ghana, and Nigeria. It does not seem to flourish in countries that have little or no recent history as colonies. English is widely used as a medium of instruction in Ethiopia, yet I have never heard of an Ethiopian proposing that an Ethiopian variety of the language be taught in his country's schools. An Afghan will probably be greatly pleased if you tell him he speaks English like an Englishman or an American; an Indian may be quite disconcerted by the same remark (1968: 460).

We think Prator is very much mistaken here; maybe, he talked to people who talk about 'Indian English' in near-native RP or GA. Any Indian who is not involved in the politics of 'Indian English' will be pleased to hear that he/she speaks English like a native speaker of English. It is the dream of many to speak English like an Englishman or an American, and as somebody remarked: 'If native English could be packed into a pill, it would be the single most widely prescribed and beneficial medicine in the world.'

Prator cites an Indian linguist who said:

> The Americans don't speak like Englishmen; they have their own kind of English. The Scotch, the Australians, the South Africans each speak their own particular brand of English. Why shouldn't we have our own variety? We studied the language in our schools for many years now and shall probably continue to do so. Many educated citizens of this country speak English better than some Americans and Englishmen. We prefer to learn to speak the language as our educated countrymen do rather than as you speak it. It's much more important for us to understand one another well than outsiders (op. cit.: 460).

It is obvious that Prator understands fully well the implications of what was written by the Indian linguist. But in the same article Prator says:

> After 20 years of testing the English of hundreds of incoming foreign students semester after semester at the University of California, I am firmly convinced that for the rest of the English-speaking world the most unintelligible educated variety is Indian English. The national group that profits least from the University's efforts to improve their intelligibility by classroom instruction also seems to be Indians; they can almost never be brought to believe that there is any reason for trying to change their pronunciation (op. cit.: 473).

May be, Prator lives in a different world. For, in the very same California that he talks about, there are hundreds and hundreds of Indians working in areas like computer sciences, management, medicine and health care, motel management, etc., and some Indians teach English in the colleges and universities. If they are so unintelligible, as Prator says, how do they interact with their employers and the people around them? Fortunately for Indians, Prator is not incharge of any testing programme for employment purposes! But Prator's prejudices are to be taken into account in studying the doctrine of local models of English because there are many others who carry such colonial attitudes — the rulers as well as the ruled.

2.13 De-prejudicing the Outlook

Kachru's circularity, the 'otherness' syndrome, bias for or against the non-nativeness of 'Indian' English, are the outcome of a combination of many factors — a colonial past, English education bequeathed by the colonizers, and political freedom that did not generate indigenous thinking, to name the most obvious ones. Instead of pitting the 'two faces of Indian English' (to use Kachru's phrase), into a sea of complexities (and India has oceans on three sides!), let us plunge them into inter-active contemplation.

In the chapter that follows, our investigation of English in India is routed through an examination of colonization and hegemony, the notion of nationality, and the Indian multitudes' relation with the English language through chronologically compiled data and its analysis.

Chapter Three

The Technology of 'Power' and the Power of the Weak

> But whereas the scientific apparatus (ours) is led to share the illusion of the powers it necessarily supports, that is, to assume that the masses are transformed by the conquests and victories of expansionist production, it is always good to remind ourselves that we mustn't take people for fools.
> — Michel de Certeau, *The Practice of Everyday Life*

3.1 The Technology of 'Power'

Long ago, Edmund Burke remarked, 'I know of nothing sublime which is not some modification of power'. Power is multifaceted, omnipresent and omnipotent, and has several manifestations, overt as well as covert. Power may be 'State power', 'military power', 'money power', 'muscle power', 'political power', 'media power', 'language power', 'ideological power', 'technological power', 'organizational power', 'spiritual power', 'the power of knowledge', 'the power of education', 'the power of the subaltern', 'the power of the individual', 'the power of nature', etc. All these manifestations of power have certain things in common — the position and capacity to control and manipulate, and this very condition of seekers of power enslaves them to the power of others; power, naturally and necessarily, goes with danger and destruction.

The concept of 'power' has been studied by many in the West, and these studies are known because they are available in English. This very context shows the power of English and the position of the Anglo-American World. The conventional conception of 'power' is discussed by Lukes in his book, *Power*, where he says that 'the supreme and most insidious exercise of power [lies in] ... shaping [people's] perceptions, cognitions and preferences in such a way that they accept their role in the existing order of things...' (1974: 24). In another book edited by Lukes (1986), Galbraith points out the 'rise of organization as a source of power and the concurrent lessening in the comparative roles of personality and property' which, according to him, results in 'a hugely increased reliance on social conditioning as an instrument for the enforcement of power' (1986: 214–19). Chomsky has proposed a propaganda model that focuses on the inequality of 'wealth and power and its multilevel effects on mass-media interests and choices' (1988: 2).

Foucault's analysis of power is well known. He rejects the idea of the agent exercising power and argues that 'the analysis should not concern itself with power at the level of conscious intention or decision', and says that the 'real and effected practices' of power should be studied:

> ... how things work at the level of ongoing subjugation, at the level of those continuous and uninterrupted processes which subject our bodies, govern our gestures, dictate our behaviours, etc.... we should try to discover how it is that subjects are gradually, progressively, really and materially constituted through a multiplicity of organisms, forces, energies, materials, desires, thoughts, etc. We should try to grasp subjection in its material instance as a constitution of subjects (1976: 233).

He sees power as 'something which circulates... as something which only functions in the form of a chain.... Power is employed and exercised through a net-like organization. And not only do individuals circulate between its threads; they are always in the position of simultaneously undergoing and exercising this power...' (ibid.: 234). Foucault's study of the 'technology of power' and its history shows that power is cancerous and it multiplies within itself; the various elements of the apparatus combine with each other and reproduce themselves, spreading throughout the entire strata of society. In addition, he claims that language is power in the sense that it is one of the 'multiplicity of organisms, forces, energies, materials, thoughts, etc.' (1976: 233) and people are constituted by the discourse used in their society. Thus, Foucault sees all individuals, including the most powerful and those who exercise power in some form or the other, as subject to power. Power becomes so powerful that all people are constituted by the various power mechanisms of society; he makes power omnipresent and omnipotent.

The sociologist, Pierre Bourdieu, has argued that *capital* is a form of power and capital is not only economic (a characterizing trait of capitalism) but also social and cultural.

> There is an interplay among the three forms of capital and, at one level, society is structured by the differential distribution of capital (as formulated by Bourdieu) and, at another level, individuals strive to maximize their capital. (This does not mean that they have a transitive preference ordering which they seek to maximize. Rather, unaware of some true possibilities, unable to take full advantage or conceive of other possibilities, due to their class habitus, agents nonetheless seek to maximize benefits, given their relational position within a field.) The capital they are able to accumulate defines their social trajectory (that is, their life chances); moreover, it also serves to reproduce class distinctions (Calhoun 1993: 5).

According to Bourdieu, the 'habitus' is the dynamic intersection of structure and action, society and individual, which shape and are shaped by social practice. His concept of field provides the frame for a 'relational analysis' by which he means 'an account of the multidimensional space of positions and the position-taking of agents. The position of a particular agent is the result of an interplay between that person's habitus and his or her place in a field of positions as defined by the distribution of the appropriate form of capital. The nature and range of possible positions varies socially and historically' (ibid.).

Connolly (1983: 149–50), considers various theories of power and concludes that a generally accepted definition of power is unlikely to emerge:

> The concept 'power' . . . is one of the sites of a struggle between rival ideals of the good life competing — though not on equal terms — for hegemony in our civilization. If modernity is marked by rivalries in which efficiency and community, democratic citizenship and the imperative of economic growth, utility and autonomy, rights and interests, domination and appreciation of nature all compete for primacy, it is not surprising . . . to see microcosms of this rivalry inside the concepts which help to continue that way of life.

He further adds that those who construe the standards operative in their own way of life to be fully expressive of God's will or reason or nature, with transcendental provincialism, try to treat the standards with which they are intimately familiar as universal criteria against which all other theories, practices and ideals are to be assessed. Thus, power-struggle appears to be part of existence, and is implied in the theory of the survival of the fittest. However even if we assume that power-reproduction is 'natural', we have to offer an explanation (a) for the privileged development of some elements of this apparatus over others, and (b) for the processes that develop the silent, dormant forces that lie within, 'sleeping furiously' as the potential and immense reserve constituting the beginnings or traces of other configurations.

3.2 The 'West' and the 'Rest': Some Contemplations

It is quite likely that the role of English in the contemporary world and its popularity in the Indian subcontinent, a complex and ancient civilization with a recent colonial past, may offer some insights into the concept of 'power' in general, the power of language in particular, and the play of forces that bring about socio-cultural, political, economic, and technological contexts in societies in which they are in circulation.

The English language has been widely accepted as the 'carrier of wisdom', the 'window to the world', as the tool for 'transfer of technology', and the language is invariably allied with Anglo-American hegemonic dominance which is mistakenly equated with the 'West'. Michael Binyon (*The Times*, 1989) claims that the English language has conquered Europe, though it is welcome in some areas and loathed in others. According to him all the signs on the continent are in English, and the nations speak to each other in English. He further claims: 'Europeans may be swept along by the American way of life, but on the whole they do not like the American way of speech. Most schools insist on British pronunciation and spelling, and send their pupils on exchange visits to Britain not the United States. Geography is partly the reason; so, too, is the small number of American teachers of English in Europe and the large number of British people serving as teaching assistants in schools.' As part of the internal politics of the Anglo-American world, he asserts that 'English is sold only by the pound and not by the dollar'.

For the 'rest' of us, the Anglo-American English Empire represents 'Western' imperialism. Imperialism 'has its own normality, a daily time table which unfolds in the margins of its unpublished confessions' (Mattelart 1979: 1). It is well known that imperialism is so very powerful that it can manipulate and legitimize anything — including the space it occupies. According to the English Empire, the 'world' has become a small global village through the use of English, the language of the satellite communication network, the Internet, etc. It is like the tale of the Imperial Map in Borges where the map has the same scale as the Empire itself. The English Empire sees itself as the world or the community or the village itself which ultimately comes to mean, the Empire as the First World within the First World and their agents/slaves — the First World within the Third World. It must be pointed out here that certainly there is an under-developed or undeveloped 'Third World' (if that is what it means or what it has come to mean though it was not the 'intended' meaning) in every 'First World' and that there is a 'First World' in every 'Third World' — though thinly distributed as 'agents' of the Empire. The story is very complex, more complex than the stories of the old empires, since the *avatar* has many ever-changing manifestations; there are several 'myths' that are made and floated as part of the neocolonial condition. In this new drama the players come off stage and mix with the public, making it difficult to separate the actors from the audience.

There are some who say that it is the weak who are asking the Empire to come to their rescue and 'enlighten' them through their language and technology; it is said that the 'rest' are asking the 'West' to help them in order to become 'advanced'. On the contrary, there is also the alarm raised in the West (= USA) that the white males are actually the victimized minority; the conservative cry of 'political correctness' and the 'English Only' campaign in the USA are manifestations of the kind of new hysteria and myth-making within the Empire. At least, there are some who appear to be forthright in their views; they say that there is an attempt to replace the classics of the Western culture with second rate texts from the Third World, meaning literature from the 'Orient'.

Some others argue that there is something called 'victim mythology' and that it has become customary to blame the Anglo-American hegemonic dominance and the Occident for all the degradation, loss of national and cultural identity. They point out that this 'mentality of subalternity' goes by different names — orientalism, post-colonialism, neocolonialism, cultural colonialism, language imperialism, etc. It is projected by the 'rest' as though the Western tribe of arrogant, power-hungry white males, also identified with the oppressive patriarchy, spreads like a deadly virus all over the planet and kills all other tribes and cultures that do not use English and 'Western' values. A good example of this point of view is found in Turner who asserts that those who propagate the myth of the oppressive patriarchal West claim that the central tenet of Western ideology is that there is only one overarching truth, and that this totalizing idea denies the diversity and relativity of cultural values, and the great ideals of diversity and pluralism. He argues:

> According to this myth, the traditions of Western art, literature, science, and philosophy are riddled with hidden justifications for oppression, and thus politically poisonous, except for some works, which were either composed by persons of non-Western ancestry or influenced by non-Western sources. Western mathematical, physical, and chemical sciences reduce the living world to a passive and inanimate colonial victim, to be exploited and raped by technology for the sake of power.... The purpose and net result of all these Western techniques has been to keep the masses of people in the third world and their brothers and sisters, the minority populations in the West itself, in a state of poverty, misery, and powerlessness (1995: 145–6).

Turner's argument is that the West is not unique in its ethnocentricism, xenophobia, and racism;

> ... all three are culturally universal.... Racial and ethnic prejudice is a normal feature of every society, from Serbia to Brazil, from China to Honduras, from Lebanon to Australia, from Sri Lanka to Azerbaijan .... Indeed, prejudice and stereotyping could be seen as the essential mechanism of all human (and perhaps all mammal, vertebrate, even animal) perception and information processing.... The West is not unique in the practice of conquest and imperialism. The imperialistic exploits of Islam and the Han Chinese, the expansionism of the great Mesoamerican and Andean empires, the epic conquests of the old African kingdoms and the odyssey of the ancient agrarian peoples of Taiwan who swept through the East Indies on their way to Polynesia and

Madagascar, are now under study by historians, archaeologists, and linguists. . . . There are no human beings anywhere who live where their ancestors always lived; we are all the children of interlopers, conquerors, enslavers, aliens, as well as of their victims. There is also no cultural purity anywhere in the world, no set of simple and unadulterated folkways, no authentic wellspring of human innocence]. . . . Any moral accounting of the story as told by the myth should lead to all Westerners committing suicide in part payment for their crimes. But it is despair also for the 'third world' and the 'minorities', as losers either in the game of values or in the game of power. If the West is as bad, as powerful, as cleverly conspiratorial, secret, and selfaware, as the myth proposes, then there is no way that it will give up its power, and no way to force it to do so. Indeed, the only intelligent recourse would be to give up the struggle and learn to enjoy the doubtful pleasures of the oppressed: the satisfaction of physical desires, the oppression of those even weaker than oneself, the relinquishing of any attempt at objectivity, the sense of complete irresponsibility for one's own condition, the loss of anxiety about the past and future, and the feeling of solidarity with others who have likewise given in (op. cit.: 146–54).

The question is, whether we, in the Third world, are doing what Turner has suggested in accepting English and justifying it in the name of World Englishes. But let us hear out Turner on oppression by the West. He further justifies his position by pointing out the 'shaking down' and integration of ideas:

Colonial peoples such as those of India and Africa were sometimes unaware that they had contributed some of the key ideas that their colonial oppressors now used against them. Now at last the relatively isolated cultures of the Americas, of sub-Saharan Africa, and of Oceania began to pour their own contributions into the great stream of the human plenum . . . . The great virtue of this emerging world civilization, falsely called the West, was that it was passionately interested in other cultures, and could so profoundly imagine the world of the other that the other was no longer the Other. Orientalism, despite the sneers of the likes of Edward Said, was a movement of extraordinary imaginative generosity . . . . One paradigmatic expression of the new world integration is Peter Brook's *Mahabharata*, whose cast contains members of almost every major ethnic group. But we can find it also in many contemporary phenomena: 'World Music', the international financial markets, the worldwide concern with environmental issues, telecommunications, the World Health Organization, international science, the worldwide interest in the space program, and throughout the arts. The media link the world in nanoseconds. Japan has outdone Europe and America at their own industrial game, and the 'little dragons' of the Pacific rim are doing so too. Huge common market areas emerge. The last legally racist regime, South Africa, has dissolved itself. One of the special characteristics of the information age is that the artists of it are no longer predominantly European or American, exercising an imaginative sympathy for other peoples. They are of all backgrounds, and live within a world where there is no privileged center of initiative or special insight. Indian anthropologists study white American natives. Kurosawa gives us the definitive Shakespeare, Yo-Yo Ma the definitive cello, Midori the definitive Mozart. The Latin American novel sets the fashion in fiction, West African Griots set it in music. The co-authors of scientific papers read like an international directory of names. When the Berlin Wall came down there was a great performance in Berlin of the *Carmina Burana,* with a black American soloist, a Jewish conductor, a German orchestra, and a Chinese choir.

This story of the emergence of world culture might also have been told with some plausibility from the viewpoints of the Indian subcontinent or from that of the coasts of the South China Sea, rather than from that of the Mediterranean, as I have done here. Europe was a backwater at the very beginning and during the Dark Ages. It would be harder to tell it as if its center of intensity were anywhere else, and those three nodes were themselves closely connected for thousands of years. Today its center is everywhere on the globe, though there are still places where, because of concentrations of wealth, education, population, and tradition, the fire burns most brightly. But the point is that for any self-styled local culture to set itself against the 'West' — that is, against the composite world culture — is pathetically futile and self-destructive . . . (op. cit.: 159–61).

Though there is some truth in what Turner says regarding the cumulative nature of world culture, the point is that the 'West' is equated with world culture, and Turner is writing the history of the 'world culture' from the point of view of the victorious West. The same line of argument can be constructed for the growth and spread of the English language which has become a 'world language', absorbing contributions from various sources — probably Latin, French, Spanish, Arabic, Sanskrit and other

Indian languages — and is fast converting the world into a 'global village'. To some extent it is true that English is no longer the language of the English or the Americans. But for every myth that is constructed there is a counter-myth and it is well known that history has always been written by the victors and 'reality' is what is perceived by those who have power. Turner will never know that all this talk about 'world culture' and 'world music' means nothing to those whose only 'culture' is their survival and their main problem is the next meal. It is just beyond his imagination because he lives in a different world and he simply does not know the experience of the 'colonized', in every sense of the term, from inside. But, at the same time, some of the issues raised by Turner are worth considering. Are the weak so helpless that they have no other course than accepting English as the international language and Western culture as 'world culture' and 'enjoy the doubtful pleasures of the oppressed', as suggested by Turner? Is there no 'escape' or hope for the weak? How did the West emerge from the Dark Ages and become a powerful force? Nothing is stagnant forever; history is a story of budding, blossoming, and withering. A study of the driving forces that bring about changes in history and an understanding of the nature of power and dominance may be helpful in understanding English as the world language.

From what one can see in the Indian subcontinent, the victims who say that they are victimized are a part of the culture of complaint, and are really fascinated and lured by power and the Western way of life. That section of the population, the English educated urban elite, have become the colonizers though they were the colonized under the British rulers. Even today, the departments of English continue to be the 'colonies' of British literature, and elsewhere the colony of the multinationals and pop-culture is fast expanding. As Mattelart (1979: 231) says, 'National culture, in the era of multinationals, has to guarantee the dependence of these bourgeoisie on the United States at the same time as that of their own hegemony as the ruling class in a particular nation.' The study of English in India may, therefore, serve as an interesting case study to illustrate how the common people in a multilingual, multicultural, multiracial, and now 'multinational' context handle so many conflicting forces and somehow manage to live, carrying so many layers of control and oppression. May be, they learned to live in a multiverse as part of their existence over centuries in an area that has evolved a complex civilization; the theory of everyday practices and the role of English in the Indian subcontinent offer an interesting interface.

3.3 The Power of the Weak

In a way, the answers to some of the questions raised about 'power' are proposed by Certeau in *The Practice of Everyday Life*:

> Thus the spectacular victory of Spanish colonization over the indigenous Indian cultures was diverted from its intended aims by the use made of it; even when they were subjected, indeed when they accepted their subjection, the Indians often used the laws, practices, and representations that were imposed on them by force or by fascination to ends other than those of their conquerors; they made something else out of them; they subverted them from within — not by rejecting them or by transforming them (though that occurred as well), but by many different ways of using them in the service of rules, customs or convictions foreign to the colonization which they could not escape. They metaphorized the dominant order; they made it function in another register. They remained other within the system which they assimilated and which assimilated them externally. They diverted it without leaving it. Procedures of consumption maintained their difference in the very space that the occupier was organizing.
>
> Is this an extreme example? No, even if the resistance of the Indians was founded on a memory tattooed by oppression, a past inscribed on their body. To a lesser degree, the same process can be found in the use made in 'popular' milieus of the cultures diffused by the 'elites' that produce language. The imposed knowledge and symbolisms become objects manipulated by practitioners who have not produced them. The language produced by a certain social category has the power to extend its conquests into vast areas surrounding it, 'deserts' where nothing equally articulated seems to exist, but in doing so it is caught in the trap of its assimilation by a jungle of procedures rendered invisible to the conqueror by the very victories he seems to have won. However spectacular it may be, his privilege is likely to be only apparent if it merely serves as a framework for the stubborn, guileful, everyday practices that make use of it. What is called 'popularization' or 'degradation' of a culture is from this point of view a partial and caricatural aspect of the revenge that utilizing tactics take on the power that dominates production. In any case, the consumer

cannot be identified or qualified by the newspapers or commercial products he assimilates; between the person (who uses them) and these products (indexes of the 'order' which is imposed on him), there is a gap of varying proportions opened by the use that he makes of them. . . . Statistics can tell us virtually nothing about the currents in this sea theoretically governed by the institutional frameworks that it in fact gradually erodes and displaces. Indeed, it is less a matter of a liquid circulating in the interstices of a solid than of different movements making use of the elements of the terrain. Statistical study is satisfied with classifying, calculating and tabulating these elements — 'lexical' units, advertising words, television images, manufactured products, constructed places, etc. — and they do it with categories and taxonomies that conform to those of industrial or administrative production. Hence such study can grasp only the material used by consumer practices — a material which is obviously that imposed on everyone by production — and not the formality proper to these practices, their surreptitious and guileful 'movement', that is, the very activity of 'making do'. The strength of these computations lies in their ability to divide, but this analytical ability eliminates the possibility of representing the tactical trajectories which, according to their own criteria, select fragments taken from the vast ensembles of production in order to compose new stories with them. . . . A distinction between strategies and tactics appears to provide a more adequate initial schema. I call a strategy the calculation (or manipulation) of power relationships that becomes possible as soon as a subject with will and power (a business, an army, a city, a scientific institution) can be isolated . . . a tactic is a calculated action determined by the absence of a proper locus. No delimitation of an exteriority, then, provides it with the condition necessary for autonomy. The space of a tactic is the space of the other. Thus it must play on and with a terrain imposed on it and organized by the law of a foreign power. It does not have the means to keep to itself, at a distance, in a position of withdrawal, foresight, and self-collection; it is a maneuver 'within the enemy's field of vision,' as Von Bulow put it, and within enemy territory. . . . In short, a tactic is an art of the weak . . . clever tricks of the 'weak' within the order established by the 'strong', an art of putting one over on the adversary on his own turf, hunter's tricks, maneuverable, polymorph mobilities, jubilant, poetic, and warlike discoveries. . . . These practices present in fact a curious analogy, and a sort of immemorial link, to the simulations, tricks, and disguises that certain fishes or plants execute with extraordinary virtuosity. . . . Tactics are more and more frequently going off their tracks. Cut loose from the traditional communities that circumscribed their functioning, they have begun to wander everywhere in a space which is becoming more homogeneous and more extensive (1984: 31–40).

Certeau has been quoted at such length for two important reasons. Firstly, he provides a basic framework for the analysis of English in India; secondly, an authority is needed to lend support to the claims that are going to be made even if they are based on common sense. At present, only an author from the West like Turner can say that his own book 'relies upon no authority but its own; and it comes into the world naked of any scholarly apparatus', and that 'the references to authors and books in the body of the text indicate an indebtedness to them, rather than an attempt to subdue the reader with the eminence of my sources' (1995: v). Certeau presents what are called 'survival tactics' or the 'human will to live', the art practised by the 'weaker section' in any society — women, children, servants, slaves, etc. or anyone who is put under some control for the sake of their own survival. They know intuitively, as part of their survival, how to 'manipulate' and even 'destroy' the enemy, using all kinds of tactics. Not only fishes and plants but also human beings (from palace-women to school children, for example) know the 'survival tactics' which sometimes take the form of subversion even under adverse circumstances. In order to understand how the voice of the voiceless is articulated, and to articulate the everyday practices of our common 'hero', we need to study the subtle forms of domination and remote-control mechanisms in the modern world. Two such forms that have become powerful concepts in the modern world, developing under Western influences, are the 'masks of nationalism' and print capitalism.

3.4 The Masks of Nationalism

Group-loyalty and patriotism, which are difficult to define, have now taken the form of nationalism, which is equally difficult to define, because all the three are based on feelings and romantic themes. Scholars who have attempted to uncover the origins and development of 'nationalism' consider it a recent development in world history. Gellner (1983) testifies to the creation of a modern 'high culture' as the important sociological condition that has activated the nationalist imagination; but, Anderson (1986) defines 'nation' as 'imagined political community'. From any point of view, the origin of 'nation' was not a sudden phenomenon, nor was it a replacement of feudal, cultural or religious systems; though based on antiquity, it is a notion with a difference. As Anderson emphasizes, 'It would be short-sighted, however, to think of the imagined communities of nations as simply growing out of and replacing religious communities and dynastic realms. Beneath the decline of sacred communities, languages and lineages, a fundamental change was taking place in modes of apprehending the world, which, more than anything else, made it possible to "think" the nation' (op. cit.: 28). By 'thinking the nation' Anderson means constructing an abstraction called 'nation', and he argues that one crucial factor which precipitated the imagining of 'nation' was print-capitalism which is related to the emergence of the bourgeoisie. Print-capitalism is linked with literacy and education which created the educated class, the administrative class, and a middle class bureaucracy. Thus, in a way, the systems centred around privileged sacred languages were replaced by print-capitalism and 'nation' as a non-dynastic political entity where the systems of governance and power are controlled by some people in the name of 'masses' came into being. In an imagined community called nation, a section of the community — people unknown and unrelated to each other — control others in the imagined community in the name of nationalism. Powers — old or new — and their agents and agencies always cleverly manage their authority, and in contemporary societies they have very subtle and closely-knit procedures at their disposal to make people believe that the masses are the masters. Several belief-systems like nationalism, ideologies, political parties and many other social networks like education, schools, police, the administrative apparatus, the media net-work, etc. have become the instruments of control and maintenance of authority. At the same time these systems have become polluted like any other commodity in the present-day world. Nationalism, which is a belief-system, is no exception to this principle.

The case of the imaginary institution called India and Indian nationalism is very closely linked to the story of English in India or 'Indian English'. As Kaviraj (1992) rightly points out:

India, the objective reality of today's history, whose objectivity is tangible enough for people to try to preserve, to destroy, to uphold, to construct and dismember, the reality taken for granted in all attempts in favour and against, is not an object of discovery but of invention. It was historically instituted by the nationalist imagination of the nineteenth century. The exact form this reality took was one among many historical possibilities in that situation, though the fact that only this line of possibility came to be realized is so overwhelming that it is now difficult even to conceive of some of the others (p. 1).

Kaviraj cites Gramsci to show some similarities between Italian nationalism and Indian nationalism:

There is nothing of the sort [a national history] in Italy where one must search the past by torchlight to discover national feeling, and move with the aid of distinctions, interpretations and discreet silences. . . . The preconception that Italy has always been a nation complicates its entire history and requires anti-historical intellectual acrobatics. . . . History was political propaganda, it aimed to create national unity — that is, the nation — from the outside against tradition, by basing itself on literature. It was a wish, not a move based on already existing conditions (Gramsci in Kaviraj 1985: 9).

Kaviraj further argues:

The British could write 'histories of India' much more unproblematically than their Indian imitators, for they wrote of an India that was externally defined, a territory contingently unified by political expansion. To define the boundaries of British India was a simple operation; this merely required looking at the latest map of British annexations. By contrast, the India that Nehru so painstakingly discovered was an India more difficult to define, for the nationalists he represented sought to demarcate its boundaries by a more elusive internal principle. To give itself a history is the most fundamental act of self-identification of a community. The naming of an Indian nation, I wish to suggest happens in part through a narrative contract. To write a history of India beginning with the civilization of the Indus valley is marked by an impropriety. An India internally defined, an India of a national community, simply did not exist before the nineteenth century; there is, therefore, an inevitable element of 'fraudulence', in Gellner's sense, in all self-constructions. 'The history of India' is a massively self-evident thing to write about and this powerful transformation of something that is fundamentally insecure into something aggressively self-evident is precisely the mark of an ideological construct. It is ideological because there seems to be no other reasonable way of writing the history of these historical objects (op. cit.: 16).

The discovery of the nation-India is partly colonial and partly anti-colonial because the hostility against colonialism brought together regions, religions, linguistic and ethnic groups. Ever since that hostility has faded the forces that got united are struggling to establish their identities, and Indian nationalism is getting more and more weakened. This is why one is a Bengali or Punjabi or Tamilian while in India; only when one goes outside India, he/she becomes an 'Indian' because the outside world and the passport say so. No one in India feels he/she is an Indian.

In this context, it is easy to understand why the construct 'Indian English' is easily defined by outsiders like Peter Strevens or Larry Smith and Indians like Kachru who live outside, and so elusive to those who look at it from inside. Like Indian nationalism, 'Indian English' is 'fundamentally insecure' since the notion 'nation-India' is insecure. One can argue that insecurity is a property of not just Indian nationalism but of nationalism in general. Anderson, Homi Bhabha and others point out that nations are imagined communities but the essential difference is that the subcontinent that later became India, Pakistan and Bangladesh was essentially amorphous — not based on any single concept or relations of religion, language, community, culture or economy. It was essentially a feudal society where anything that could be named — language, religion, region, caste, etc. — was used more to divide and exploit people than to unite them. Nationalism came in as a handy instrument to divide and exploit them. Nationality has a sentimental side which may or may not be based on race, language, religion, natural frontiers or what is known as geography, or a combination of these. Renan argued almost a century ago that 'the United States and England, Latin America and Spain, speak the same languages yet do not form single nations. Conversely, Switzerland, so well made, since she was made with the consent of her different parts, numbers three or four languages' (Bhabha 1990: 16). But the case of Switzerland is more of an exception than the rule and the size and geography of Switzerland is very different from that of India. India is not a monolithic whole but a curious mixture of many things. It defies any kind of classification, and the methodology needed to study the situation in the Indian subcontinent is at present not available. The study of English in India, therefore, necessitates a reinvestigation of several concepts currently used by scholars.

3.5 Print-Capitalism in the Indian Context

Anderson points out that in the West, the feudal system and religion, which were centred around privileged script-languages, were displaced by print-capitalism, which 'created' the vernaculars. The vernaculars operated below the privileged realm of Latin and in effect, certain 'dialects' became more powerful due to a new kind of fixity and access to masses, gained through printing.

In the East, printing was known in the fifth century and printing with wooden blocks was in use in China and India but it was not practised as a commercial activity. The earliest printed texts found in the subcontinent were religious texts; printing was also used in the area of textiles, printing cards and paper money (see *Encyclopaedia Britannica*, vol. 18. 'History of Printing', pp. 541–3). Printing was not involved in learning because education was imparted through the oral mode. The concept of a book that could be bought and read did not exist until the Europeans brought the printing press to India in the sixteenth century.

The written mode, of course, offered a patterning principle in the evolution of the civilization of the Indian subcontinent. Coulmas (1989) and Goody (1986, 1987) have discussed writing with special reference to India but they differ in their purposes and consequently, in their arguments. Coulmas examines the relationship between writing and the Indian society, and Goody pursues the question whether the Vedas represent purely oral literature or orally composed literature of a society that knew writing. Goody argues that in the Vedic period literature was entrenched in writing although composition and transmission of literature was done through the oral mode, and that writing preceded oral literature; but Coulmas maintains that writing came long after the awareness about the cultivation of language, and as a result writing was deployed for purposes different from those of the spoken mode. He says: 'Notice first that a highly conscious and normative attitude towards language was present in India before the advent of writing . . . writing was soon instrumentalized for the already recognized purpose of language cultivation, and it was the cultivated forms of language that were reduced to writing' (1989: 194). Coulmas assumes that oral literature preceded writing. Though this seems to be a controversial issue, it is certain that the tradition of oral composition and oral transmission continued even after writing was used. For a long time teaching and learning was done through the oral mode but the formalization and codification of knowledge was done through the written mode. The written mode must have been instrumental in cultivating and preserving the best in language. Moreover, as Coulmas rightly points out, Sanskrit became a language whose spoken realization was dependent on rules committed to writing. Sanskrit was a language that very few learnt and fewer still learnt to write it; yet it was upheld as the repository of all that is best in language. Prakrit, considered a 'corrupt' spoken form of Sanskrit, served the purposes of daily existence. Prakrit was also used as the language of administration by the Mauryan dynasty for some time but it neither replaced nor eclipsed Sanskrit as the 'high' prestige language.

The history of writing in India shows that the written mode was assigned high functions and spoken vernaculars continued to exist but were not committed to writing for a long time. This 'functional diglossia' created a kind of linguistic environment wherein it was not thought necessary to bring writing close to speech, and the spoken mode was to be guided by writing in formal and rhetorical situations. Thus, writing was a means for high functions ('high' in the sense of repository of the best, and not in terms of the hegemonical 'high' status), and speech was meant to face the vicissitudes of daily existence (in that sense 'low' functions, and not in the demeaning sense). Even when the modern Indian languages were committed to writing, the written mode was used for 'high' functions (chiefly, literary) and their distinct scripts did not lead to mass illiteracy, nor to a large-scale use of the written form by the masses. This was the environment in which modern Indian languages evolved without displacing Sanskrit from its prestigious position.

But this situation is very different from the European situation; in Europe the written mode in print was instrumental in the assertion of the modern European languages against the hegemony of the written mode of Latin. The diminution of the hegemonic power of Latin is referred to by Goody as the democratization of the concept of language in Europe. In the history of Europe, mass production of the written mode by printing and its dissemination through the print market demolished the privileged status of Latin, the first 'written' language of Europe. In the history of the subcontinent, however, an interrelated hegemony of language-religion-polity did not exist; but, writing, Sanskrit and repository prestige functions came to be interlinked in the Indian subcontinent. Irrespective of what came first, written or oral literature, it can be said that the written mode participated in the patterning of functions in pre-British India. Initially, some domains of human activity were assigned to the written mode; these domains were restricted to literary activity and pursuit of knowledge in areas like philosophy, grammar, astronomy, mathematics, aesthetics. Later on, the administrative and legal domains were also assigned to the written mode. It is essential to remember that the functional patterning was done by the written mode per se, and not by any particular written language. In the history of the subcontinent it is not just one language but always more than one that has performed the written functions. Sanskrit and Persian are the most prominent ones that were used for long periods of time by various rulers for administrative and legal written functions. The history of the process of extension of the written mode from repository prestige functions to administrative and legal functions has not been studied carefully but it appears that it was necessitated by the Mauryan Empire and later, by the Mughal Empire. In other words, a new patterning which did not depend on lineage and feudal loyalty was evolved, and it may be called 'the State' (Thapar 1984). The relationship of the people and 'the State' was mediated in terms of the economic functions of paying revenue which was carried out through the functionaries of 'the State' who articulated their roles through the written mode. Thus, the two factors which were interrelated were 'the State' and the written mode.

In addition, as Kesavan (1985, 1988) indicates, the problem faced by printers in India was not how to represent Indian languages in the written form but how to adopt Indian scripts to printing; not all languages in India had their scripts but the point is that the concept of the written mode was evolved prior to the introduction of the printing-press in the sixteenth century. Therefore, it cannot be said that Indian languages and printing form a homogeneous field as they did in Europe. In India, the printing press that came with the Europeans, in a way gave more stability to the nation-transplant through the English language that came with the British and helped colonialism and later, anti-colonialism. Both made use of printing as well as the English language, but, in that process the vast majority of people, the millions brought up in the oral tradition and in the indigenous educational systems, got marginalized and became 'illiterate'. Maybe, this is the implication of what Mahatma Gandhi says: 'The British administrators, when they came to India, instead of taking hold of things as they were, began to root them out. They scratched the soil and began to look at the root, and left the root like that, and the beautiful tree perished. The village schools were not good enough for the British administrator; so, he came out with his programme' (Mahatma Gandhi cited in Dharampal 1983). They not only destroyed the indigenous educational system but also created a new system which made the British and, after their departure, the English-knowing Indians all powerful. Thus, English-education and print-capitalism created a new urban-class of Indians thereby cutting out the rural masses, their oral traditions, and the Indian languages and their literature from the mainstream. Mahatma Gandhi stated in October 1931, that 'India to-day is much more illiterate than it was before fifty or hundred years ago' (cited in Dharampal 1983) and, as Dharampal rightly points out, even those who wrote about the Indian educational system before the British came did not take the oral traditions seriously because there were no printed documents to support the claims and historical research had to rely only on printed sources.

Even after fifty years of political independence, very little has been done to change the situation created by the British because the nation — 'India' came about as the result of colonialism as well as anticolonialism, but more importantly, it came about by replacing the British. How in the Empire called 'India', English education became a mask for exploitation has been narrated by Gauri Viswanathan in her *Masks of Conquest* (but, to be authentic, the unmasking had to be done only in Columbia University in the USA and that too in English).

That is only one part of the story. How a section of Indians too asked for English education, though for a different purpose, and how the class of English-educated Indians, when the 'moment of arrival' came in the 'nation' called India, not only took over the reins of power but also got the 'masks of conquest' and repainted them with nationalistic colours has not been told though this part of the story is known to the common people. Leaders like Jawaharlal Nehru equated the nation-India with the Congress and the Congress with the Congressmen mostly from the northern part of India, though the southern part of the subcontinent participated actively in the independence movement. In a way, leaders of that generation were conscious of the gap between the nation-state and the nation-people and Nehru discovered India in 'people like them and me, who were spread out all over this vast land. Bharat Mata, Mother India, was essentially these millions of people, and victory to her meant victory to these people. You are parts of this Bharat Mata, I told them, you are in a manner yourselves Bharat Mata . . . ' (Nehru 1946: 49). But the 'leaders' that came later made a clear distinction between 'us' and 'them'. Nehru himself pointed this out with reference to some 'irresponsible' leaders like Ramachandra, a peasant leader of Uttar Pradesh. This observation is true of all 'leaders' now: 'Having organised the peasantry to some extent he made all manner of promises to them, vague and nebulous but full of hope for them. He had programmes of any kind and when he had brought them to a pitch of excitement he tried to shift the responsibility to others . . . he turned out later to be a very irresponsible and unreliable person' (Nehru, p. 53). This statement of Nehru is true of all 'leaders' and politicians in contemporary India whether they are from the north or the south, the east or the west. English education in India has become one of the masks of nationalism, and it serves as a powerful tool which turns the vast majority into illiterates — into a 'silent majority' which is marginalized while the English-educated minority from the urban areas is centralized.

Certeau refers to writing as a 'modern' mythical practice and discusses in detail the ideology of 'informing' through books and education in general. He says:

> In the eighteenth century, the ideology of the Enlightenment claimed that the book was capable of reforming society, that educational popularization could transform manners and customs, that an elite's products could, if they were sufficiently widespread,

remodel a whole nation. This myth of Education inscribed a theory of consumption in the structures of cultural politics. To be sure, by the logic of technical and economic development that it mobilized, this politics has led to the present system that inverts the ideology that formerly sought to spread 'Enlightenment'. The means of diffusion are now dominating the ideas they diffuse. The medium is replacing the message. The 'pedagogical' procedures for which the educational system was the support have developed to the point of abandoning as useless or destroying the professional 'body' that perfected them over the span of two centuries: today, they make up the apparatus which, by realizing the ancient dream of enclosing all citizens and each one in particular, gradually destroys the goal, the convictions, and the educational institutions of the Enlightenment. . . . This text was formerly found at school. Today, the text is society itself. It takes urbanistic, industrial, commercial, or televised forms. But the mutation that caused the transition from educational archaeology to the technocracy of the media did not touch the assumption that consumption is essentially passive — an assumption that is precisely what should be examined. . . . The result of class ideology and technical blindness, this legend is necessary for the system that distinguishes and privileges authors, educators, revolutionaries, in a word, 'producers' in contrast with those who do not produce (1984: 166–7).

But Certeau further adds that the consumers are not as passive as they are supposed to be:

Formerly, the Church, which instituted a social division between its intellectual clerks and the 'faithful', ensured the Scriptures the status of a 'Letter' that was supposed to be independent of its readers and, in fact, possessed by its exegetes: the autonomy of the text was the reproduction of sociocultural relationships within the institution whose officials determined what parts of it should be read. When the institution began to weaken, the reciprocity between the text and its readers (which the institution hid) appeared, as if by withdrawing the Church had opened to view the indefinite plurality of the 'writings' produced by readings. The creativity of the reader grows as the institution that controlled it declines. This process, visible from the Reformation onward, already disturbed the pastors of the seventeenth century. Today, it is the sociopolitical mechanisms of the schools, the press, or television that isolate the text controlled by the teacher or the producer from its readers. But behind the theatrical d'ecor of this new orthodoxy is hidden (as in the earlier ages) the silent transgressive, ironic or poetic activity of readers (or television viewers) who maintain their reserve in private and without the knowledge of the 'masters' (1984: 172).

He concludes this section by saying that 'we mustn't take people for fools'.

What Certeau says of reading, writing and education in general is true of English education in India. The British introduced English in India for 'enlightening' the natives and the colonizers wore English education as a mask to establish their empire; during the struggle for independence, local elites used English as a tool against the colonizers (Kachru 1986: 7). However, after independence, the same practices — the dominant system of administration, the same educational system — are being continued by the 'leaders', politicians, local elites who plotted to oust the British, the teachers of English, and the media in the name of technological development and modernization. 'Invisible strategies' can play a more important role than organized language policies (Kachru 1991: 8). As noted by Ahmad (1992: 75), 'India has numerically by far the largest professional petty bourgeoisie, fully consolidated as a distinct social entity and sophisticated enough in its claim to English culture for it to aspire to have its own writers, publishing houses, and a fully fledged home market for English books.' The non-resident Indians too, who live outside the country (particularly in the West) for their own personal comfort and convenience and talk about the Indian diaspora, post-colonialism, American imperialism, Indian culture, Indian English, etc. in their own 'foreign' accent, make use of these areas and their English-education as commodities; they act as 'double agents' and 'work' for both the cultures — Western as well as their own — making use of both to further their own cause. As Ahmad says:

> Those who came as graduate students and then joined the faculties, especially in the Humanities and the Social Sciences, tended to come from upper classes in their home countries. In the process of relocating themselves in the metropolitan countries, they needed documents of their assertion, proof that they had always been oppressed. Books that connected oppression with class were not very useful, because they neither came from the working class nor were intending to join that class in their new country.... What the upwardly mobile professionals in this new immigration needed were narratives of oppression that would get them preferential

treatment . . . (op. cit.: 196). (This is true of many, including Ahmad himself!)

These practices are not very different from what happened in the earlier stages in the Indian subcontinent. Brahmanic education was very much elitist and whole classes of people were excluded from the study of Sanskrit. Buddhist education, which started as a revolt against the elitism of Brahmanic education, preserved a number of elements it opposed, and ultimately it did not reach those whose interests it advocated. Similarly, Muslim conquests of India produced another kind of religious education parallel to the Hindu system of education. All these resulted only in layers of elitism and helped only certain groups and their agents. As a result the vast majority of people remained illiterate. The role of elites in language movements (Annamalai 1979) and the competition between emerging elites after the departure of the 'foreign elite', the British, have been discussed by some (Selma Sonntag 1995). English education added one more layer — a class layer — well fortified by the print media and the publishing trade, and a layer that cuts across the existing caste and religious layers. As Ahmad says, 'what is at issue at present is not the possibility of its ejection but the mode of its assimilation into our social fabric, and the manner in which this language, like any other substantial structure of linguistic difference, is used in the process of class formation and social privilege, here and now' (1992: 77). We must see what the vast majority of people must be doing — maybe, something else without the knowledge of their 'masters', but the 'masters' too are not fools.

That is where we have to consider another important factor, the quality of education. Not all sections of the population receive the same quality of English education. Tollefson (1991) shows how the English taught to lower-class students in the Philippines is both qualitatively and quantitatively insufficient for those who want to apply for higher-level jobs. In India too, like in many other developing countries, those who can afford, send their children to the best English medium schools in the country from where they go to the best universities like the MIT, Stanford, Harvard in the USA and other 'advanced' countries; others send their children to the so-called English medium schools that have mushroomed in every part of the country. Most of these 'English medium' schools teach not only other subjects like physical sciences and social studies but also English through the regional language, and the teachers who 'teach' are themselves products of such educational institutions. The degrees that the teachers hold are not necessarily the indicators of their competence. All teaching and learning, if there be any, is examination-oriented and the examination system tests nothing except the learner's capacity to reproduce it. As a result of all these factors, people are only being exploited in the name of English education. English education has created a distinction between the 'convent' educated products of the most expensive and the best public schools, and the rest. The quality of English that is taught in the name of 'English' is not to be ignored while considering the role of English in India. Those who can afford, get imported whisky and the best English education; at the next lower level, people go in for 'Indian-Made-Foreign-Liquor' (IMFL) and better English education; at the lower levels, most people will have to be satisfied with the government-approved locally brewed liquor sold in 'toddy shops' and government-run English medium schools; and still lower are those who consume the illicit arrack, the least expensive but the deadliest, while their children learn how to say 'Daddy and Mummy' in some 'teaching shops' which pretend to be 'English medium schools'. The basic rule is the same — one for the Master who can afford it, and one for the poor boy/girl who lives down the lane!

Thus, in the subcontinent, a linguistic area deeply entrenched in oral traditions, religious and caste structures, the print-publishing trade along with English education in recent times established the colony of the written word over the 'voice' of the people. A written constitution, written rules and regulations gave the English-educated administrators, in a sense the class of 'interpreters' envisaged by Macaulay, a splendid opportunity to become interpreters and manipulators of the written word. The modern 'scriptural' system, print-technology and print-publishing trade, and the authority to interpret the written word by the 'educated elite' and the semi-elite partly replaced the status of the Scriptures, the authority of the old orthodoxy and its hierarchies, while adding new social stratifications and class relationships that cut across all other hierarchies.

The politics of 'interpretation and reading' must be understood against the backdrop of the practices that have been in operation, making the 'new' practices politicizable. Like the print-media, the electronic-media too uses the 'verbal and/or iconic' writing, and the ideology that a society can be produced and moulded by a 'scriptural' system, and that 'the efficiency of production implies the inertia of consumption'. The following passage becomes very significant in the context of what has been said so far:

> The installation of the scriptural apparatus of modern 'discipline', a process that is inseparable from the 'reproduction' made possible by the development of printing, was accompanied by a double isolation from the 'people' (in opposition to the 'bourgeoisie') and from the 'voice' (in opposition to the written). Hence the conviction that far, too far away from economic and administrative powers, 'the People speaks'. This speech is alternately seductive and dangerous, unique, lost (despite violent and brief outbreaks), constituted as the 'Voice of the people' by its very repression, the object of nostalgic longing, observation and regulation, and above all of the immense campaign that has rearticulated on writing by means of education. Today it is 'recorded' in every imaginable way, normalized, audible everywhere, but only when it has been 'cut' (as one 'cuts a record'), and thus mediated by radio, television, or the phonograph record, and 'cleaned up' by the techniques of diffusion. Where it does manage to infiltrate itself, the sound of the body often becomes an imitation of this part of itself that is produced and reproduced by the media — i.e. the copy of its own artifact. It is thus useless to set off in quest of this voice that has been simultaneously colonized and mythified by recent Western history (Certeau 1984: 131–2).

From the mere sketch that has been presented so far, it can be understood that the invention and development of writing and printing has changed the very concept of language in such a way that the praxis of a given 'lect' has come to be entrenched in the written mode though in contemporary linguistics it is often repeated that speech is primary and writing is secondary. Jacques Derrida has said that 'they have as their ultimate reference . . . the presence of a value or of a meaning (*sens*) that is supposed to be anterior to difference'; but in the context of the culture of control that we are considering, we must not forget that the anterior intention is, in the words of Jean-Francois Lyotard 'to arrest the meanings of words once and for all, that is what Terror wants' and to establish scriptural imperialism. Reading and writing have become evangelical; new belief-systems or 'religions' like nationalism, print-capitalism, politics, media-control, and pop-culture have displaced old religions and their scriptures.

3.6 The Native-Speaker Myth

It is in this context that we have to critically examine another concept — the concept of the 'native-speaker'. A new myth has been created by monolingual users of English that a native-speaker is the centre of all decision-making in a language. In multilingual societies where different languages are allocated different functions, learners acquire two or three languages simultaneously as 'native' languages, and it is very difficult to say which one is the mother tongue or the first language. Such linguistic richness is an asset and it becomes part of the user's linguistic competence. Sociolinguistics must include multilingualism in its formulation of communicative competence, and it should be able to integrate synchrony and diachrony, speech and writing, inductive and deductive approaches which are treated as separate compartments by modern linguistics. It is obvious that the social context of language use is created by dynamic social forces, but the social forces in multilingual/multicultural societies have not been properly studied and incorporated in formulating the notion 'native-speaker'.

The question 'who is a native-speaker?' has not been satisfactorily answered. Medgyes (1994) shows that all the criteria that have been proposed to describe/define a native-speaker are fuzzy. He argues that a child born in an English-speaking country who acquired the language during childhood can move to a non-English speaking country and forget the language acquired. It is also difficult to specify the duration of childhood — will it be 3, 9, or 12 years? What about a child in a family where the mother speaks English and the father French/Hindi/Chinese? What about a native-speaker of English who cannot read or write the language? Such a person will literally be a *speaker* and not a reader or a writer. Paradoxically, when we talk about teaching a foreign/second language, four skills — listening, speaking, reading and writing (LSRW) are taken into account but in formulating the notion 'native-speaker', reading and writing are left out. Can we consider an illiterate or semiliterate person, whose linguistic competence is only partial and not comprehensive, a native-speaker? What about creative writers like Joseph Conrad, Wole Soyinka or Nobokov? Are they native-speakers? Can there be persons who are native-speakers of two or three languages? Many such issues can be raised but we take for granted that a native-speaker is one who has a 'native-like' command of the language.

It is so very obvious that even in monolingual communities all native-speakers of a given language are not 'native-writers'; speech is 'caught' and picked up as part of one's growth in a linguistic environment but writing must be learned and cultivated. It is assumed that the entire language, including reading, writing, and stylistic competence, comes naturally to the native-speaker, and there is nothing to be learned. This is not really so: some areas of any language are 'foreign' even to its native-speakers.

Though writing brought about standardization, it created illiteracy and helped the literates to dominate over the illiterates. Even in English-speaking countries like the UK and the USA, there is a lot of illiteracy, functional as well as total. A considerable number of native-speakers of English are literally *speakers* of English and not writers though to a certain extent, readers. People become speakers without much effort; for example, the ordinary speaker of a language, who has been *speaking* the language of a particular community, at the age of twenty-four or twenty-five, may be about twenty-three in terms of his/her *speaking-age* but three or four in terms of the *reading-age,* and only one or two in terms of the *writing-age* because of the fact that very little reading or writing has been done. The 'age' in a particular area of competence is to be determined by the duration of exposure and use in that area. In addition, in the majority of cases, apart from professional writers, the writing of the native-speakers is speech-oriented and they write as they speak, i.e. they do not distinguish between *there* and *their, his* and *he is, he has* and *he is* and they have very little knowledge of spelling and punctuation. Just like the amusing specimens of non-native English collected by the English rulers, it is possible to collect 'amusing specimens' of written English by native-speakers. Given below are some examples from the written English used in the USA:

In the hospital:	Visitation Hours (for Visiting Hours)
At the Grand Canyon:	View Points (for 'Viewing Points')
In a motel:	All Rooms $35 (for any room)
In an aircraft:	Press the button for flotation

> Parking Lots: Parking Restricted 24 Hours A Day
>   (Is the meaning clear?)
> Circular issued by American Diabetes Association:
>   Driver do not carry change.
> In the novel *Native Son* by Richard Wright, 1940/1987/1989:
> i. Gentlemen, let's don't be childish . . . (p. 340)
> ii. All his life he had been knowing that sooner . . . (p. 255)

What is 'recommended' as standard usage in grammar books is not followed by native-speakers. For example, in American English *enjoy* is used intransitively (*Go and enjoy*); Americans *purchase* a pencil (though the verb is recommended for bigger things). It has been the experience of many who teach English in the USA (and Prator should note this) that college level students do not have even high school level proficiency in written English though many of these are native-speakers of English. Given below is an actual specimen of the written English of a native-speaker in one of the universities in the USA on a topic that the undergraduate students like and are comfortable with; so, the readers need not be taken aback by the topic.

> I think when sex is combined with love it is an essential way to have self fulfillment, and it confirms the love between two people. Having intercourse is special act of sharing and intimacy, I find it more than a genital feeling. I also believe that premature leaps to sex without a love base will ruin a love base from ever happening I find. Todays society has extremely changed from the sexual revolution of the 60's that I wasn't even around for it 'dam . . . .' The many different views of love and sex have more open and easier to talk about. Due to our changing sexual culture there are many views and expectations about love. People are free to create their own morals and values about love and sex. Each idea about sex will differ from person to person. Since outlook on our society, this proves that there is no moral obligations about love and sex only expanded ideas. Sexual decision are unfortunately one's own moral worth, and for some people it rests in this superstition that sex is the best way. Many of my friends find dating and having a variety of relationships is the best way to achieve there self-fulfilment. There is no universal obligation to link sex and love in any one way. There are varieties of moral ideals dealing with sex that are perfectly acceptable. Basically ideals create obligations to fit there individual needs.

The competence of the native-speaker, unless it is *idealized*, is not uniform even in the case of a monolingual native-speaker. In the case of native-speakers of English, the majority of them are monolinguals because even during the colonial or neo-colonial periods, as the rulers, they did not feel the necessity of learning any other language. As rulers they distorted all other languages (for example, even expressions like *Ya Hasan Ya Husain* became Hobson-Jobson and names of places like *Kanyakumari* became Cape Comorin), and 'borrowed' whatever fascinated them. On the contrary, a non-native user's speech is writing-oriented since in the process of learning, writing comes first and speech is learned through writing; that is why many Indians 'speak English like books' but their spelling and punctuation is generally better than that of *native-speakers* of English and, as far as the written mode is concerned, the competence of the non-native user of English is more rule-governed than speech-governed.

Moreover, most Indian users of English are bilinguals and multilinguals. Even among the famous leaders, some of whom were educated outside India, there has been 'a great tradition of bilinguality and polyglot ease in communication' (Ahmad 1992: 76). Nehru could speak Urdu and Hindi well but wrote only in English and, it is said that J. Krishnamurti sobbed and called aloud for his brother in Telugu when he heard of his brother's death. Though some leaders like Jinnah could not function beyond English, there were others like Maulana Azad, an erudite scholar of Arabic and Persian and a great master of Urdu, who read English only haltingly. The 'national' intelligentsia, according to Ahmad, 'is now rooted much more decisively in English than in any of the indigenous languages' (op. cit.: 76) but there are a number of 'leaders' who cannot function in English and some are Chief Ministers at the State level; bilinguality is not on the decline. It is but natural that in the case of bi-/multi-linguals, the use of any one of the languages gets domain-restricted unlike in the case of monolinguals. And it is in this cultural-linguistic context that we must investigate the use of English by Indians.

3.7 One for Transaction and One for Contemplation

It is obvious from what has been said so far that Western linguistics and pragmatics have not been able to capture the dialogism, the epistemological mode of a world dominated by heteroglossia (Bakhtin 1981). Though Western theories and thought are projected as *the* most 'scientific', they reflect only the Western point of view and thinking. In Western linguistics and pragmatics, for example, it is commonly said that language is meant for communication which, obviously, over-emphasizes the transactional culture of the Western society that encourages more external transactions. Language is also meant for contemplation; in India and generally in the East, one is encouraged to go inwards in search of the real meaning after understanding the futility of external transactions; the symbolic function of language and its arbitrariness gives way to the intrinsic sound-sense relationship as a result of one's contemplations. This has been dismissed as 'unscientific' and false by Western thinking. Though weak, Western theories are considered powerful because of the 'power' and the dominant role of the West.

In bi-/multi-lingual communities, users switch from language to language according to the demands of occasions, and the functions and roles they play in a given context. They switch from code A to code B, and from code B to code C, and so on, and produce a chain of codes. Quite often they use one code for contemplation and another for transaction, one for intimate situations and another for formal contexts, one for technical and academic areas and another for non-technical areas, and so on. They not only code-switch but also culture-switch, and this happens very naturally in multi-lingual and multi-cultural societies. Monolinguals may consider these processes as contradictions, interference or inter-phenomena but multi-linguals perform very well in their world, using verbal tactics like creative artists and effortlessly switching codes, cultures, levels and styles.

How people in the Indian subcontinent, the users of different linguistic systems, have used English, and what tactics they have adopted in handling different systems over the years will have to be studied carefully. The next chapter documents the use of English by Indians to see if the texts cited are only amusing specimens, or representatives of Indian English, or illustrations of Indians' 'tactics'.

Chapter Four

Indians' English: A Sociolinguistic Contemplation

> 'There is something even more challenging and puzzling than change, and that is the absence of change.'
> — William Labov, *Language and Variation*

4.1 Five Phases of the History of English in India

The history of English in India begins on 31st December, 1599, the day the East India Company was granted permission to trade in the 'East Indies', as the subcontinent was then referred to. In order to develop a profile of a sociolinguistic history of English in India, the time span is divided into five phases, and five landmarks in the history of the subcontinent are used to demarcate the five phases. They are:

- 1600 — the year the East India Company was started;
- 1813 — the year the East India Company's Charter (for trade in the subcontinent) was renewed;
- 1857 — the Mutiny year — this was also the year the first three universities were set up at Bombay, Calcutta and Madras;
- 1904 — the year the Indian Universities Act was passed, which gave the British government a tighter control over colleges and universities;
- 1947 — the year India became politically independent.

These landmarks demarcate the following five phases:
  i) 1600–1813 : the pre-transportation phase,
  ii) 1813–1857 : the transportation phase,
  iii) 1857–1904 : the dissemination phase,
  iv) 1904–1947 : the institutionalization phase, and
  v) 1947–1990 : the identity phase.

Each phase in the following account contains a threefold presentation: (a) a profile of the history of English in India, (b) specimens of English used by Indians, and (c) what the data shows: some observations on the salient features of the specimens given in b; c tries to relate a and b.

4.2 An Investigation of the Written Mode

The data for this study consists of specimens of English written by Indians from 1600–1990. The specimens that comprise the data have been analysed in terms of users, uses and styles of use, types of documents, and attitudes reflected in the use of English. However, in order to make it readable and non-technical we have included only a representative sample of the analysis here; a comprehensive analysis is given in Burde 1992. The chronology of events that go into the delineation of the profile of the history of English in India is given in the Appendix at the end. The Appendix consists of five sections which correspond to the five phases of the presentation in the text. Though 126 specimens were collected for analysis for a Ph.D. thesis, due to limitations of space, at least one specimen that is representative of each domain is given in full for each phase (for more specimens, see Burde 1992).

The British merchants did not assume political power on the Indian subcontinent immediately after their arrival in 1600 AD. They remained merchants for almost a century and a half. Their language too was not a codified and standardized language at that time, and those who came to India were mostly uneducated merchants, sailors, and soldiers. Some of them might have had some sort of schooling which did not include learning the English language. The missionaries and scholars who came a little later were learned in the sense of having received classical education which again did not include English language and literature because only by 1580 AD. English was acknowledged (in England) to have literary potential. The Latin stronghold on the English literary writing may be said to have loosened in the sixteenth century. As late as 1687 Newton preferred Latin to write his 'Principia' and Dr Johnson's dictionary was published in 1755. English was not taught in the schools in England till the nineteenth century. Thus, when the British came to the Indian subcontinent, England and the English language were still in the making. It was only in the nineteenth century that 'English-educated' Englishmen interacted with Indians (some of them English-educated) in India.

Therefore, it can be said that the concept of 'governing' the Indian subcontinent took a definite shape for the British merchants only towards the end of the eighteenth century. England's own political development, the Industrial Revolution, the utility of India as a 'market', and political supremacy over Mughals and other Europeans on the Indian subcontinent shaped the British policy of ruling the colony and establishing 'the State' only by 1800. As far as English is concerned, the period between 1600 and 1813 can be regarded as the pre-transportation phase.

4.2.1 Phase I: 1600–1813 — The pre-transportation phase

(a) The profile
The pre-transportation phase was the period of power struggle to secure for Christendom the supremacy over the 'gorgeous East'. The Portuguese, the Dutch, the French, and the English in their race towards domination did not take any active interest in transporting their languages. Even the East India Company (EIC) imparted English education only to the children of Anglo-Indians and the children of the European employees of the Company. The Patashalas, the Madrassahs, the Persian schools called 'Maktabs', other schools teaching through the modern Indian languages, and domestic instruction formed the basis of what the British termed as 'indigenous education' almost till the end of the eighteenth century. Only when the Company became a political power, as part of its 'tendency towards endearing Her Majesty's Government to the natives, some centres of learning were started and Christian missionaries were allowed to undertake educational activities to spread Western light and knowledge and 'to instruct the Gentoos that shall be servants or slaves of the same Company or of their agents, in the Protestant religion.'

The EIC had the status of 'jagheerdars' under the Mughal sovereigns till 1757. The victory at the Battle of Plassey gave them political strength, and with the Diwani Act of 1765 the British became the virtual rulers of Bengal. Subsequently, they fought many battles but rarely won any till 1798; they had to sign peace treaties but by converting these into 'Subsidiary Alliance' they were able to weaken the Indian rulers and make them dependent on the British for defence, political support and internal security. It was only by the end of the eighteenth century that the British were able to bring the Indian subcontinent (except the Punjab and Sindh) under their control.

The missionaries became active in the eighteenth century. Their main aim was proselytization and the means to this end were the Indian languages, not English. For example, William Cary, an English missionary, brought out a book on Sanskrit grammar, and an English translation of the *Ramayana* and started a newspaper in Bengali in 1818. Sporadic emergence of educational institutions, mostly managed by the missionaries, marked the latter half of the eighteenth century but the medium of instruction was not English. There is no evidence of English being taught as a subject before 1800, and there was no clear policy on education until the EIC was forced to do so by the Charter Act of 1813.

In the first phase of the history of English in India, the interaction in English was between two disparate systems. On the one hand were the Indian rulers with their politicking, intrigues and internal feuds for maintaining territorial control, and on the other, the British merchants who were trying to become rulers. The interlocutors were mainly the feudal chiefs, their courtiers, the higher rung of the feudal court hierarchy, and the East India Company; the locale was the urban and the feudal power centres. The interaction mainly related to political usurpation of the Indian States which gave the EIC the territorial control necessary for trading. The political usurpation led to the emergence of the British bureaucracy which induced the use of English for certain restricted written functions. The written functions (writing petitions, commercial dealings, advertisements by Indian merchants, etc.) were earlier performed in Persian. Wherever the British gained control, some of these functions had to be performed in English. Since there was no formal education in English available during the first phase, the inadequate knowledge of English, the use of Persian for royal, administrative, and legal purposes with its royal ostentatious formality, and the deeply entrenched feudal mentality in the Indian subcontinent must have resulted in the 'affective vocabulary' which is found in the petitions written during this phase. The ornate style used in the earlier forms of English must have also contributed to this register. It should be noted here that the ostentatious formality in written correspondence, especially in official correspondence, is found even today in the Indians' use of English.

Indians' English • 83

(b) The data
Domains: political and its extensions — bureaucratic and commercial

Specimen I: Political (diplomacy)
An extract from Raja Manikchand's letter to Colonel Clive
(Source: *Indian Records Series.* Bengal in 1756–57)

23 December 1756

I have had the pleasure to receive your most friendly letter. To hear you are in good health gives me the sincerest pleasure. Your sending a copy of your address to the Nobob enclosed in your letter to me for my perusal I esteem as an instance of your friendship. Finding in it many improper expressions and concluding that by sending me the copy you desired to know my sentiments upon it, I have, therefore, made some alterations in it and return it entrusted to Radakissen Mullick, who will deliver it to you. You will write your letter after that form and dispatch it again to me, and I will forward it to the Nabob. You write that you are desirous of peaceable measures. I likewise am as desirous, as nothing is better than peace. To take away every cause of ill-will or contention this is the part of a good man. For the rest you will be informed from Radakissen of my further sentiments. You write that you send three (letters) for the Nobob, one from yourself, one from Asephad Doula, one from Anarvedi Cawn. Two of these I have received, but that from Anarvedi Cawn is missing. Perhaps by some mistake it may not have been sent. This I have thought proper to acquaint you with. I hope you will continue to inform me of your health, and look upon me as your well-wisher.

Specimen II: Political — Bureaucracy (petitions)
Kissenbuxey's Petition
(Source: *Home Dept., Public Proceedings Volumes, 1757*)

Year : 1757
The Humble Petition of Kissenbuxey,
Inhabitant of Calcutta

To
The Hon'ble Roger Drake Esqr.
President & Governor & c. Council

Mostly Humbly Sheweth,
That your Petitioner being an old Resident of Calcutta whose dwelling House is situated in Govindpore which House has cost your petitioner a large sum of money and as your Honour & C as : Orders for pulling down the same, will be soon put in Execution. Therefore

most humbly Request your Honour & C as Orders may be permitted to those Gentlemen who has been Estimators for the Houses already pull'd down, or any others to view that Building & Sett a just Value upon the same & your petitioner further prays your Honr. & c. will take this case in consideration as your Petitioner is Reduced to great Necessitys by the Capture of this place & without this humble supplication be granted by your Honr & c. your petitioner must be entirely Ruined & Reduced in utmost misery And so forth.

Specimen III: Political (conspiracy)
Two letters by 'natives' enclosed in
Colonel Sir John Cumming's letter
(Source: *Poona Residency Correspondence, Volume I*)
No. 1. (From Goordat Singh and Man Singh
to Colonel Cumming.)

14th May 1785

Pateel makes this negotiation and engagement with us that being united together we should attach the country of the English gentlemen and of the Nawab Vizier, and that before upon the same advice we had plundered Chandausi & c. As the Nawab Vizier is our neighbour and you gentlemen are men of truth and are steadfast to your engagements and this stranger having become strong in this country will injure the whole world, if you gentlemen should be desirous of friendship, the Chiefs of the Khalsa are not separated from you, they wish for mutual connection. We also are ready from our hearts and souls; we will settle all their engagements conformably to your advice, and 30,000 horses belonging to us have crossed from Manhā — Know them also to be united with you — In the end he will be alarmed. Whatever may be your opinion write it thro' Shewa Sing, who is going to your presence: from his discourse you will learn all particular and reply on their truth.

No. 2. (From Banga Singh Bahadur, Goordat Sing,
Baksh Sing Bahadur and Joda Sing to Colonel Cumming.)

At this time between us and Pateel Saheb a negotiation of friendship is in hand. He is desirous that uniting us to himself he should raise commotions on the other side of the Ganges. We before also entirely from his advice marched to that quarter and destroyed Chandausi. We from this idea that perhaps he was trying to unite us for the attack of Alygarh and that when he should have done his own business he would deceive us, answered him that it should not happen that after the business of Alygarh he should deceive us. Pateel Saheb positively asserts that his friendship is not for the business of Alygarh, that the removal of the gentlemen is the most important object of his mind, because the gentlemen are both his and our enemies and will one day make war; that the remedying of that beforehand is advisable. We therefore write from our friendship that if the gentlemen's pleasure should be inclined to this point, we are ready from our hearts and souls. We have no connection with these strangers. By the blessing of God great advantages are obtained by mutual union. This stranger will be soon expelled. You have the option from our friendship. We have given this information.

Specimen IV: Political – Commercial (an advertisement)
(Source: *The Bombay Times and Journal of Commerce*, Saturday, March 14, 1840)

Year : 1810

An advertisement

SACRAM BAPOOJE, the Mail Contractor, begs leave to apprize the Public, that he has been obliged to make an addition of two Rupees to his rates of Travelling, in consequences of the Toll levised by Government on the Bore Ghaut on each trip of a Palanquin furnished by him for the accommodation of Passengers ascending and descending that road.

No. 1. Mail Buggy between Panwell and Poona, and General Post Office and Mazagaum, and Mail Boat between Mazagaum and Panwell.

1st — The Buggy by which the Post Office Mails are conveyed, leaves Panwell every night for Poona upon the arrival of the Bombay Mail, and can accommodate one Passenger with 10 lbs. of Baggage. Any Gentlemen to avail himself of this conveyance, must be at the Panwell Post Office at 10 P.M., which could at all times be done, were Gentlemen leaving Bombay to take a seat in the Mail boat. The Mail buggy leaves Poona at 5 P.M. and Bombay at half past 6 P.M.; fifteen minutes are allowed for refreshment at Panwell Khandalla, that being the time required by the Government clerks for arranging the Mail cannot on any account be delayed without subjecting the contractor to the penalty fixed by Government in such cases.

SACRAM BAPOOJEE
MAIL COACH PROPRIETOR

Bombay Mail Contractor's Office,
9th March, 1810

(c) What the data shows: Some observations
The marked features of English during this phase, particularly in the political domain are, an ostentatious formality — the use of

'Lordship Register' with its 'friendship and humbleness' vocabulary. This variety is meant to meet the diplomatic needs; it also marks political motives. The following examples illustrate the 'Lordship Register':

(i) I hope you will continue to inform me of your health, and look upon me as your well-wisher (Sp. I)
(ii) your most friendly letter (Sp. II)
(iii) your Lordship's friendly letter and overjoyed at hearing of your health
(iv) your Lordship has written ...
(v) all these troops that are (mine are) are also your Lordship's
(vi) your Lordship without scruple will inform me
(vii) your Lordship will always write me friendly letters
(viii) that friendship which is of old firm between us
(ix) I have had the happiness to receive your Lordship's friendly letter and overjoyed at hearing of your health. (All from Appendix, Phase I, Sp. II.)

The lack of clarity at the discourse level and the unstable English reveal the ambivalent stance of Indians towards the British — a vague desire for some sort of political alliance with the British merchants, and a partial acceptance of the British rule. The British were perceived as potentially powerful by the Indian chieftains and their courtiers who were willing to conspire against other feudal chiefs to get more political importance because 'India' was not perceived as one unit. Bureaucracy was institutionalized by the British and certain written functions like the 'petition register' were within the purview of the British bureaucracy.

The examples given below illustrate this attitude:

(i) Finding in it many improper expressions and concluding that by sending me the copy you desired to know my sentiments upon it, ...
(ii) you will write your letter after that form and dispatch it again to me, ...
(iii) To take away every cause of ill-will or contention this is the part of a good man. (All from Sp. I)
(iv) Most Humbly Sheweth,
(v) Therefore most humbly Request your Honour & C. as Orders ...
(vi) ... your Honr. & C. will take this case in consideration as your Petitioner is Reduced to great Necessitys by the

Capture of this place & without this humble supplication be granted by your Honour & c. . . . (All from Sp. II)
(vii) Know them also to be united with you, . . .
(viii) from this discourse you will learn all particular and reply on this truth.
(ix) He is desirous that uniting us to himself . . .
(x) By the blessing of God great advantages are obtained by mutual union. (All from Sp. III)
(xi) from unavoidable losses together with the Badness of the Times . . .
(xii) . . . your Honars will be pleased to take their hard & Lamentable cases into your serious & charitable considerations & thereby . . . (from Appendix, Phase I, Sp. I)

The use of English in advertisements (Sp. IV) was an extension of the bureaucratic domain and Indian merchants used it for advertising in the newspapers published from Calcutta and Bombay. The advertisements resembled bureaucratic notices. The English language was constitutive of the print-media which made its beginning during this phase, and gradually got entrenched into the use of English in India. The EIC encouraged a small section of Indian entrepreneurs to undertake commercial ventures catering to the needs of the EIC; not only newspapers but also the related systems of government control came into being, and the expression 'Government of India' occurred in official documentation of information. The print-media linked the important cities of the British colony.

The English language did not make any significant impact on the lives of the people in the subcontinent till 1813. In short, political/official/bureaucratic use of English was the prominent feature of the first phase of the history of English in India.

4.2.2 Phase II: 1813–57 — The transportation phase

(a) The profile
The second phase was a period of expansion and consolidation. There had been no clear administrative policy, which was evolved during this period. For example, the recruitment for civil services was not systematic; it was done by higher officials of the EIC. With the Charter Renewal of 1853, open competition system (public examination) was established. Oriental learning was given

encouragement, and the education policy was formulated in 1854 as part of the political policy. By that time, missionary schools, private schools, District English Schools by the EIC had begun to provide English education at the school level. As a result, the education policy became a 'top-down' policy; colleges and universities, and a few high schools started English education, and primary education suffered neglect. There was a wide gap between English-entrenched higher education and the inadequate (or the lack of) English at lower levels. The link between English education and the British bureaucracy was established during this period. Print-media and creative writing in English started earlier than formal English education in India. Moreover, most of these developments took place at the three Presidency cities — Bombay, Calcutta and Madras; the locale was typically urban. Thus, 'intellectual and creative writing', which was a common link between urban centres, English education, bureaucracy, and the print-media, came to be established. As a result, the urban, 'minority-use' nature of English was entrenched in the use of English in India from its very beginning.

The first noticeable feature of the second phase of this history is the weakening of the political domain, and along with it the political communication (communication between the two disparate systems — the Indian rulers and the EIC/British) also diminishes. Instead, more communication takes place inside the domain of bureaucracy although most Indian interlocutors do not yet figure inside this domain. Moreover, the bureaucratic correspondence in the second phase does not reflect the influence of the Persian conventions of writing as it did during the first phase. The British bureaucracy usurped the powers of the native-rulers. Consequently, English became the language of the British bureaucracy.

The second feature to be noted is the relatively higher degree of comprehensibility of bureaucratic writing. One of the reasons for the increasing degree of comprehensibility of Indians' English during the second phase may be the availability of English education and changes in the policy of the EIC, resulting in the opening up of bureaucratic jobs to Indians. The Indians employed for these jobs were the recipients of English education. The non-bureaucratic correspondence with the British bureaucracy was confined to intellectuals like Rammohan Roy, or the merchants.

The elite had access to English education, and for the mercantile class, writing petitions in English had become a necessary and habitual skill.

Thus, English education and bureaucracy emerge almost simultaneously and become a decisive combination for the use of English in India. English education enabled Indians to use English, and the only way of putting it to use was to get a job in the government and write bureaucratic documents. The use of English in the bureaucratic domain was the beginning of Indians' English. It is not surprising, therefore, that the bureaucratic manner of writing dominated even the non-bureaucratic writing in the second phase.

English education opened up two other domains: print-media communication and creative writing. The print-media was used for publishing essays of school boys, annual reports of colleges, and write-ups that deal with topics like criticism, defence of an English teacher and English education, bad influence of English education on Indian youth, proposals for publishing translations of some ancient Hindu texts, etc. A review of a play staged by Indian youth, where the reviewer emphasizes that after putting up plays of Shakespeare for a long time, the youth aristocrats of Calcutta put up a Bengali version of the Sanskrit classic, Shakuntala, is quite revealing. What must be noted is that most of the topics are connected with English education, and it may be said that this type of writing is induced by English education.

Thus, on the one hand, were the British bureaucracy induced economic-administrative needs which were to be met through English; on the other hand, English education, besides feeding into the bureaucratic domain, induced communication needs for which the space of print-media was made available to Indians. In this way, these domains induced communication within themselves, thereby creating a need for English-use which was dependent on these domains for sustenance.

All the major domains of the use of English which are evidenced throughout the history of English in India emerged in the second phase.

(b) The data
Domains: bureaucracy, education, print-media communication and commercial, and intellectual/literary writing.

90 • *The Politics of Indians' English*

Specimen I: Social–Commercial (an advertisement)
(Source: *The Days of John Company:*
Selections from Calcutta Gazette 1824–32)

Year : 1827

THURSDAY, SEPTEMBER 20, 1827
GRAND NAUCHES
Doorga Pooja Holidays
BABOO PRANKISSEN HOLDAR
of Chinsurch

Begs to inform the Ladies and Gentlemen, and the Public in General, that he has commenced giving a Grand Nauch from this day, that it will continue till the 29th Inst. Those Ladies and Gentlemen who have received Invitation Cards, are respectfully solicited to favour him with their Company on the days mentioned above; and those to whom the Invitation Tickets have not been sent (strangers to the Baboo), are also respectfully solicited to favour him with their Company.

Baboo Pran Kissen Holdar further begs to say, that every attention and respect will be paid to the Ladies and Gentlemen who will favour him with their Company, and that he will be happy to furnish them with Tiffin, Dinner, Wines, & c., during their stay there.

PRANKISSEN HOLDAR

Chinsurch, September 14, 1827.

Specimen II: Education
A report of the Annual Meeting of the
Banares College by Brahma Gupta
(Source: *The Days of John Company:*
Selections from Calcutta Gazette 1824–32)

Year : 1827

THURSDAY, MARCH 8, 1827

To the Editor of the Government Gazette

Sir, — If you are not already provided with an official report of the Banares College Proceedings, you may, perhaps, allow insertion to the following imperfect description of the Annual Meeting, and oblige.

Your constant reader,

Brahma Gupta

Siddhisvari Mehalla, Kashi

February 24, 1827, Day of the Sivarathri

On Friday last, the 23rd instant, the Superintending Committee of the Banares Patasala, or Hindu College, was convened, according to the annual custom, for the purpose of witnessing the public disputations of the scholars of that institution, and of dispensing rewards to such as had signalized themselves during the year.

The meeting was held in the central hall of the New Mint, a room well adapted for the purpose:

A Sanskrit Programme of the subjects discussed, was handed about, and with the assistance of Pundit, who sat near me, I elicited therefrom, that the disputations were in five different classes. The Nyaya or logic, the Sankhya system of philosophy, the two Byakurna, and the Sahitya or poetry and general literature.

An English report upon the present state of the College, was also circulated, — a rapid glance over it convinced me that the progress of education had been highly satisfactory in most of the branches of knowledge; I regretted to observe, however, that the Astronomical class had been abolished by a resolution of the Committee, 'None of the students having made much proficiency.' And that the classes of the Vedas — those sacred volumes, which may not be opened in the presence of the profane or uninitiating, — were handled with unusual severity: If I understood correctly, the teachers of the Vedas were stated to be so inferior in respectability and learning to the rest of the Pundits, that their signature was never permitted to any of the law cases submitted to the Banares College for opinion. The report, I believe, proposes to pension off these teachers of the Veda classes, leaving them to give their instructions at their own houses. This will appear to many as severe a blow to the theology as the abolition of the Astronomical classes is to the science of the Hindus: — in the latter, however, it may be hoped that the step taken has been only a prelude to the introduction of a better system of scientific instruction, such as is now making very rapid advance in the Calcutta Native College.

A new class for the study of Puranas, or History, was also mentioned, — but the chief attention of the Committee has been apparently occupied in improving the Law classes, — a wise precaution, when it is reflected, that besides giving decrees upon important knotty points of law, the college is expected eventually to supply Law Officers for the different Zillah and Provincial Courts.

In conclusion, prizes were distributed to about hundred pupils, who had distinguished themselves during the past year, and at the same time a purse of 2,000 Rupees, was subscribed by the Raja and other respectable Native gentlemen present, to be devoted to a similar laudable purpose at the next Annual Examination.

92 • *The Politics of Indians' English*

Specimen III: Print-media communication
The Editor cites a school boy's composition
(Source: *The Days of John Company:
Selections from Calcutta Gazette* 1824–32)

Year : 1830

THURSDAY, DECEMBER 30, 1830

A Report has been handed to us of a private examination of the two first classes of the Parental Academic Institution. The Examination, it is stated on the cover of the pamphlet, was undertaken and conducted by the Master of each class for the purpose of ascertaining the comparative progress of each pupil.

We can afford room for one specimen of Composition — which we give with pleasure, the sentiments it conveys being very creditable to the author of it, a native boy.

'O mortals! you are made superior in this lower world; if you do not preserve your rank, you are less worthy than the beasts. Cultivate your minds, without which a soul is like a diamond in the rough; partake the sorrows of your earthly brothers, by giving tributes to pity; assist them, who, without your assistance, cannot get what may be very advantageous to them; love every one as you love yourselves; treat them with kindness; your servants without cruelty, for they do for you those things, which, without them, cannot be done; your domestic cattle without severity, for some feed you, and others save you from the intensity of the winter, & c. Forgive others since you are aware that you may commit the same crime, or others; besides, if you do not forgive, how should you expect forgiveness from Him, who sees everything — from whom nothing can be hidden? Be not drunken with wine, which shortens the life over which none has any right, and which not only brings misery upon him who drinks, but also upon his whole family. Tell no lies, for they are the most detestable of vices; nor commit similar vices which are injurious to the world . . .

SUMBHOOCHUNDER SEAL

Specimen IV: Education
A faculty member of the Madras University
writes a report on students' performance.
(Source: *The Eighth Annual Report from
The Governors of the Madras University* 1848–49)

Year : 1849

To the Head Master,

Dear Sir,

My opinion having been desired of the respective merits of the youths studying in the highest class under your care, as to their proficiency in the science of Astronomy in which I had the pleasure of examining them, I beg leave to assure you that they have not in any way fallen short of my expectations, and that they have gained a familiar acquaintance with the most interesting portions of Astronomy, must be manifest to every one from the readiness and facility with which they answered when interrogated in the viva vice examination. In their written replies to the questions I set them, they discover a pretty intimate knowledge of some of those processes in which the application of Mathematics is necessary for the development of the most important Astronomical phenomena. They understand the details of many calculations, only the principles of which are sketched out in the work of Hershel, which forms their class book. Some of their written replies are not of course altogether free from errors and inelegancies, many of which, I have no doubt would not have occurred had more time been allowed for the collection and arrangement of their ideas. The relative merits of the youths may be easily ascertained by a reference to the marks I have given to their written replies. No lad has, I think discovered such a decided superiority over the rest, as to merit an individual mention.

I remain,
Dear Sir,
Your's very sincerely,
T. Madava Row

Specimen V: Bureaucracy — (a formal letter)
Letter from Baboo Taruk Chunder Lahory, Sub-Assistant Surgeon, to the Secretary, Government of Madras, dated Moorsheedabad, 31st March, 1857
(Source: Madras Record Office, Government of Madras, Public Department)

Year : 1857

Sir,

I beg to despatch by book-post to-day a copy of my work on the principles and practice of Surgery in Urdoo, with a hope of getting some assistance from the Government of Madras. The Government of the N.W.P. has taken 100 copies, the Chief Commissioner of Scindh 25, and the Chief Commissioner of Oude 20 copies. The price of each copy is five Rupees (5 Rs) the English preface of the work will point out the nature and utility of the book.

(Signed) Taruk Chunder Lahory,
Sub-Assistant Surgeon

Specimen VI: Print-media communication
A review of a play
(Source: *Selections from English Periodicals of 19th Century Bengal Volume IV: 1857*)

Year : 1857

THE HINDOO THEATRE

It is not long since Calcutta was regaled with histrionic exhibitions under the auspices of native amateurs when some of the best plays of Shakespeare were acted upon the stage by young Hindoos who appeared to enter into the spirit of the characters they personated. Although the full measure of success which was anticipated could not be realized, yet the public, and specially the native community, showed a taste for such performances which promised the best results, if the managers of the Theatre had only the tact to profit by the happy opportunity. Instead, however of fostering by repeated and well got up performances the taste thus created, they permitted minor jealousies and a spirit of contention to demolish the good they had achieved; and the curtain fell upon their stage to be lifted up no more. Years rolled away. We had well nigh forgotten that we ever had such a thing as a theatre, when an invitation card surprised us with the fact that another Bengallee stage had risen like a phoenix upon the ashes of its predecessor. The announcement had the further attraction that the play announced was a genuine Bengallee one, being a translation of the well-known dramatic execution of Kally Dass — the Sacoontollah. We were still more delighted to learn that the theatre had been got up by the grandsons of the late Baboo Asutootsh Dey, the stage having been erected at the family residence of the deceased millionaire, and the partaking of the character of a private theatrical. It is not every day that native gentlemen of wealth and position are observed to spend money on amusements of a rational kind. It is altogether a relief to contemplate our youthful aristocracy apart from the low and grovelling pursuits which too unfortunately constitute the normal condition of many of that body. The drama has in all ages and with all nations formed one of the principal sources of a pure amusement. In India, it had at one time attained the highest state of perfection. But a combination of disastrous circumstances tended to annihilate the freedom of our race, and simultaneously with loss of liberty we lost every blessing which chastened manners and embellished life. Foreigners contemplate with ecstasy the genius of our poets. The universities of Europe are not tired of pouring over the musty tomes of ancient Sanskrit literature. The Sacoontollah of Kallidas has undergone the most finished translations in Germany and in England. But amongst the people for whose forefathers the immortal bard taxed his genius, his admirable work is a sealed book almost. A few only have read it in the original, and a very few contemptible number in the diluted form even of a translation. The play is admirably fitted for the stage. We had abundant evidence of the fact from the performance which came off on the night of the 30th instant. The young gentleman who personated Sacoontollah looked really grand and queenly in his gestures and address, and did great justice to the part he was enacting. The other amateurs also succeeded in creating an effect. We are told that the performers have not had the benefit of any lessons from practised actors, and this circumstance enables us to accord great credit to exertions polishing the corps dramatique will be able to make a brilliant debut.

From: *Hindoo Patriot*, 5 February 1857

Specimen VII: Literary writing

Year 1828–57

To the Pupils of the Hindu College

Expanding like the petals of young flowers
I watch the gentle opening of your minds,
And the sweet loosening of the spell that binds
Your intellectual energies and powers
That stretch (like young birds in soft summer hours)
Their wings to try their strength. O how the winds

Of circumstances and freshening April showers
Of early knowledge and unnumbered kinds
Of new perceptions shed their influence,
And how you worship truth's omnipotence!
What joyance rains upon me when I see
Fame in the mirror of futurity,
Weaving the chaplets you have yet to gain,
Ah then I feel I have not lived in vain.

Henry L. Derozio

(c) What the data shows: Some observations
The most outstanding feature of English during this phase is the emerging bureaucratic register with its officialese and the formulaic use of English within and outside the bureaucratic domain. Though the 'Lordship Register' is not very widely used, the 'most humbly beg' variety gets established in the petition format. 'Sir' and 'Honoured Sir' are used as customary salutations and 'humbly beg . . . ' as the customary ending.

(i) Begs to inform the Ladies and Gentlemen, . . .
 . . . further begs to say . . . (Sp. I)
(ii) Dear sir,
 . . . I beg leave to assure you that . . . (Sp. IV)
(iii) Sir,
 I beg to despatch . . . (Sp. V)
(iv) My Lord,
 Humbly reluctant as the natives of India are (Appendix, Ph. II, Sp. I)

Passive constructions and fixed phrases are frequently used even in reports and advertisements:

(i) My opinion having been desired . . . (Sp. IV)
(ii) . . . has been abolished . . . (Sp. II)
(iii) . . . respect will be paid . . . (Sp. I)
(iv) in consequences of
 for the purposes of
 undermentioned
 undersigned
 the public are hereby respectfully informed
 respectfully solicited

During this period, English education seems to be gaining ground slowly replacing indigenous education. Socially, English is gaining the 'high' status.

The language has been accepted for bureaucratic functions. The editorial — Salam Sabb — and the examples of students' writing (Sp. II and III in the Appendix) very clearly show that the English used by 'natives' has improved; even long sentences are well formed; shorter sentences are used; the first person pronouns are found in correspondence. The following examples illustrate these:

(i) Many other instances of this kind could be mentioned, all of which would tend to prove, that if the Natives have from religious motives kept at a distance from the Christians, the latter have from much worse motives discarded them from their society. (Appendix, Ph. II, Sp. II)
(ii) In Egypt, India, and China where nature bestows her blessings in spontaneous profusion, the human intellect was first called to paly... (Appendix, Ph. II, Sp. III)
(iii) Notice that the entire advertisement (Sp. I) consists of only two long sentences.
(iv) On Friday last, the 23rd instant, ... (Sp. II)

Odd usages continue to occur:

(i) to furnish them with Tiffin...
(ii) to favour him with their Company
(iii) furnish the guests with dinner... (all from Sp. I)
(iv) ... signalized themselves during the year...
(v) ... may allow insertion to this report...
(vi) ... the students having made much proficiency... (all from Sp. II)

The language used in the print-media communication is verbose and ostentatious with archaic words and odd expressions; maybe, they were used in English during the early 19th Century.

(i) Calcutta was regaled with histrionic exhibitions...
(ii) ... the curtain fell upon their stage to be lifted no more.
(iii) ... partaking of the character of a private theatrical...
(iv) ... of the deceased millionaire... (all from Sp. VI)

The attitude manifested in the review of a play — The Hindoo Theatre — shows that Sanskrit, Hindoo, and Indian are sought to be linked together, and that the native pride is asserted in English. The school boy's composition (Sp. III) mentions a 'native' boy, and credits him for the use of English. It indicates that the ability to write in English was considered an accomplishment worth giving publicity. Rammohan Roy's letter (Appendix, Ph. II, Sp. I), and the editorial 'Salam Sabb' (Appendix, Ph. II, Sp. I) show the appropriate use of English.

In the area of creative writing the genre that seems to have captured the imagination of Indian writers in poetry; the writers and readers were products of English-education and were based in urban centres. The poem given (Sp. VII) is a good example of how Indian writers imitated English poets:

soft summer hours
freshening April showers
joyance rains upon me
weaving the chaplets you have yet to gain

The same poet, a Christian convert, has written other poems like a 'Hindustanee Maid' which are ostensibly 'Indian'. The poem 'Satan' by Madhusudan Dutt does not have any trace of 'Indianness' — no Indian loan words and no Indian images.

4.2.3 Phase III: 1857–1904: The dissemination phase

(a) The profile
The Crown took over from the EIC and the British Government with its departments and bureaucracy gradually got established in the subcontinent, resulting in the expansion of the use of English and its 'show-off' value in the society. English became the language of the Government and Indians as 'subjects' accepted the governing authority and the language of the rulers.

The result was further stabilization and expansion during the third phase of the history of English in India. All the major domains and features observed in the second phase (1813–57) became stable during the third phase. In other words, the restricted nature of the domains of the use of English got stabilized and a new domain was added. The other domains and the induced use of English were the same as in the earlier phase but there was expansion and stabilization within the domains. There were more Indians using English within the domains. A certain amount of diversification is also seen within the domains; for example, there are more compartments within the bureaucracy. More departments were formed and Indians took over the bureaucratic network at various levels. This led to an increase in the number of Indian bureaucrats. The content of education was European and the British controlled the system through the written word, though the management and teaching was done by Indians under the British rule. There was rapid expansion in higher education resulting in an increase in the number of Arts colleges. The interdependence between education and the bureaucracy got consolidated during this phase. English education generated its own socio-intellectual activities in the urban areas which can be seen in the literary activity (the emerging Indo-Anglian Writing), debating societies and associations formed by English-educated Indians in cities, particularly in Calcutta. For example, 'the Academic Association' was founded by the young Indian graduates of Calcutta. These associations and societies catered to the induced needs for using English (for activities induced by higher education). Indigenous education was completely obliterated, and primary education totally neglected.

English does not seem to involve the entire Indian subcontinent into its self-created domains; nor does it interact with the native civilization of the subcontinent. There is no indication of the finer areas of life like religion, arts, social customs, etc., interacting with English. We can only say that the restrictedness of the use of English in India got consolidated during this phase of history. The induced use of English by Indians becomes established with a higher degree of comprehensibility during the third phase and, at the same time, with the increase in numbers a cline of comprehensibility in the use of English is noticeable. Indians do not vacillate between acceptance and rejection of English; they perceive certain advantages in the use of English but they want to reap the advantages without being excommunicated from their own sociocultural milieu. The problem for the English-using Indians seems to be how to accommodate English with its socio-economic advantages within the native cultural pattern. Apparently, the use of English in the bureaucratic domain is treated as a convenient way of using English for formal impersonal communication in English-induced areas. The bureaucratic use of English thus becomes an impersonal module of communication, and this modular function of English is an important pointer to the developments in the later years wherein English comes to be treated like a module in the outer areas of life according to the needs of Indians.

But English began to serve another purpose during this phase. The Indian National Congress was founded during this period (1885), and there were some militant associations like The Indian Association, which was formed by an expelled ICS officer, Surendranath Banerjee, in 1876; Indians began reacting to the British Government using the language of the rulers.

(b) The data
Domains: bureaucracy, education, print-media communication and commercial, intellectual/literary writing, and social

Specimen I: Commercial
(Source: *The Delhi Gazette*, Thursday, March 17, 1859)

Year : 1859

An advertisement

MESS PRESIDENTS of Her Majesty's forces are hereby informed, that if they have in their Messes empty glass, soda-water bottles for sale, they are requested to send early intelligence to the undersigned who will pay 15 Rupees a hundred for them, and have them brought on his own expenses if they are found within the following stations, viz:-

Agra, Allahabad, Azimgurh, Banda, Barielly, Benares, Fategurh, Jaloun, Jhansee, Lullutopore, Meerut, Nagoda, Nowgong, Oude, Shajehanpore, or all places within 300 miles of this.

SHEUPERSAUD, Banker,
Son of the late Tantee Mull

Cawnpore, 12th March, 1859.

This notice shall appear up to a fortnight, and the bottles shall continue to be purchased till the hot season.

Specimen II: Bureaucracy
A petition of zemindars
(Source: *Papers relating to the Indebtedness of the zeminders of the Muncher Lake in Sind*)

Year: 1872

To
His Excellency The Honourable
Sir Philip Edmond Wodehouse, K.C.B.,
Governor of Bombay

the Petition of the Zemindars of Sehwan Taluka

We humbly desire to make known to your Excellency some of the difficulties under which we labor. We are landholders, we have lived on the produce of our land. We do so still and must continue to do so, but to our sorrow we see men of ancient and respectable families so reduced in means as hardly to have the means of living remaining; very few of us landholders are far from debt incurred not by our own fault but to unavoidably. By concurrence of circumstances we have lost everything, our lands have gone and going out of hands, and ancient and respectable families are being reduced to a state of destitution. We have now reached the extreme verge of poverty.

We fear that if we say anything in respect to the settlements or our ignorance the delicate feelings of many officers may be offended. We do not attribute our poverty, to any Act or Acts of Government, but we blame our own bad luck. We have suffered losses for a series of years. Although the Government have always assisted us by granting remission, the loss of seed, labor and expenses incurred in the cultivation, and the cost of maintenance of ourselves for the year of the loss and the succeeding one are without any means of relief cannot be covered by an entire or partial assessment of revenue.

We are sure that your Excellency's auspicious visit to this Province and the kind enquiries you are making about us will soon alter our circumstances. We now pray for one great kindness at your Excellency's hands that a special enactment be passed in our behalf prohibiting until such time as we regain our former position, the sale by the Civil Court in execution of its decisions of our implements of husbandry, bullocks and seed as also the lands which were secured at the cost of thousands of rupees and have been in our possession from a very long time, and which are now valueless. Arrangements should be made to pay our debts and allow us sufficient maintenance from the produce of our fields. The revision of settlements now in progress should be made with great consideration and liberality, and until complete arrangements are made for the supply and drainage of the Muncher, the settlement assessment should be levied on such fields only as may be cropped. The rights which we possess over lands and of which the present system of settlement deprives us should be continued to us.

We submit this petition knowing that the Government is more kind to its subjects than what the parents are to their children.

(signed) Gulam-Russul Shah and other zemindars

Specimen III: Print-media communication

From: *The Statesman*
(Source: *Selections from English Periodicals of the 19th Century Bengal, Volume VIII: 1875–80*)

Year : 1878

'EUROPE-RETURNED' HINDOOS

To the Editor

Sir, — It is well known that at the present moment the position of those native gentlemen who have visited Europe, as regards their families and orthodox Hindoo relations, is anomalous and unsatisfactory. On the one hand, the orthodox Hindoos, however they wish to do so, cannot receive their 'Europe-returned' relatives into their houses, until the young men have performed the usual rites and ceremonies for being purified. On the other, the young men consider it infra dig and hard to be called upon to perform outrageous ceremonies when they assert that, in visiting Europe for education and improvement, they have not discarded the faith for their fathers. The consequence is that there is an estrangement between father and son, between brother and brother, between uncle and nephew. To bridge over the gulf, which is gradually widening, between the young men and their relatives, and to place the former in their legitimate positions among their countrymen, some of the leading men of the orthodox native community, who are well known for their enlightenment, patriotism and sympathy for the progress and well-being of their country, and who are fully alive to the necessity of allowing an opportunity to those native gentlemen who have returned from Europe to be taken back into the bosom of their families, have placed themselves in communication with some of the principal pundits and adhyapaks of Calcutta, in order to obtain from them some authority from the Shastras, some vyavastha, which will enable both parties to come to an understanding on the vexed point without infringing caste rules, or violating the provisions of the Shastras. A very favourable opinion on the case in point has been received from that profound scholar and experienced propounder of Hindoo law, the venerable Bharat Chandra Siromoni, and it is expected that our worthy Principal of the Sanskrit College will, in a few days, give a similar favourable opinion. We thank both these gentlemen for their high public spirit, their encouragement of progress and for the absence of party feeling in their minds upon so momentous a question . . . .

Doorga Mohan Doss

22 February 1878

Specimen IV: Print-media communication
From : *The Statesman*
(Source: *Selections from English Periodicals of 19th Century Bengal, Volume VIII: 1875–80*)

Year : 1879

An Appeal to Bengal

To the Editor,

Sir, — Baboo Amrita Lal Mitra Breathed his last in January 1879 in Banares. He was a man of rare qualities. Those who knew him must unhesitatingly admit that India has suffered a great and irreparable loss. Possessed of vast information on various subjects yet devoid of pride, uncommonly intelligent yet humble, charitable yet unostentatious, full of energy yet inoffensive, outspoken yet mild, truthful yet prudent, loving liberty yet tender hearted, active yet gentle, just yet not severe — he had in short all the good qualities that become a great man. The number of such persons in this world is very few. To gain a name and become famous is the principal object of most men in this world; but that was not the object of his life. He was never ambitious, else he would have very easily become famous. He sought not the praise of men. The aim of life was so noble, that few could attain it. Slowly and silently he worked a great deal for the good of the world. Love for his native land was predominant in his breast. It will not be a hyperbole to say of him that he was an ornament of Bengal, a pride to India, and a model character in this world . . . .

L.N. Maitra

78, Dhurrumtollah,
26 November 1879

Specimen V: Education (an advertisement)
(Source: *Letters to Gooroodas Banerjee*)

Year : 1886

THE ALYGARH INSTITUTE GAZETTE
With which is incorporated the 'PROGRESS'
Vol. XXI SATURDAY, MARCH 6TH, 1886 No. 19

NOTICE

An English Teacher is required for Narora School, who can prepare boys for Anglo-Vernacular Middle Class Examination. Pay of the post is Rs 20 to 35 per mensem. Preference will be given either to a retired School Master or to a man who has passed Entrance Examination of Calcutta University.

Apply, stating full particulars and sending copies of certificates, to

KADIR BUKSH,
Honorary Secretary,
Garo School,
NARORA

Specimen VI: Social
A letter from Syed Shamsul Huda to Gooroodas Banerjii
(Source: *Letters to Gooroodas Banerjee*)

5th November 1888

My dear Sir,

I read in this week's Calcutta Gazette of your appointment as a judge of the High Court. Allow me to offer you my most sincere congratulations on your accession to the bench. It is remarked in some of the native papers that the appointment has caused great heart-burning to the Mohamedans. It is singularly unfortunate that attempts should be made by those who ought to know better, to turn anything and everything into a race question. I may however assure you, if indeed such assurance is needed, that whatever others may think, those at least among the Mohamedans who have the privilege of knowing you personally, cannot but feel that a happier choice could not have been made. Hoping you will live long to enjoy these honors.

I remain
Yours Sincerely
Syed Shamsul Huda

Specimen VII: Bureaucracy
An official letter written by K. Seshadri Iyer, the Diwan of Mysore
(Source: *Karnataka Letters, Volume I, 1883–1901*)

GOVERNMENT OF MYSORE

Bangalore, 30th May 1895

My Dear Mr Whiteley,

Some time in the later part of March I communicated to you the Resident's wish to have monthly reports regarding H.H. the Maharaja's Education. I don't know whether I sent you Mr Lee Warner's letter. If I sent it to you please return it and also send me a copy of any letter I wrote you on the subject.

I sent you a telegram asking you to expedite the reports and enquiring when I may expect them. Your best plan will be to put your monthly report into a memo and write at the bottom 'Submitted to the Resident through the Diwan' when I receive it I will at once send it on to the Resident.

I think your first monthly report will be the one for April and the second that for May.

The monthly report should hereafter be submitted irrespective of trips and vacations, and as soon as possible after the close of the months to which they relate.

Yours sincerely,
K. Seshadri Iyer

Specimen VIII: Social (semi-official)
A semi-official but non-bureaucratic letter written by a Congressman to Dadabhai Naoroji
(Source: *Papers of Dadabhai Naoroji*)

The Congress Reception Committee Office
Madras, 16th April 1896

My Dear Sir,

I am in receipt of your letter. The question of sending a witness was fully discussed at the last Congress — Mr Mehta was against the proposal and hence it was dropped — We will revive the question. Will you kindly send me a complete set of all the papers you submitted to the Commission and oblige — I am glad to tell you that at a meeting of the Mahajana Sabha it has been resolved upon that you be requested to represent the Sabha at the Imperial Institute for the next two years —

>With my great regards
>I am
>Yours truly
>M. Viraraghavochariar

Specimen IX: Print-media communication
From the column named 'News of the Week'
(Source: *The Moslem Chronicle* —
An English newspaper published from Calcutta)

1st February 1896

There is a rumour afloat that His Majesty the Ameer has decided to have the streets of Cabul lighted with electricity.

The French Cabinet has agreed to grant either a site or a sum of money for a mosque to be erected by subscription in Paris.

The Canadian Government has voted half a million sterling to be expended in drilling the entire militia of the Dominion this year.

The death is announced of Mr Alexander Macmillan, the publisher.

Mr G.C. Kilby, Deputy Superintendent and Remembrancer for Legal Affairs, has been granted an extension of leave for six months.

Specimen X: Literary Writing
(Source: *The Golden Treasury of Indo-Anglian Poetry: 1828–1965*, Edited by V.K. Gokak, 1970)

A Hymn to Surya

Chasing darkness, light thou sendest,
And our mortal frame thou mendest
Source of joyful rainy season,
Gladden hearts and whet our reason,
Hymns we sing, we sing thy praises,
Yes! thy sight our spirit raises,
Dismal darkness dreads thy presence.
Life is light — thy glorious essence.
Move our minds, our souls inspiring,
Move our hearts, our feelings firing.
Lord of skies! of light the centre,
Come, we pray, our spirits enter.
Face of gods! a light surprising.
Eye of heaven — is he not rising?

Moves he not fire — the earthly power,
And the god that waters shower? . . .

A.M. Kunte

(c) What the data shows: Some observations
The extension of the bureaucratic use of English outside the bureaucratic domain, and the competent handling of the language by English-educated Indians appear to be the prominent features of Indians' English during this phase. The extension of the use of English in non-governmental and social contexts is noticeable; though urban areas continue to be the power centres, the network of offices begin to extend beyond the cities and the British Government's bureaucracy is institutionalized and departmentalized; communication among Indian bureaucrats, between Indian and British bureaucrats, and between non-bureaucrats and bureaucrats begins to take place in English.

The specimens analysed in the bureaucratic domain contain officialese but the correspondence is handled with more flexibility to suit the content as well as the degree of formality. Specimen VII written by an Indian shows that the elite are at ease with the language:

(i) My Dear Mr Whitely,
(ii) Yours sincerely,
(iii) I sent you a telegram asking you . . .
(iv) I think your first monthly report will be the one . . .
(v) The monthly report should hereafter be submitted
(vi) . . . please return it . . .

The use of personal salutations, the first person pronoun 'I' and the helping verbs show that the writer has handled the language competently. At the same time expressions like 'to communicate' (instead of 'to write') and 'to expedite' (instead of 'to send') are also found.

English officers are addressed as 'Honoured and Dear Sir' (Appendix, Ph. III, Sp. I) but among Indians 'My dear Sir' (Sp. VI) is used.

Specimen IV (Appendix, Ph. III) represents the continuation of the old petition format:

To
His Excellency the Viceroy and Governor-General in Council

The humble memorial . . .

Respectively Sheweth

. . . as in duty sound shall ever pray . . .

your Excellency in Council be pleased to . . .

The first person pronouns are avoided; long sentences are used but they are not very well-formed.

In other petitions too (Sp. II), the use of 'humbleness vocabulary' and odd usages are found.

We humbly desire . . .

We submit this petition knowing that the Government is more kind to its subjects that what the parents are to their children.

We fear that if we say anything . . .

your Excellency's auspicious visit . . .

We now pray for one great kindness at your Excellency's hands . . .

But the tone of the discourse is different from what it was during the first phase; the plaintive appeal of the earlier phases is replaced by courteous citizenship and the governed feel justified in making requests. Roles and the contexts of their enactment has been stabilised, and so have the petition format and bureaucratic convention of writing.

English meets the need of formal non-personal communication arising out of official but non-bureaucratic contexts. The letter written by a Congressman (Sp. VIII) to Dadabhai Naoroji is a good example of the use of English in the social domain; it combines personal and bureaucratic conventions.

(i) My Dear Sir,

> with my great regards
> I am
> Yours truly

(ii) I am in receipt of your letter . . .
(iii) Will you kindly send . . . and oblige
(iv) . . . that you be requested to represent . . .

The congratulatory letter is another example of the use of English in social/personal domains; it also shows that Indians are able to handle English well in formal situations but not in informal contexts:

(i) My Dear Sir,
                                              I remain
                                         Yours sincerely
(ii) a happier choice
(iii) anything and everything
(iv) a race question
(v)   my most sincere congratulations
(vi) hoping you will live long to enjoy these honors

Specimen I shows that the British opened up new commercial possibilities for Indian entrepreneurs. The advertisement is written in English since it is for the 'MESS Presidents of Her Majesty's forces'; though it is an advertisement, it has the features of bureaucratic writing:

(i)   hereby informed
(ii) bottles shall continue to be purchased
(iii) items sought by the advertiser
(iv) to send early intelligence to the undersigned

Specimen IX shows that journalism in English is fairly established, and mostly Englishmen were the editors or they had the editorial control; that is why the English used is clear and comprehensive except for some occasional oddities. Specimen III, written by an Indian (may have been edited) is a good example of the competent handling of the English language. The topic necessitates the use of words from Indian languages: shastras, some vyavastha. Certain features are prominent:

(i) Adjective piling:
anomalous and unsatisfactory; infra dig and hard; profound scholar and experienced propounder
(ii) Some quaint and odd expressions:
party feeling; bosom of families; looked upon with to prevent the meeting

The text reflects the predicament of English-educated Indians; there is a high premium on a visit to Europe but Hindus are contaminated' and 'polluted' by it, and Hindu orthodoxy treats Europe-returned Hindus as outcastes. The text shows how Hindus are trying to work out adjustments in their social system so as to accommodate not the English culture but the coveted status gained through contacts with Europe, Britain, and the English language.

In the domain of literary/creative/intellectual writing, there is a deliberate attempt to transcreate Indian concepts in the English linguistic system with the help of universal symbols and Indian loan words. Kunte's poem 'A Hymn to Surya' (Sp. X) and many more in the *Golden Treasury of Indo-Anglian Poetry* are examples of such attempts; but the process of transcreation is restricted to the lexicon. In literary writing too the piling of adjectives and a verbose style are prominent but some of them may be part of the literary strategy. The number of writers in the literary domain is on the increase during this phase.

4.2.4 Phase IV: 1904–47 — The institutionalization phase

(a) The profile
The two World Wars, English going international, the intense political activity during this period, and the Swadeshi Movement changed the role of English in India. After 1900 the English language got gradually detached from the British rule, and more and more Indians started using it as the medium of communication in the domains in which it got stabilized during the third phase. One can say that from a foreign language, English gradually became a second language in the subcontinent. If stability was the main feature of the third phase of history (1857–1904), then 'detachability' must be acknowledged as the main feature of the fourth phase.

What emerges during this phase is the desire to accommodate the advantages of English within the indigenous orthodox socio-cultural frame work but not the culture of the English language. In the fourth phase, Indians seem to have taken a definite stand on the meaning and role of English in India; they make it obvious that they will use English for certain purposes but their identity remains rooted in their cultural heritage. In that sense, English in India has been detached, in a way from the polemics of cultural confrontation, and is treated as a module to be used according to people's needs. This does not mean that English does not pose cultural problems to its users in India. By 'detaching' it from the main socio-cultural stream and treating it as a module, they have changed the dimensions of the problem and extended their strategy of restricted interaction, a strategy which they had used to contain all other languages and other forms of invasion during the earlier periods, to the English language. Converting it into a module is a way of restricting the invasion, and is part of the strategy in an ancient civilization that accepts *heteroglossia*. Sanskrit, Persian, Urdu, Arabic and even religious and cultural forms have been treated in the same manner in the subcontinent. By extending the same strategy, Indians have come to terms with English by restricting the domains of English.

The Indian subcontinent under the British Government needed many English-knowing Indians at various levels of bureaucracy — the government network with its departmentalized bureaucracy, legislature, judiciary, various governing bodies (some elected and some appointed by the Government). The management of railways, press and mass communication also spread to more cities, towns and districts. Though the highest functionaries were British, many 'British trained' Indians entered the various levels of administration. Indian Civil Service (ICS) attracted many Indians who became the servants of the Government; only those whose proficiency in English was high could get into the Civil Service and get trained by the British.

Indigenous education went into oblivion and only 'minority institutions' like Madarassahs continued to function; primary education was neglected. The number of students in the English education system increased. Even the semi-urban population situated near urban areas came under the influence of English education; the teaching and administration were done by Indians (except in some missionary institutions) but the system was controlled and supervised by the British Government.

With more Indian entrepreneurs in business, more Indians as readers and writers of English, the number of English newspapers increased; with the increasing circulation and sale of English newspapers, the advertisements in these papers also increased. The use of English in the commercial domain and print-media brought in many more Indian users of English — editors, journalists, reporters, correspondents, printers, publishers, writers and readers. Political activity involving national leaders and members of political parties, and political awareness made the print-media powerful. It became a forum for expressing and creating opinion, and a channel to reach out to people in the urban areas opened in the subcontinent.

Indian writing in English — prose, fiction, poetry, and non-literary intellectual and academic writing got well established; publishing centres were started in cities like Bombay, Calcutta, Delhi and Madras.

In the social domain, more and more Indians used English for communication among themselves; formal and informal correspondence took place in English. Members of the Indian National Congress, lawyers, political activists, and other prominent Indians started using English in their social communication.

However, the number of Englishmen as interlocutors in the domains mentioned got reduced (even in the bureaucratic and educational domains) on account of the quantitative expansion in the use of English, and the social domain which emerged within the elitist section of urban Indians became more exclusively Indian. Print-media and literary activity gained more prominence. In all the domains the attitude to English is the same; it is the 'detachability' which anticipated the fate of English in India after 1947 when Indians put into operation the 'nation' module along with the English language.

(b) The data
Domains: bureaucracy, education, commercial, print-media communication, intellectual/literary writing, and social.

Specimen I: Print-media communication
An extract from an article in an English journal
(Source: *The Hindustan Review*, vol. XLV, no. 272, May 1922 — An English monthly published from Allahabad)

Year : 1922

HINDU NATIONAL EDUCATION

It is needless to say that the present system of education in India has been condemned by a general consensus of opinions as inadequate, halting, imperfect, unsatisfactory and barren of high results. It is neither national making for the physical, intellectual, moral and religious advancement of the people nor practical and useful in the worldly sense, calculated to develop their material and economic prosperity. It tends more towards materialism than towards the material success and prosperity of the people. It was born at a time when our foreign rulers just arrived in the country and unable to learn the language of the people and unacquainted with their manners and customs, wanted numbers of English-knowing clerks to carry on the every day work of government in their (ruler's) own tongue. The later generations of British Officers, following the example of their predecessors, continued to administer the affairs of the country through the medium of their own tongue and did not care to learn the language of the people and thus to make the administration popular and less costly. The ugly system of education devised in haste by the first comers has thus been perpetuated and contingents after contingents of English-knowing Babus fit only for serving their foreign masters have been turned out — the supply far exceeds the demand . . . .

No education which is based on foreign ideals and imparted through a foreign medium can be satisfactory. A country that forgets its past glorious achievements, its lofty national ideals, its noble traditions and well-tried customs, cannot fulfil its destiny. None can deny that India has a lofty Mission to carry out, a high destiny to achieve, but these can hardly be accomplished so long as it remains a slave to the present system of education, so long as it does not introduce its own national system of education. A nation that does not feel pride in its glorious past and holds light its national ideals, cannot make its future bright, nor can it aspire to occupy a high place in the hierarchy of civilized nations. It is my intention to give in this short paper, an outline of the programme of national education according to my own light. I do not claim for it any perfection or even all-India suitability but if it could be of any use in evolving a better scheme, it will not have been written in vain.

Kanoomal

Specimen II: Social
About a local festival of Eastern Bengal
(Source: Man in India, A quarterly record of Anthropological Science with special reference to India. Ranchi, vol. III, nos 3 & 4, September & December, 1923)

Year : 1923

Notes on Kali-Nautch in the District of Dacca in Eastern Bengal
by
Dhirendra Nath Mazundar, B.A.
and
Sarat Chandra Mitra, M.A.

The Hook-swinging festival has been popular in the district of Dacca in Eastern Bengal from time immemorial. Although it has now disappeared on account of legislation, its place has been taken by another festival which is differently designated in different parts of the district. The names commonly applied to this festival are Nila Puja and Pata-Puja. It is celebrated on the last day of the Bengali month of Chaitra which corresponds to the English months March-April.

The customs associated with this Puja or worship-festival are varied and numerous. I shall describe one of these customs, namely, a *nautch* or dance which is performed by the rustic people of the district, on the same *tithi* or lunar date as the day fixed for the holding of the hook-swinging festival.

Just a fortnight previous to the aforementioned *tithi* or lunar date, the people come out in bands and armed with sticks, and, with drums beating, parade the whole neighbourhood and collect rice and other contributions towards the expenses of the nautch or dance. This dance is somewhat similar to that performed in connection with the Muharram Festival. The people, particularly the boys, arming themselves with sticks or *kanchis* of different shapes and devices, dance up and down the streets, and are welcomed by all the people of the locality through which the party parades. The dance is held in honour of the goddess Kali who is the presiding deity of this festival. I have learnt from the devotees — the celebrants of this worship-festival — that, when they fall ill, they usually pray to the goddess Kali, vowing that, in case they will recover from their illness, they will actually take part in the *nautch* to be performed in honour of her deityship. It, therefore goes without saying that this *nautch* or dance is the outcome of sincere faith and of devotion; and the devotees indulge in it whole-heartedly.

Specimen III: Print-media communication
(Source: *The Times of India*)

Year : 1924

READER'S VIEWS
THE BOLI CHUMUZ

To
The Editor
The Times of India

Sir, — I recently paid a visit to Bijapur in company of a few friends who were desirous to see the famous building of the town. We went to see the Boli Ghumuz or the Whispering Gallery which is reputed to be one of the most wonderful works of art in India. I need not add that tourists from Europe and America go down to Bijapur specially to see this Whispering Gallery and that it justly enjoys reputation which is only next to that of the Taj Mahal of Agra. This was not my first visit to Bijapur. I have seen it twice or thrice before. This time, however, I was painfully surprised to find that repairs on an extensive scale were going on at the Boli Ghumuz. Something is wrong with this great building and when I discussed the matter with some friends I came to know that the close proximity of the railway station to the Ghumuz was the cause of the repairs. The constant shock that the building receives owing to the railway traffic are too much for it and it appears to be the opinion of men who understand the subject that unless the railway line is removed at a safe distance the Boli Ghumuz will come to permanent harm before long. I am a layman and I cannot say anything authoritatively on the subject, but I venture to bring the matter to the notice of the government so that necessary steps might be at once taken to preserve this admirable monument of Mahomeden art. I remember that when, during the Viceroyalty of Lord Curzon, some cracks were observed in the Taj Mahal at Agra, that eminent lover of arts and ancient monuments lost no time in setting things right. In fact, Lord Curzon's services in the matter of preserving the ancient monuments have been unique and I hope the spirit that prompted Lord Curzon still prevails in the Government. The Boli Ghumuz is one of the greatest show places of our country and it will be disgraceful if any harm comes to it. If the proximity of the railway line is the cause of the mischief, then the line ought to be removed at a safe distance. The Government will, I hope, attach greater weight to the need of preserving this ancient monument intact.

M.D. Altekar,
French Bridge, Bombay,
January 21, 1924

Specimen IV: Literary Writing (Prose)
S. Srinivasa Iyengar's 'Foreword' to a book by K. Iswara Dutt
(Source: Dutt, K. Iswara (1929), *Sparks and Fumes: Pen-Pictures of Andhra Leaders*, Madras: Current Thought Press)

Year : 1929

FOREWORD

It is a difficult and risky thing to attempt the piquant portrait of contemporary men of note about whom there must always be some controversy. It is more difficult in India than elsewhere where the skin is still sensitive to criticism but gluttonous to flattery. In his pen-pictures of Andhra Worthies, Mr Iswara Dutt of *Swarajya* has set himself a task which is by no means easy and requires considerable judgement and skill. His phrasing is crisp and convincing, his style has both vigour and freshness, and his delineation is characterised by shrewdness and subtlety. I have spent an enjoyable hour and I should like others to have the same pleasure.

S. Srinivasa Iyengar
Amzad Bagh,
Mylapore
April 12, 1929

Specimen V: Bureaucracy
A handwritten application for the post of a teacher
(Source: *B.S. Moonje Papers*; Sub file: Bhosla Military School — Applications for various posts in the Bhosla Military School)

Year : 1936

To
Dr B.S. Moonje,
General Secretary,
Central Hindu Military Education Society, Nagpur

Sir,

I beg to offer my services as a teacher in the proposed Bhonsla Military School, to be started next July.

I am a B.A. of the University of Bombay. I passed the said examination in 1927 from the then New Poona College (Now Sir Parashurambhau College), with English and Marathi as my voluntary Subjects. Since then I have been working as a teacher and thus acquired vast experience in teaching. At present, I am working in the Parle Tilak Vidyalaya, Vileparle, where I am in charge of English of the Matriculate class and Sanskrit & Marathi of Std. VI. The testimonials attached hereto will speak regarding my experience and ability in teaching.

It will not be out of place, I believe, if I say a word about my aim in life. I have willfully taken this line when immediately after my graduation I had ample chances of getting a job either in the Revenue or Postal Departments.

Believe me, Sir, if I say that nothing would please me than serving a public educational institution like the one you are going to start next July.

I may add that it has been my honest endeavour to find a suitable field wherein to use my talents and ability to the best, and I will be highly obliged to you if you will kindly give me scope by taking me up.

I may assure you that if taken up, your choice in my case will be amply rewarded.

Thanking you in anticipation.

I beg to remain,
Sir,
Your most obdt. sevt.
. . .
(D.N. Bhagwat)
Dt. 12th January 1936

Specimen VI: Bureaucracy
An extract from a bureaucrat's report of an accident
(Source: *Railway Accidents:*
Reports and Inquiries for the half-year ending 31st March 1937)

Year : 1937

Eastern Bengal Railway

No. 94 Down Passenger train running into a sand humped isolation dead-end at Dum Dum Junction on the 3rd December 1936

From Mr R.B. SETH, GOVERNMENT INSPECTOR OF RAILWAYS, CIRCLE No. 2, CALCUTTA, LETTER No. 48/1010/ 83, DATED THE 18TH JANUARY 1937 (6849-T.)

Description of the Accident. — While approaching Dum Dum Junction Khulna Branch Train No. 94 Down, Dattapukur Local, ex-Dattapukur to Calcutta, entered sand humped isolation dead-end provided at the North end of the station to isolate the Khulna Branch from the Main Lines. The engine and the vehicle next to it, a bogie Third and Brake Van No. 1788, went through the sand hump down a 20 feet high bank. The engine capsized completely and lay with chimney down and wheels up. The body of the bogie Third and Brake Van was wrenched off the under-frame, thrown lower down the embarkment (near a tank of water) and was smashed, the under-frame was on the slope of the bank and was twisted and bent. The remainder of the train was on the rails and suffered no damage except the head stock and buffers of the second vehicle from the engine.

The train consisted of 6 bogie passenger vehicles with a four-wheeled coaching goods wagon in the rear drawn by a 2–6–4 Type Tank Engine (B.T.C. Class No. 647) running chimney first. The weight of the engine and train was about 300 tons and the overall length about 494 feet. The vacuum brake was in operation on all wheels of the vehicles and on the coupled wheels of the engine, brake power being about 83.3 per cent.

The train was well filled with passengers, the vehicle next to the engine was crowded chiefly with vendors. I regret to report that one passenger received fatal injuries, 19 passengers were admitted as 'In-door' patients in Hospitals at Calcutta and 7 received treatment as 'Out-door' patients. Of the Railway employees, the driver, both the firemen and a Khalasee of Engineering Department received minor injuries.

The amount of damage to rolling stock is estimated at about Rs 25,000. There was no damage to the Permanent-way.

The injured received early medical attendance. First Aid was given by the Guard of the train and a local medical practioner. The Chief and District Medical Officers of the Railway reached the scene of the accident within an hour of the occurrence.

The relief Train arrived at the site of the accident at about 8–02 hours and line was cleared for through working at about 8–52 hours.

The weather was fine and clear and the rails dry.

Specimen VII: Social

A handwritten letter received by
Shanta Bhalerao, Asst. Secy., A.I.T.U.C.
(Source: *All India Trade Union Congress Papers.* Sub-file: Letters received by Shanta Bhalerao)

Dalal Bhawan,
Nadiad,
8th April 1943

Dear Miss Bhalerao,

Do you remember me? Well, we met at Broach and once again in Bombay. Though rather belatedly, I would like to congratulate you for the fine impression you created on everyone at Broach. I wish the A.I.T.U.C. could circulate you more. Can't you possibly train up few more wholetimers like yourself?

This is to thank you for have given your co-operation to Dr Trivedi and Mr Shah. They have just written to me praising to the skies. Of course, I can assure you that I shall take this with a pinch of salt because I want you to be even more helpful to them. I asked them to keep in touch with you and to work in consultation with you. I do hope you will get Mr Joshi to get a close interest in the matter.

Isn't it fine that the Broach teachers have won? Now we should do something to organise teachers all over Gujarat and thus capitalise the victory of the teachers of Broach. I am seeing teachers here and asking them to wake up. Have you any suggestions to make?

With best wishes,

Yours Sincerely,
(Sd/ Rajani Patel)

Specimen VIII: Bureaucracy
A letter of complaint
(Source: *Hyderabad Residency Correspondence.* File No. 371, 1946)

Bownpally, Secunderabad Dn.
Dated 6th Feb. 1946

To
The District Supdt. of Police,
SECUNDERABAD DECCAN.

Respected Sir,
    I beg to bring a few following lines under your kind consideration.
    I am a pensioner of 81st Pioneer, Madras, in which I was a Havildar and also I am a retired Head Constable of S.D.P. I am residing now in Pedda Thokatta, Comsary Bownpally. The place where I am residing, there is a undesirable party, who call themselves as Arya Somagists as they do not act according to the rules and regulations of the Samaj, but they used to hit poor people and do bad things in village and they want other people of the village to be always under their control. Like this they were pressing my son A. Ramuloo from one & half year to join their party and many a times Deshmukh B. Pratapa Reddy of this village also pressed my son, but being myself a pensioner and my son a government employee, I made my son not to join the Samaj of the party. He listened to me and refused to join the party or Samaj.
    Having not listened to them and not joined in the party they determined to kill my son, on Sunday the 3rd instant at 10.00 o'clock in the morning at my premises in my presence in my house, my son was standing in my house at that moment the Deshmukh of the village gathered all the party and asked them to rush on us. With his instructions they came with lotties and Swords and rushed into my house and hit me and my son, in the meantime my son escaped from them and ran straight to the Police Station of that village and reported this matter. This was happening until and after the police to this place. They called me and my son to Deshmukh's house and taken down the statement of me and my son and went away saying that they will call the party and us to the police station the next day, but till now they have not yet taken any action for the above matter.
    Now what the party and Deshmukh of the village determined is that they are going to kill me or my son on the way of going for duty in the day or night time, and another thing what the Deshmukh is doing is, he is forcing the person called Marri Ramaswamy who sold the house to me on 22–7–1938 for Rs 425/- H.S. in which I am staying now to stand as witness for Deshmukh, that he has not sold the house to me but has given to me for rent. Like this the Deshmukh want to go myself from the village leaving the house to them.

So as my life is in danger, and they are behaving with me like this, I can't bear. I hope your honour would take necessary steps into the matter as my life is in danger.
Thanking your goodself for the same.

I beg to remain,
Respected Sir,
Your most obedient Servant,
(Sd/-) . . . .
(Sd) Madurappa Thevar
Ex-head Constable &
Ex-Havildar,
Pensioner, 81st Pioneer Madras.

Address:-
Madurappa
127, Pedda Thokatta,
Kamsary Bazaar, BOWNPALLY
SECUNDERABAD DECCAN

Enclo : 2

Copy to:-   1. The Hon'ble Resident at Hyderabad,
               Residency Court, Hyderabad Dn.

            2. The Welfare Officer, HQ 172 (Sec'bad)
               Sub Area, Bolarum

Through :   The Soldier's & Sailer's Board
               HQ 172 (Sec'bad) Sub Area, Bolarum

Specimen IX: Print-media communication
(Source: *The Star*. An English journal published from Bombay)

Year : 1946

A THOUGHT FOR THE DAY

The Editor,
The 'Star'
Bombay

Dear Sir,

    Healthy criticism adds to progress. And every one who aims at progress invites criticism. I trust you will not think otherwise when I write you the following, which is only a suggestion or rather a poser.

    I am keenly following the progress and greatly interested in the healthy growth to fame of our little baby 'Star' and always pray for its success. From its first publication I am reading 'The thought for the day' just over the Editorial. Each time I found that quotations are taken from some other source and not from the Holy Qoran. Qoran is the only Sacred Book on the earth which contains and covers all the subjects. Plenty of quotations, thoughts and instructions to suit any day and any occasion. I am not in any way against your publishing quotations from anybody. What I want to convey to you in this letter is that we are Muslims first and everything next. Our Qoran first and others next. Your paper is read mostly by Muslims and Muslims always like and respect quotations from the Holy Qoran. Not only that even others who belong to other religions will have the chance of knowing what is in Holy Qoran. Why not we concentrate on what is best and what is our own?

I will wait for the next issue of the 'Star' with a brighter twinkle and with a 'Qoran touch'.

Yours truly,
Mohamed Ashraf Rangoonwalla
Bombay, 4th March, 1946

Specimen X: Education
An official letter written by an Indian Vice-Chancellor to a British bureaucrat
(Source: *Hyderabad Residency Correspondence.* File No. 371, 1946)

Vice-Chancellor
Osmania University, Hyderabad Deccan.
April 15, 1946

My Dear Dr Sargent,

In pursuance of the suggestion made by you in successive communications the Osmania University has decided to have a Student's Advisory Bureau for the objects which you have indicated from time to time. Before the fact is notified for the benefit of the public, it is essential that the Bureau should be so equipped with up-to-date information with regard to studies abroad as to be able to effectively fulfil the object of advice or information. So far, no information appears to have been placed at our disposal and you would be assisting us considerably by sending us copies, whether in book form or in the form of Circulars, of all such up-to-date information with regard to admission, academic and other facilities, names of particular Universities and institutions for particular subjects etc., as may be in the possession of the Government of India. Such information will be carefully docketed and used by our own Advisory Bureau and we would, therefore, welcome receiving it as early as possible, as we are anxious to provide the machinery immediately for advising non-sponsored students in the state.

I would much appreciate your throwing light also on another matter, viz., whether you would suggest including in the scope of the

Student's Advisory Bureau, the giving of information or advice with regard to train of technical personnel in factories and works — a subject with regard to which the different Universities and Governments have been approached by the Department of Labour of the Government of India. If that subject is also included it would prevent duplication which would otherwise result through establishment of another Bureau of some sort for advising technical personnel on the question of receiving training abroad in factories and works. I would much like to know your reactions in this matter.

Yours Sincerely,
Sd/ — Ali Yavar Jung

Dr John Phillip Sargent, C.I.E.,
Educational Advisor to the Government of India,
New Delhi

(c) What the data shows: Some observations

Apart from the general features in the domain of bureaucracy and the allied areas like education, judiciary and legislature, there are some department specific formats and lexical items in the bureaucratic writing.

Specimen VIII, a letter of complaint, contains a sentence which is attitudinally important; the format follows the conventions found in the earlier phase:

Respected Sir,

I beg to bring a few following lines under your kind consideration

. . . .

Thanking your good self for the same.

I beg to remain,
Respected Sir,
Your most obedient servant,

The writer says, 'being myself a pensioner and my son a government employee, I made my son not to join the Samaj of the party.' The party refers to a local association. The writer considers that being a government employee is reason enough for staying away from local associations; he may be afraid of losing his pension. The attitude is that government employees form a distinct class, and that they should not get involved in local politics.

The letter is full of mistakes, unacceptable and odd expressions like 'like this the Deshmukh want to go myself from the village', 'hit poor people and do bad things in village', 'they determined to kill my son', etc.

Specimen IV is an example of the language used in the railways:

Sand humped isolation dead-end; Main lines; engine capsized; under-frame; head stock and buffers; a four-wheeled coaching goods wagon; 2–6–4 Tank Engine; rolling stock; the relief train ...

Mostly passive constructions are used: was twisted: was smashed; is estimated; was given by; was cleared

The odd construction is: The train was well-filled with passengers.

The 'railway register' is continued even now with all its oddities.

Specimen V, an application for a job, is also an interesting piece the features of which can be found even in the application written today:

(i) I beg to offer my services

(ii) I'll be highly obliged if you will kindly give me scope by taking me up.

(iii) I may assure you that if taken up, your choice in my case will be amply rewarded.

(iv) I have willfully taken this line ... I had ample chances of getting a job in the Revenue or the Postal Departments.

(v) Thanking you in anticipation;

> I beg to remain,
> Sir,
> your most obdt. sevt.

The letter shows that government jobs are sought after and to forgo them to become a teacher is a sort of 'sacrifice' which vouches for the applicants commitment to the teaching profession.

These letters show that English is used for all these purposes because there is no other language that is known to both the parties; in addition the connections and functions in the use of English have been so institutionalized that they resemble the official/impersonal faces of bureaucracy.

Specimen III & IX (letters to the newspaper editors) share a number of features, appropriate as well as inappropriate; the topics chosen by the writers indicate that religious and socio-cultural identity is attempted through English though there are instances of inappropriate usages.

The article, 'Hindu National Education', is an indication of the awareness of being 'Indian' and of the emergence of 'Nation-India' though it is equated with 'Hindu'. The predicament of this article (Sp. I) is that the protest against English education has to be articulated in English. Expressions like 'national making' (what is meant is 'nation making'), 'national ideals', 'national system of education' have been used. Though there are a number of mistakes in the essay (e.g. numbers of clerks, according to my own light, etc.), attitudinally it is important.

Specimen X is an official letter written by an Indian Vice-Chancellor. The ease with which educated Indians handled the English language is amply reflected in this letter; another example of the competent handling of English is found in Specimen IV.

(i) My dear Dr Sargent,
. . .
Yours sincerely,

(ii) In pursuance of . . .
. . . placed at our disposal . . .
. . . as may be in the possession of the Government of India.
(These are officialese found in the letter.)

(iii) With regard to train of technical personnel (maybe a mistake in typing!)

Specimen IV is short and crisp; the choice of vocabulary and syntax is appropriate.

The emerging 'cline' is the most prominent aspect of the use of English in the subcontinent; some used it effectively with a high degree of competence but quite a few use the language inappropriately. Specimen VII is a personal letter full of mistakes:

Circulate you more

train up more wholetimers

for have given your co-operation

The cline of intelligibility exists even today in the use of English.

Specimen II is an example of another kind of incomprehensibility arising out of a restricted cultural context, though the Indian words are paraphrased in terms of 'either-or':

Bengali month of Chaitra which corresponds to the English months March–April;

Puja or worship-festival; nautch or dance; tithi or lunar date

There are other expressions like 'hook-swinging festival', 'deity-ship', 'drums beating', etc. The writer has translated and/or trans-literated word by word and image by image but has not been able to communicate the ethno-cultural context of this 'festival'; it is low on the cline because of its low communicability.

The poem 'Sita-Rama' (Appendix, Ph. IV, sp. VII) uses Indian linguistic repertoire to create an 'Indian rhythm of the Indian' milieu:

Ram he Ram; Sita-Rama, Sita-Rama Ho!

The imagery has two levels; descriptive (which can be comprehended by anyone), evocative (which is not easily comprehensible to readers unfamiliar with Indian culture). Yet, the language is creatively used. When Indian poets want to convey uniquely Indian themes, they incorporate items of Indian linguistic repertoire into the English linguistic system and interweave English lexical items into images that communicate at the two levels: descriptive and evocative. This is part of the 'creative bending', in the literary writing of Indians using English. Indian writing in English also found an international market during this phase.

4.2.5 Phase V: 1947–90 — The identity phase

(a) The profile
The two important legacies of the British rule in India are
 (i) a full-blown bureaucratic network, and
 (ii) an institutionalized English education within the framework of the Macaulean system of education; in both, English continues to be the dominant language. In the post-1947 India, the Indian elite who struggled to oust the British have established their power over the vast majority. According to the 1981 census only 23.31 per cent constitute the urban population and that percentage includes the migrant workers from rural areas, labourers and other poorer sections of the society who are either illiterate or barely educated (school dropouts). This section of the population does not come under the English-educated category. Thus, the urban population itself is a minority and the English-knowing section of

the urban population is a minuscule minority. It is this section of the population that controls education and the bureaucratic network through their knowledge of English and the printed word. Education feeds into the domain of bureaucracy which in turn governs and regulates education. Academic, intellectual and literary activities are overlapping and interdependent domains in the unified communication space of the written word, and bureaucracy too intersects the field of the printed word in the form of government and control.

The full-blown bureaucratic network covers the socio-economic areas of governance and planning in the form of advisory boards, committees and commissions, ministries and the various government departments, the legislature and the judiciary, government controlled non-governmental set-ups like the educational institutions, autonomous bodies, trusts, banks, registered companies, social organisations, and societies, etc. In all these areas, the 'Baboo culture' continues though the country is ruled by Indians for Indians; the 'ruling Indians' have only replaced the British rulers but the system has not changed. The 'ruling Indians' expect the same 'most humbly beg' variety from the ruled. However, attempts to accommodate Indian languages in education and administration have started creating a 'hybrid tradition' that is yet to get stabilized.

There has been a phenomenal expansion in areas like education and mass communication in the recent past. There is an international market for English and materials in English in print as well as electronic media — and newspapers, newsmagazines, advertising agencies have all the paraphernalia, 'producers' and 'consumers'. Mass media, information technology and communication network have brought about radical changes in national and international contexts; access to the international market has brought in new pressures on post-1947 India. All these developments have reinforced English and English education and there is a great demand for English and Western technology which in turn re-introduces English as an international/second language. India is forced to catch up with the West and English in India has become more 'internationally oriented' than 'British oriented'.

The boom in literary areas like Indian Writing in English and in intellectual areas like Indian culture and philosophy, post-colonial studies, herbology and alternative medicines demonstrates that outside India, 'India' sells very well in English.

While all these 'explosions' are taking place in the English-knowing world, the 76.69 per cent of the rural population combined with the illiterate section of the 23.31 per cent of the urban population is becoming more and more illiterate. These people, who were brought up in the oral traditions of the social milieu, became illiterate even in their mother tongue with the introduction of the printed word. They again became illiterate vis-à-vis English and English education; now they are becoming 'incomputerate', an even worse disadvantage than illiteracy and English illiteracy; 'computeracy' is again pushing them to the margins.

The gap is widening; as in the socio-economic area, in the knowledge and use of English, there is an ever increasing (de)cline of intelligibility in each domain. There are levels of English-knowing bureaucrats, educationists, business persons, media persons, teachers and students, writers and readers; there is a continuum of English: from 'Bazaar-English', 'Butler-English', 'Baboo-English' to 'near native English'. Where there is quantitative increase, qualitative decline is unavoidable.

In the social domain, particularly in the recent past, English has induced what may be called the 'imitative function' — a tendency to imitate the successful English-educated elite. As a result, quite a few people have started using English even in areas where it is neither necessary nor appropriate. The 'imitative use' has an element of parody in the case of some but in most cases it shows the desire to be successful in life.

English and English education have been with a section of the urban population so long that it has uprooted quite a few, and the result is that they are neither here nor there; this section of the population has no mother tongue and no cultural roots in the conventional sense; they are comfortable only with English but that English is not 'native'. These displaced people — linguistically and otherwise — are in their 'camps' or 'settlements' in the urban areas and such settlements are on the increase. There is nothing derogatory about displacement or the hybrid culture that is being created; maybe, these are products of attempts to integrate cultures and languages; maybe, such people do not adopt the modular strategies of the common people.

(b) The data

Domains: bureaucracy, education, print-media communication and commercial, intellectual/literary writing, and social

Specimen I: Bureaucracy: Resolution passed by the Kandla Port Advisory Committee on 8th June, 1950
(Source: *Sardar Patel's Correspondence 1945–50, Volume 10*)

Year : 1950

III. Town Planning

1. The Committee resolved that:
   (a) pending finalisation of arrangements mentioned in sub-paras below planning should continue under present arrangements;
   (b) to avoid costly mistakes, it is necessary to utilise the best available talent and to the fullest extent, even though that might involve extra expenditure of a few lakhs of rupees;
   (c) the services of a firm of unquestioned repute should be utilised for the preparation of all plans of the entire area, on a well co-ordinated and well-planned basis;
   (d) Seth Kasturbhai Lalbhai, Chairman of the Committee, be entrusted to settle terms with M/s. International Basic Economic Corporation. This firm, in the opinion of the Committee, are not merely a firm of town planning consultants, but have on their staff well-known experts on water supply, drainage, power supply, road building, etc. and are therefore in a position to evolve a well balanced Master Plan on a sound basis of overall economy.
2. The Committee further resolved that a substantial portion of the cost of town planning should be borne by the Government of India, a moiety being borne by the Sindhu Resettlement Corporation.

Specimen II: Print-media communication
(Source: *The Times of India* —
Special supplement of some news items from 1921 to 1960)

Year : 1956

A film review
ON THE INDIAN SCREEN
SHANTARAM'S 'JHANAK JHANAK'
DELIGHTS PACKED HOUSES
By Our Film Critic

February 1, 1956

Mr Shantaram's new picture, 'Jhanak Jhanak Payal Baaje,' produced and directed by him, was premiered with considerable eclat at the Metro and the Royal Opera House in Bombay on Friday.

The picture stars Sandhya with Gopi Krishna in the romantic leads and a brilliant supporting caste including the famous character actor Keshavarao Date.

The story is a saga of the Indian dance. Supported by sumptuous sets of massive grandeur displaying a refined artistry of the highest order in colour as well as design.

A feast of Kathak at its best, displayed in a series of sparkling vignettes and gorgeous ensembles with delightful glimpses of occasional folk-dances. A truly brilliant movie. Entirely rewarding.

Specimen III: Literary-writing (Prose)
An ex-army General's foreword to a book about Indian Army
(Source: Dharam Pal (1961), *Traditions of the Indian Army*,
New Delhi: National Book Trust)

Year : 1961

Foreword

When respect for 'Traditions' and the observance of certain unwritten rules of Society seem to be on the wane, the publication of a book like this, the Traditions of the Indian Army, is indeed very timely. Respect for and the application of, 'Traditions', in the things we say and do in life in the service of our Motherland do help build esprit de corps and this is helpful in stimulating the spirit of loyalty and team work thus producing efficiency all round. Mere 'talking' and 'reading' of traditions alone will not help in any way. We must be their practical respecters and not just theoretical devotees.

This is the very first book of its kind I have seen so far. The Officers in our army today, old and young — indeed our youth as a whole, owe a deep debt of gratitude to the author, Dr Dharam Pal, for this yeoman service he has done them and to those millions to come after. For the publication of this book the author certainly has done a great research and wide study. Its pages are a crowded gallery of the accounts of heroic deeds of our grand soldiers, past and present, on and off the battlefields all the world over, with a clear evaluation of the characteristics of the various classes of our people who are members of this glorious Team — Our Army.

I do hope this book will be read very widely by our people everywhere, for they should know what stuff our gallant Officers and Men are made of and what they should do to see that standards are kept higher than before. I do hope too that a copy of *Traditions of the Indian Army* will have a place in every library in our Country.

I earnestly hope that our youth of today will, by reading this book, be inspired to emulate the spirit of devotion to duty, selflessness in their service to the country and preparedness to make every kind of sacrifice for the cause of the country, so inherent in every Officer and Man, in all that they will do as architects of the India to be — a Land of plenty and peace for all.

K.M. CARIAPPA,
General (Retd.)

Roshanara
Mercara
May 24, 1961

Specimen IV: Print-media communication
A letter published in a newspaper
(Source: *The Times of India*, 13 January, 1961)

Year : 1961

To
The Editor
The Times of India

Sir, — The Five-Year Plans of our nation are at present being launched on April Fool's day, which surely is not a very auspicious beginning for them. Would it not be a better idea to launch them at the time of Diwali-Laxmi pooja, when the Goddess of Prosperity is worshipped and propitiated?

13 January, 1961   G.B. Singh

Indians' English • 131

Specimen V: Commercial (An advertisement)
(Source: *The Eastern Economist.* An English Journal published from New Delhi, vol. 55, no. 17, Oct. 23, 1970)

Year : 1970

YOUR CARGO in our Safe deposit vault! Air transportation is not just for small goods. We're anxious to tell you that we carry heavy and bulky cargoes across oceans and continents with skill, care and speed.

We uplift heavy and massive items of machinery, ships spares and generators, computers and other delicate equipment, requiring very special handling.

On our palletised flights we carry seven thousand kilos on three pallets, all cabin loaded. In addition, we carry four thousand kilos in our holds.

If you're fighting for time, contact us. We'll fly your consignment on our palletised service swiftly, safely, sufficiently. Use Air-India and profit!

Cargo by
AIR-INDIA

Specimen VI: Bureaucracy
An official notice

CENTRAL INSTITUTE OF ENGLISH AND FOREIGN LANGUAGES
HYDERABAD 500007

29 December 1988

NOTICE

The physical stock verification of furniture in each room in the Hostels will be taken up on Saturday 31st December 1988. Participants occupying those rooms where the physical stock verification is not taken so far, are requested to be available to the persons doing the stock verification that day between 10.00 a.m. and 1.00 p.m.

(Signed)
REGISTRAR

Notice Boards (Hostels)

Specimen VII: Education

An undergraduate student's answer

(Source: *Answer-sheets from the second year B.Sc. pre-final examination in English of a degree college in Secunderabad, Andhra Pradesh*)

Year : 1988

Raju was the hero of R.K. Narayan's 'The Guide'. He was born in Malgudi. He studied in a Pyol School but he stopped in middle. He studied the book of life. His mother was his natural teacher. She told him many moral stories. He acquired knowledge from books & newspapers.

Raju was very intelligent. He used to know the interest of the tourists and he also showed interest in those things. He used to know the tourists Economic status by seeing them once.

Raju was a passive hero. Things were happening in his life. He did not plan out anything in his life. They were just happened like that. He didn't want to become a tourist guide he didn't want to become a Saint but when he was sitting in his railway shop people used to ask him about the tourist places and their importance. Like that gradually he became a guide and he showed interest in the Tourists interest. He became very famous as Tourist Guide.

As a guide he met Rosie & Marco. He liked Rosie very much. She is not beautiful but she is pleasant. Marco was not bothered about Rosie. Raju showed interest in Rosie. He showed her the Cobra dance and he appreciated her art. So Rosie became closer to Raju. But he did not have any interest in her art. He loved her sincerely.

Raju after some time became an Economist and wanted to make money of Rosie's art. He acted like a manager. He showed interest in her money than her dance. He spent all money for graudier. He was imprisoned for forgering Rosie's signature.

After coming from the prison he was sitting on the bank of Sarayu. People thought he was a saint and gave him much importance as a saint. So he became a saint without his opinion. But after becoming a saint he wanted to be a saint. He wanted to lead a simple life. He started a school for the children of the village in temple. When rains were not true the Shopkeepers of the village increased the prices of everything and villagers thought that a saint like Raju observes fast then the rains will come. Villagers went ask Raju. Although he was not a saint he observed fast for the rain to come.

Raju was intelligent, lover, economist. Relationship between Raju & Rosie was money. Like this the Tourist Guide Raju became a Saint without his knowledge.

Specimen VIII: Social
A personal letter by an educated Indian (B.A.L.L.B.)
to a friend, another Indian
(Source: Personal correspondence)

Year : 1990
B — —

30th Jan

Dear A — — ,

How have you done your Exams? Its long time since I have received a letter from you. Are you still busy? Did you go home?

I have got the interview letter. The interview is on 12th Feb. I will come there in 12th morning at around 9.30 or 10 AM. If I am not troubling you I will come and keep my things in your room and have a wash. I am planning to go back the same day. If it is not possible I may have to stay for a day. I have written a letter to R — — to inform P — — to let me stay for a day. Happy that I will be meeting you all.

How are you. How are you progressing your Ph.D. I am sure you will be at least 50 per cent released after M.A. exams. When will you get the results. I pray God that you get a I Class. What news from your side. Hope to get a letter before I come there. Meet you on 12th. Convey my regards to A — — .

Specimen IX: Print-media communication
An extract from an editorial
(Source: *The Statesman,* Friday, May 10, 1991, p. 8)

Year : 1991

Reprieve in Bihar

The Centre's decision not to take any action in Patna at this stage must be accorded a welcome, for any move to dismiss Mr Lallu Prasad Yadav or to postpone the elections would only have created misgivings about New Delhi's motives, besides making martyrs of criminals. This is not, of course, to deny that Bihar has become notorious for its lawlessness and that the situation on the eve of the general election inspires little faith in the custodians of the democratic process. Pre-poll violence picked up alarmingly with the killing of Nagina Rai and the murderous attack on Mr L.K. Advani, with a belligerent Chief Minister not helping to mend matters with the inflammatory statements that pay scant heed to the code of conduct, and with his deployment of a massive number of home guards personnel whose credentials are suspect. But though this reckless attitude first drew the Election Commission's attention, the Centre's earlier reported plan either to dismiss the Janata Dal Ministry or to postpone the polls was not prompted by any altruism either. In fact, the efforts by the Union Minister of state for Home Affairs, Mr Subodh Kant Sahay, to take drastic steps may have been prompted by his inability to enthuse voters in his home constituency of Ranchi, while Mr Chandra Shekhar's critic claims that he hoped to prolong the political instability by delaying the election of the 54 members that Bihar sends to the Lok Sabha.

(c) What the data shows: Some observations
Most of the features noticed during the earlier phase (1904–47) are also found during this phase. In addition, the expansion within some domains and the absence of the British as interlocutors, show other significant features.

Bureaucratic correspondence continues to manifest the remnants of the British era though there are attempts 'to waive the formality' and to do away with the 'humbleness vocabulary'; but the absence of alternative conventions cause inconsistency. Sometimes 'Esquire' and sometimes the name with *'ji'* are used. Specimen I (Appendix, Ph. V) is an example of two interlocutors who share Hindi as a common language trying to evolve new conventions; it also shows that English has a status value for politicians and others involved in any work channelized through the government. The resolution passed by the Kandla Port Advisory Committee (Sp. I) is another example of the bureaucratic style; it consists of long sentences with passive constructions: should be utilised; should be borne; a french word 'moiety' that belongs to the legal register is used.

An official notification issued by the CIEFL (Sp. VI) is also full of passive constructions. Cliched expressions and odd usages peculiar to the bureaucratic domain since its inception in India are found in the notice: physical stock verification of furniture; are requested to be available; is not taken so far; those rooms where; doing the stock verification.

The specimens given in the domain of education clearly illustrate the (de)cline of intelligibility; the low point is seen in Specimen VII:

They were just happened like that

when rains were not true . . .

villagers went ask Raju

He studied the book of life.

Raju was a passive hero.

Raju was intelligent, lover, economist.

Relationship between Raju and Rosie was money.

He used to know the tourists Economic status by seeing them once.

It is full of uncomprehended concepts and mistakes in the use of words and sentences.

Specimen VIII and specimen II (Appendix, Ph. V) are examples of informal letters that are low on the cline:

Its long time since I have . . .

If I am not troubling you I will come . . .

How are you progressing your Ph.D.

. . . the places where the schools are there . . .

I pray God that you get 1 class.

The invites aren't ready but am wtg . . . the worse part of it

My parents 'approve but don't really approve' so you see its quite difficult!

Love lots,

The AIR INDIA advertisement (Sp. V) illustrates the use of English for commercial purposes at the international level; it is high on the scale and shows sophisticated salesmanship.

The other ones (Appendix, Ph. V, Sp. III) are not very sophisticated, maybe they are meant for the local market.

The specimen from the print-media communication shows that Indian users of English are able to adapt the language to the needs of the situation and evolve a suitable style. Specimen II, a review of an Indian film, shows 'verbosity' and 'pomposity' — qualities found in the English of the subjects of the ex-colonies of England: with eclat; a saga of the Indian dance; sumptuous sets of massive grandeur; sparkling vignettes and gorgeous ensembles.

On the other hand, Specimen IV, is more balanced; there are no oddities though the sentiment expressed is Indian; so is Specimen IX.

Specimen III clearly shows the Indian identity of the writer since nationalistic pride is expressed in relation to the Indian army; otherwise, there is nothing particularly Indian as far as the language is concerned.

Enough has been written about the intellectual/literary writing that has been subjected to 'creative bending' in order to create an Indian milieu; often a blending of Indian words, symbols and images with the English linguistic system is used. This represents the creative use of English. An expanding international market for Indian writing in English has generated more creativity in this domain; even here, linguistic features — especially at the level of grammar — are less significant than the subject matter expressed. In creative and intellectual writing comprehensibility depends on the writer's ability to adapt English to suit the subject matter and the inability to do so results in ineffective texts. (Burde's Ph.D. thesis (1992) contains many examples and their linguistic features.)

4.3 Summary: Restricted Domains and 'English Sustained' Features

Even a cursory glance at the data and the observations given clearly reveal that the use of English has been contained by restricting its domains. This is just an extension of the survival tactics of the Indian subcontinent; whenever there was a 'foreign' invasion, this 'mode of moduling' happened naturally as part of the survival tactics in a multilingual and multicultural society.

One can see from the data and its analysis presented that the political domain, the 'Lordship register', and the petition register seen during the first phase (1600–1813) fade during the second phase; even the quaint usage influenced by Persian conventions of writing is not very prominent after mid-19th century. The purposes for which English is used begin to cluster in the bureaucratic network which slowly expands and absorbs most areas of public life, bringing them under the written mode. It is the bureaucratic centre called the government of India (set up by the British and taken over by English educated Indians after 1947) that became a vehicle for the entity of the polity; the English language was the instrument for the setting up of the 'State' by the British, for the formation of 'nation-India' (partly through the bureaucratic network and mostly through the struggle for freedom), and for the political freedom and the transfer of power that was wrested from the British. English was the natural choice because it was the only language that the Empire understood and 'nation-India' could not be linked to any one language of the subcontinent. It is quite paradoxical that the very plurality that is celebrated by all, necessitates the use of English in the Indian subcontinent. It was, therefore, no coincidence that the constitution of the politically free nation named 'India' came to be written in English and modelled on the British system of government. The infrastructure of the 'State', its bureaucracy, judiciary, the written functions institutionalized and expanded by the British through the English language remain intact. English education functions as the base for bureaucracy, academic work, science and technology, intellectual and 'management' activities in which basically the English educated and English-knowing urban population participates. This is seen in the domains of English-use around 1900 and during the twentieth century.

The course of the history of English in India charted out so far is sketched below to show the texture and growth of the four/five domains and the domain-restricted use of English.

Phases		Domains
I	: 1600–1813	Political and its extensions: bureaucracy and commercial
II	: 1813–57	Bureaucracy, education, print-media communication and commercial, intellectual/literary writing
III	: 1857–1904	Bureaucracy, education, print-media communication and commercial, intellectual/literary writing
IV	: 1904–47	All the six listed above
V	: 1947–90	All the six listed above

138 • *The Politics of Indians' English*

Profile I
Phase I: 1600–1813 Domain — Political Correspondence

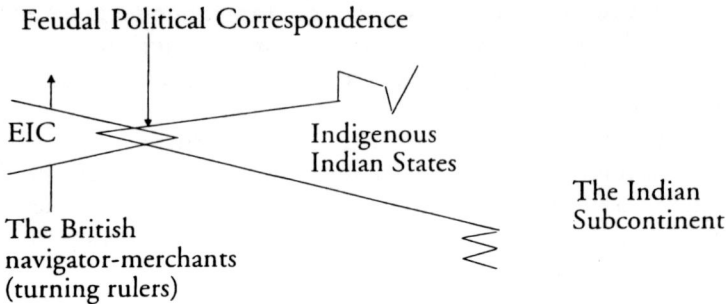

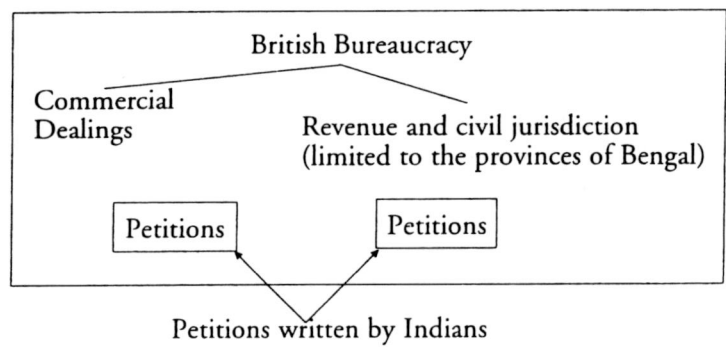

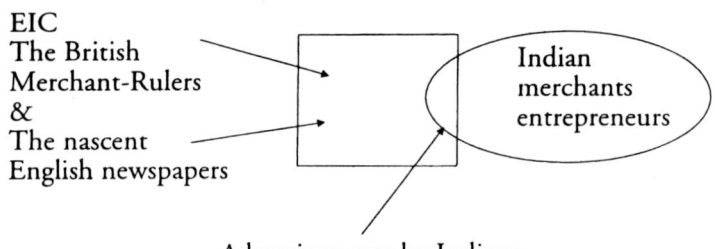

Note: All representations are to be treated as analogical presentations of the spread of English; not to be mistaken for empirical quantitative representation.

Profile II
Domain: Bureaucracy

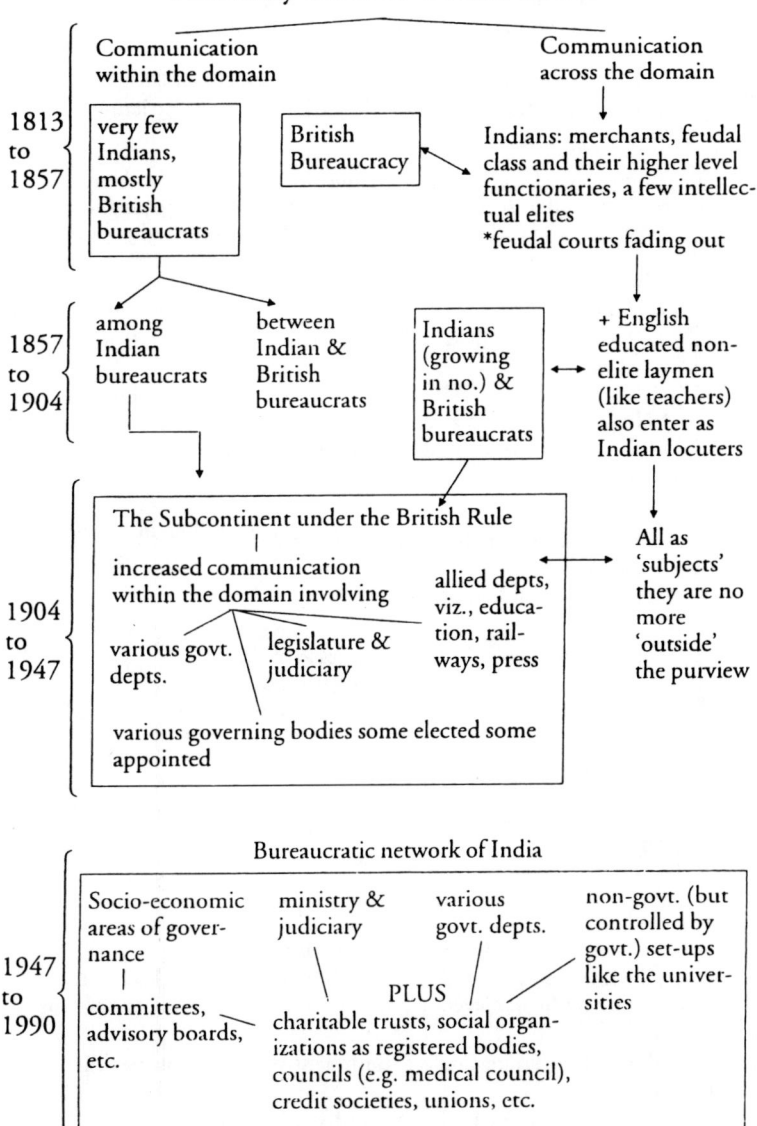

140 • *The Politics of Indians' English*

Profile III
Domain: Education

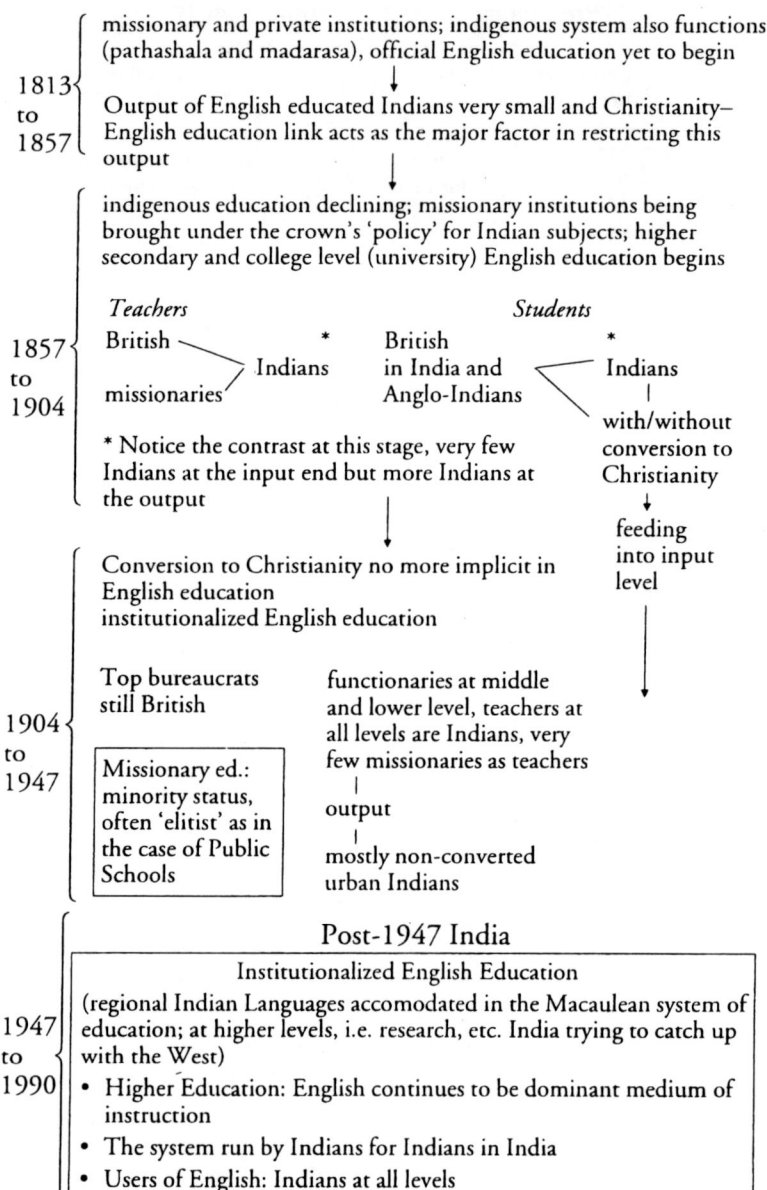

Indians' English • 141

Profile IV
Domain: Print-media communication and commercial (advertising)

	Content	interlocuters	locale	relationship
1813 to 1857	news, ads., editorials, letters to editors, occasional essay(s)	proprietors; editors; contributors of news, letters, essay(s) — British (mostly in India) > English educated Indians	Bombay, Calcutta, Madras	urban readership — British (mostly in India) / English educated Indians
1857 to 1904	+ Socio-cultural and political issues, intellectual debates thru' letters to editor, 'nation' related topics	*Same* But the proportion changes, British < Indians, national leaders, intellectuals, literati, professionals	Spreads to Delhi, Lucknow, Madurai, Patna, and other cities	*Same* But the proportion changes British < Indians
1904 to 1947	• increase in number — newspapers, Indian staff, Indian proprietors, Indian editors, correspondents, Indian entrepreneurs, Indians taking over and growing in number • readership — growing no. of English educated Indians, beyond cities, in towns, district headquarters; overseas readers — both British and Indians; socio-political issues • printing still an urban activity but distribution and sale extends to semi-urban areas • change in terms of quality and a cline			
1947 to 1990	pan-Indian commercial enterprise	journalists, reporters, editors, columnists		professional media men

users of English

(Cont'd on next page)

(Profile IV cont'd)

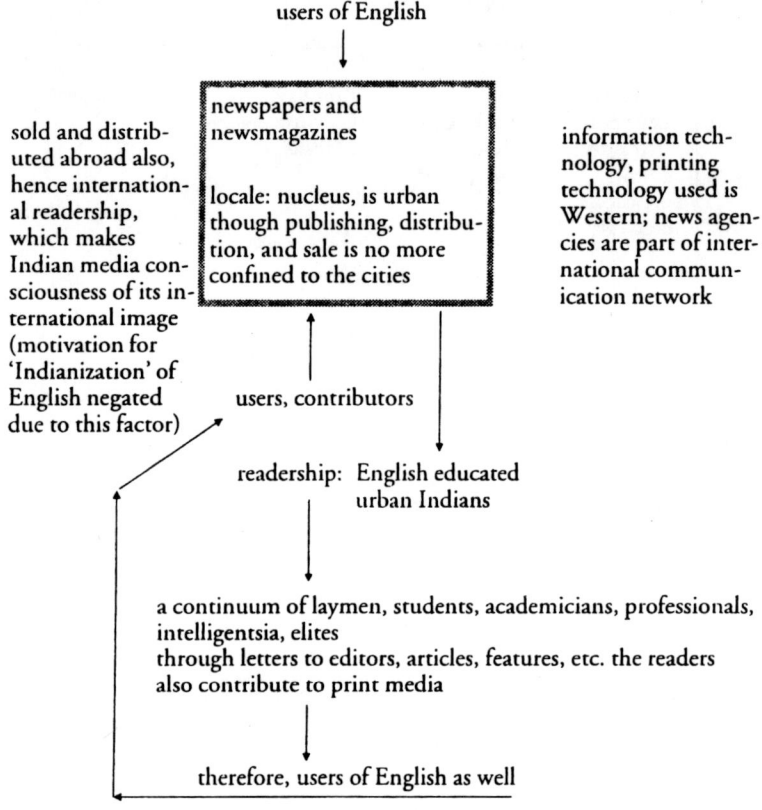

Note: Territory drawn in grey lines indicates that the use of English is not rigidly intra-national; it is open to international pressures.

Indians' English • 143

Profile V
Domain: Intellectual and literary writing

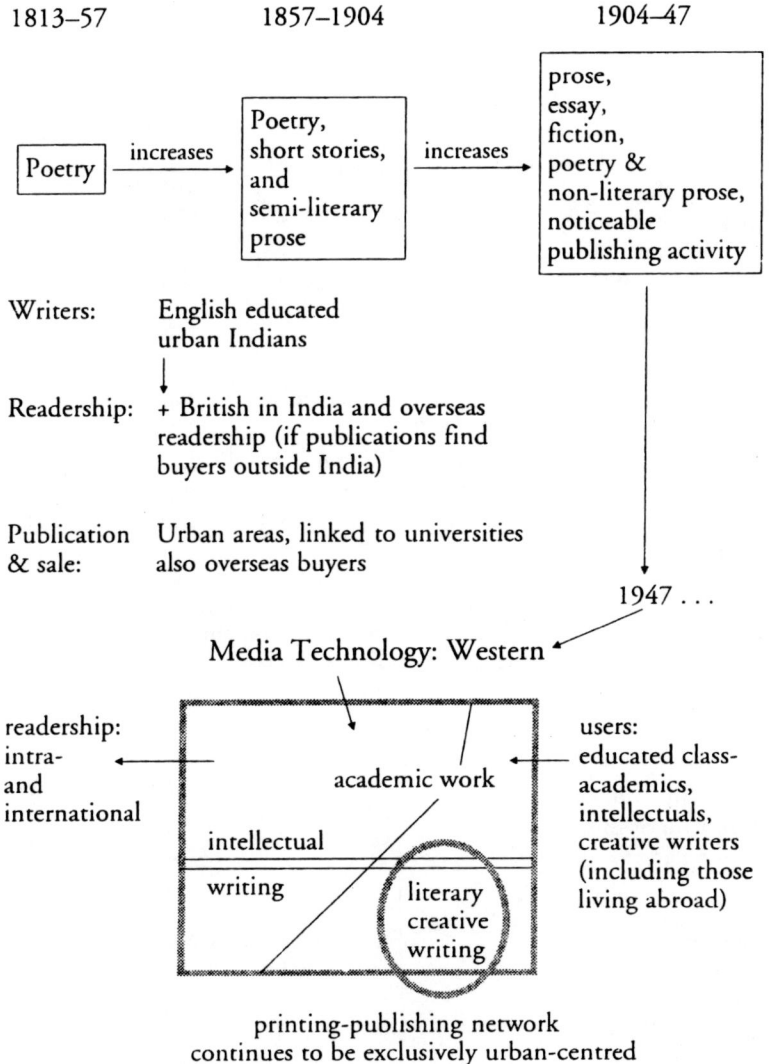

Note: Grey lines indicate international pressures.

Profile VI
Domain: Social (1857 ...)

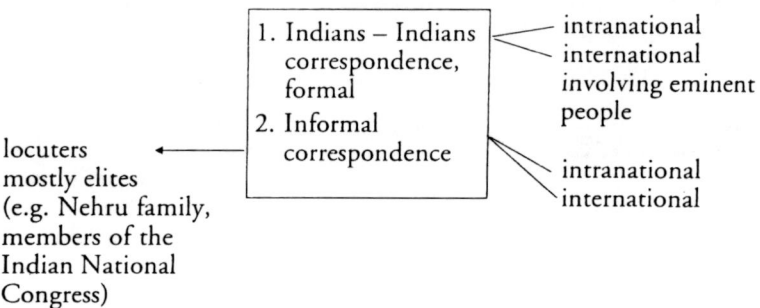

[Sometimes British were involved when eminent Indians wrote to their English friends or vice versa.]
* Users: Urban, English educated Indian elites, leaders, other prominence-gaining Indians. viz., lawyers, political activists
* This domain emerges clearly in the fourth phase and may be called the social domain

Though it does not comprise the socio-cultural milieu of the sub-continent, the number is on the increase — students, professionals and some sections of the upper and middle class.

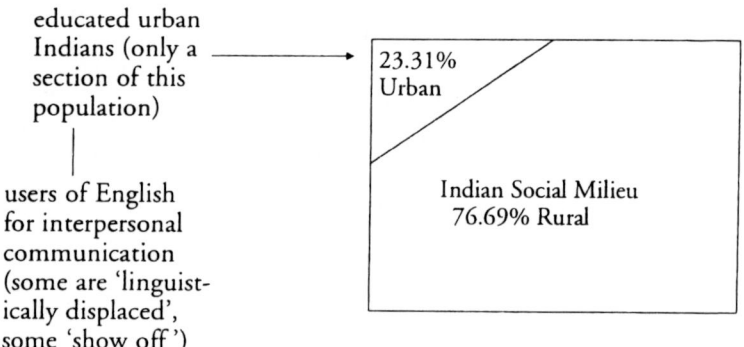

(* Rural–urban ratio as per 1981 census.)

Chapter Five

Indians' English: A Modulect

> India, the perpetual paradox, challenges the imagination in a way no other country does in the world today.
> — Sasthi Brata, *India: The Perpetual Paradox*

5.1 Is there a Case for Indian English?

Consider the passages given below:

(a) What did we mean by 'rediscovery of the past'? Time per se had relatively little to do with it, and nostalgia nothing at all. What was 'past' might have originated long ago and still be functional or accessible — and so part of the present — like a building, a philosophy, a myth, a craft, a dramatic form, a pattern of interaction, a memory. It might be inactive, or forgotten, or discarded, for a whole range of reasons. We proposed to explore continuity and change in India from the inside, to mark the beginning to consciousness and conscious utilization of the past — which is multiple, spiritual, emotional, and empirical — for the sake of the present and the future. How did one wish to synthesize old and new — even East and West? In what ways could relearned or restructured truths be applied to defining goals for the individual and the community and to achieving them — and with what effects? Sacred groves are important not only for religious reasons but for water conservation and as gene banks. Some farmers today, recognizing that they must preserve the long-term biological diversity of their land, are turning to the re-establishment of sacred groves as part of the answer and drawing on elements of modern Western scientific resource management as well. In architecture and planning, acquaintance with historical and traditional forms has inspired among some practitioners a re-interpretation of building activity to incorporate practical respect for the environment and for cultural conditions along with modern techniques. The present grew from the past and, as the artists have described more explicitly in their essays, the two change one another.

— Writer 1

(b) Similarly, those who have been teaching a catechism based on the dogma of 'negative capability', 'primary and secondary imagination', 'spontaneous overflow of powerful emotions recollected in tranquility', and 'objective correlative', for years now claim it impossible to read the 'jargon' and the neologisms of deconstructive and psychoanalytic, or even marxist or feminist theory. The well-digested critical vocabularies of Romanticism, or of Arnold or Leavis or Eliot, are taken as prediscursive and self-evident, as belonging to no histories and staking no ideological positions: theirs are the virtues of universal concern and trans-historical and cultural meaning and value. Any other critical vocabularies, especially those that derive their fundamentals from disciplines other than Literature, and which are of comparatively recent provenance and thus demand an extra effort to learn, are rejected as motivated and partisan. Ultimately (and unfortunately), the entrenched dismissal of theory has more to do with wilful ignorance, academic prejudice and intellectual sloth, and less with an engaged, informed and rigorous response to or rebuttal of competing ideas. What is lacking is a fundamental seriousness or integrity of academic purpose: what substitutes is a series of bad faith, ex cathedra pronouncements.

— Writer 2

(c) All societies have traditions, but only a few have traditions which are central, overpowering, and vital. These are the traditional societies, the whipping boys for students of political development. Their pasts are supposed to have a stranglehold on their presents and their futures, and the pursuit of modern statehood is supposed to be outside the scope of their ancient ideas of citizenship. Yet, some traditional societies seem to take better advantage of the civilizations they represent. In these societies, the traditions are not merely dominant and living, but they are also sufficiently pliable, sufficiently complex and sufficiently self-confident to accommodate the society's efforts to redesign its major institutions. Unlike other traditional societies these do not allow their traditions to be supplanted by modern inputs:

instead, they continuously try to give old meanings to these new experiences.

Ostensibly, such societies are impervious to externally induced changes. Their very cultural autonomy forces them to carry alone, even at the nadir of their strength and dynamism, both the immense burdens and advantages of their traditions. According to some, these societies live by an awareness of this fact; according to others, they are doomed by it. But all agree that any discussion of the culture of politics in such a society must take into account not only the indigenous categories of analysis, but also the society's own priorities and its struggle to learn from its own history whenever possible and to free itself from that history whenever necessary.

— Writer 3

(d) In one of his less celebrated articles, John Plamenatz has talked about 'two types' of nationalism: in both, nationalism is 'primarily a cultural phenomenon' although it often takes a 'political form'. One type is 'western', having emerged primarily in Western Europe, and the other 'eastern', to be found in Eastern Europe, in Asia and Africa, and also in Latin America. Both types depend upon the acceptance of a common set of standards by which the state of development of a particular national culture is measured. In the first type, however, although there is the feeling that the nation is at a disadvantage with respect to others, it is nevertheless already 'culturally equipped' to make the attempt to remove those deficiencies. Thus, although the new global standard of progress may have been set for the rest of the world by France or Britain, they were based upon a set of ideas 'about man, morals and society' which, in their social and intellectual origins, were Western European generally. Britain and France may have been the cultural, economic and political pace makers, and may have been envied or admired for this reason, but simultaneous with the process of their emergence as world leaders, there had emerged a 'comity of nations' in Western Europe 'which had already learned to think of itself as ahead of all others'. Consequently, when nationalism emerged in the other countries of the West, despite the fact that it was the product of a sense of disadvantage with respect to the standards of progress set by the pace makers, there was no feeling that the nation was not culturally equipped to make the effort to reach those standards.

Germans or Italians, for instance, already had the necessary linguistic, educational and professional skills that were deemed necessary for a 'consciously progressive civilization'. They had therefore 'little need to equip themselves culturally by appropriating what was alien to them'. That is to say, although the acceptance of a universal standard of progress had produced an awareness of disadvantage, that universal standard itself was not seen in any fundamental way as being alien to the national culture.

'Eastern' nationalism, on the other hand, has appeared among 'peoples recently drawn into a civilization hitherto alien to them, and whose ancestral cultures are not adapted to success and excellence by these cosmopolitan and increasingly dominant standards'. They too have measured the backwardness of their nations in terms of certain global standards set by the advanced nations of Western Europe. But what is distinctive here is that there is also a fundamental awareness that those standards have come from an alien culture, and that the inherited culture of the nation did not provide the necessary adaptive leverage to enable it to reach those standards of progress. The 'Eastern' type of nationalism, consequently, has been accompanied by an effort to 're-equip' the nation culturally, to transform it. But it could not do so by simply imitating the alien culture, for then the nation would lose its distinctive identity. The search therefore was for a regeneration of the national culture, adapted to the requirements of progress, but retaining at the same time its distinctiveness.

— Writer 4

(e) Imperialism theory will be expounded more fully later. Prior to that, a cautionary note is needed on the implications of using a label such as 'imperialism' as a technical term. It follows from what has already been said about imperialism that individuals with possibly the most altruistic motives for their work may nevertheless function in an imperialist structure. This might for instance apply to anyone concerned with educational aid ('aid', 'educated' and many additional western concepts need to be used with critical caution). That the individuals in question would be disconcerted at being classified as cultural or linguistic imperialists is to be expected. Whereas for most of this century many Europeans were proud to be imperialists, confidently participating in the radiation of their culture, most would resent being accused of imperialism now — even if they represent a dominant culture and their role is to disseminate it. There is likely to be a gut reaction against an accusation of involvement in any form of imperialism, linguistic or otherwise. This is because there is an element of the unethical and morally reprehensible attached to the term, as there is with the words 'racism' and 'sexism'. In order for analysis of the issue to go beyond the level of individual perceptions, roles, and self-image, it is essential to dig down to the underlying structures which support (or counteract) individual efforts. This highlights the need for the elaboration of an adequate theory for this purpose, preferably one which also elucidates how individual actors can influence the structure so as to change it.

— Writer 5

(f) The setting of British administrative policy was laid at the foundations of the British domination in India. In the early period after Plassey expediency predominated. The immediate problem at that time was the manner in which the British should exercise their controlling power in the Bengal territories. At first they felt too inexperienced and unready to contemplate taking the government of the country into their own hands, and had resort to the expedient of a puppet Indian government. Even when this system broke down, and Clive obtained from the titular Mughal authority the grant of the formal right to collect the land revenue and administer civil justice (the grant of the Diwani in 1765), he was determined that the native administration and its officers should be continued, and the Company's power still held in the background. The result was Clive's famous 'double government'. The first point in his politics, as he told the Bengal Council on his departure in 1765, was that the Company's sovereignty should be masked. In this way as little interference as possible was to be made with the indigenous political system. The attitude persisted when the considerations of expediency which had prompted it were no longer so strong. As the indigenous system withered, the British were compelled increasingly to intervene in the revenue and judicial spheres, and to fashion administrative machinery of their own. But they continued to regard themselves as inheritors rather than innovators, as the revivers of a decayed system and not the vanguard of a new. Social conditions favoured this attitude. A handful of eighteenth-century Englishmen, scattered throughout the Bengal territories, without English wives, or prospects of furlough, and with no rigid moral or religious code, soon adapted themselves to Indian ways of living. Set on making their fortune before the climate or disease carried them off, they were zealots for no cause or political principle, and were content to conduct the public business according to its traditional Indian forms and in the traditional hybrid Persian.

— Writer 6

The six passages given above are in the domain of intellectual/academic writing; how many of these are by Indians? The reader is invited to see if Indian writers can be identified. If they can, then there is a case for Indian English; if it is just a matter of individual styles, then there is no case for a distinct or unique variety. Maybe, an experiment like the one suggested above carried on a massive scale can tell us something about the way English is written all over the world in the domains in which it is used. Even the limited data given above shows that there are no significant differences in the written mode between the native and non-native varieties of English in certain domains.

The data presented in the previous chapter clearly shows that the basic structure of English has not changed although Indians have been using it for more than a century now. However, it does display inappropriateness and incomprehensibility, particularly at the lower levels of the cline, and these instances have been projected by some as amusing specimens of Indian English. At the higher levels of the cline in the written mode, these instances of inappropriate usage do not appear. Therefore, a few Indian loan words and fossilized expressions found in Indians' use of English do not constitute a valid base to claim 'Indianization' of English or its pidginization/creolization.

But the data indicates other possibilities of examining English in India. The data displays that the prominent functions of English in India are:

(a) the domain specific, registral use — mostly for bureaucratic, administrative, academic, legal, technical and scientific, and for some limited social purposes,

(b) the culture-translation use that shows culture-bound associative meanings and stylistic variations,

(c) the journalistic use for print-media communication and the creative use for literary-writing with a 'creative bend'.

Though supraregional, its use is mostly confined to urban and semi-urban areas with a strong influence of the written mode.

Of late, these functions are also subject to international pressures and the market-potential available in these areas. The print-publishing trade is another important factor that has helped the spread of English in India. The availability of printed material in English and the non-availability of the same in Indian languages is also an important reason for the tardy development of Indian languages and for retaining, even today, English in education, science, and technology.

For presenting the culture-bound content of the subcontinent, Indians employ words and phrases from regional languages as part of their English, particularly in the social domain, and this process of culture translation, in turn, often affects comprehensibility. In one sense, this process of culture translation helps them to reinforce their identity and keep their roots though it affects comprehensibility; transcreating Indian concepts into comprehensible English is as difficult as the process of translation, something which is impossible but necessary.

The third feature manifested mostly in literary and 'creative' writing, and sometimes in cartoons, commercial advertisements and journalistic writing is the indigenous use of English which has its own motivations and represents bilingual creativity and 'creative bending' directed towards a particular kind of readership.

With the increase in population, particularly in the urban and semi-urban areas, and with the spread of education and the increased internationalization of English, there is quantitative expansion and increase in the number of Indian users of English; this in turn has widened the spectrum in the cline of comprehensibility. The power centres are located in the urban areas and English education that provides the human resources to the power machine is also located in urban areas, thereby justifying and sustaining its existence. Bureaucracy and print-media, which are related to the power structure and products of English education have become part of the network. Thus the intricate networking has helped the microscopic minority of English-knowing urban population to project itself as *the* Indians.

Post-1947, India continues with the same bureaucratic 'governing' system that combined in itself all political and administrative powers with the addition of the 'nation' as the constituting principle; the English educational system continues to provide the human resources to that machinery. This very fact restricts English to the political and administrative definition of 'nation-India'.

At one level, English and English education continue to dominate in spite of the resistance to their oppressive role; but at another level, (post) colonial varieties of English themselves are performing a subversive/'productive' function in a different way — sometimes with an element of parody, sometimes imitating the oppressive 'non-native' elitist variety which in turn is a 'subaltern variety'. The 'carnivalization' continues — a lesson to be learnt from dialectology and subaltern/(post) colonial varieties of English/New Englishes/World Englishes.

5.2 English as a 'Module' in India

A possible explanation could be that 'Indian nationality' is a political label and for people in the subcontinent their identity is 'multi-modular'. The name 'India' indicates only the *political identity* of one part of the subcontinent; the other parts have constituted different nationalities — Pakistan and Bangladesh. As Devy (1992: 2–3) says:

> The term 'India' may be valid in the pages of an atlas, but as a cultural label it is hopelessly inadequate and simplistic. A product of colonial historiography, the term brings with it a politically coloured self-image and the suggestion of cultural amnesia. It can be said that colonialism gave rise to an equally false image of the West in India, an image that is larger than life, static and apparently invincible. Accordingly, the Indian view of the West has remained fraught with idealization, arbitrary fragmentation and unhistorical reductions. This disfiguring colonial epistemology has created false frameworks of cultural values and has stratified knowledge into superior (Western) and inferior (Indian) categories.

If the interaction between English and the Indian subcontinent resulted in the political definition of nation-India and its 'internationalization', it stayed in the educational system that was created by English-education; 'education', which started as part of the political policies of the British rulers, has come to be linked to English-dominated careers, viz. science, technology and its allied areas like mass media, medicine, engineering, commerce, etc. English has also remained as part of the judiciary and administration that it induced. But the finer realms of life that were not involved in the interaction with English have remained unaffected by it; English has not made any serious inroads into the social customs, ceremonies connected with births, marriages and deaths, religious functions and rituals that go with festivals, worship in temples, intimate interactions in the family and in the peergroup — even in urban areas. Only a microscopic minority living in pockets that are spread all over a country of subcontinental size (but that section of the population is 'visible' because the total population of the country is very large and visibility goes with power and status) has been absorbed by English and English education; the vast majority seems to know how to handle the cultural osmosis, how to contain alien languages, how to control invading influences, and how to absorb and manipulate them to its advantage without any clash.

This complex cultural osmosis has been described differently by others — 'segmented identities' (Thapar), 'fluid identity' (Nandy), 'mosaic identity' (Burde), or 'salad-bowl arrangement'; other observers have put it differently. Ghulam Mohammed Sheik says: 'Living in India means living simultaneously in several cultures and times' (1989: 107). It must also be added that for everything that is true of India the opposite is equally true. Arthur Mayhew comments on Indian education and culture: 'The professor of English will not talk about his personal and intimate debt to that literature. For it does not intrude into his personal and domestic life' (quoted in Devy, 1992: 97). The essence of it all is that there is no 'identity' for 'India or 'Indianness' or 'Indian English' as such; at best, one can call it a *plexus*, to borrow a term from biology to mean an organic structure consisting of a network of fibres closely interwoven and intercommunicating or, better still, 'modules' as in computer technology where each one, though self-contained, performs a particular function.

These 'modules' have been developed over centuries as part of the evolution of civilization. Take for example, an inhabitant of the subcontinent who was, at the same time, an inhabitant of Bengal and a Muslim, spoke Bengali as the mother tongue, used Urdu as the language of the religion, was a trader and paid taxes to a Hindu king. Or, one could have been an inhabitant of the Punjab, spoken Punjabi as the mother tongue, been a Sikh by religion and related to a non-Sikh Hindu family, and paid taxes to a Muslim king. This has been a never ending transition, a 'multi-modular' operation. Devy in his *After Amnesia*, says something similar about English education: 'To have it was to have, figuratively speaking, an access to the life in cantonment' (1992: 97).

Even today the same transition continues; we can take, for example, the case of Mr X, a Brahmin by birth, who belongs to the upper-middle class in terms of socio-economic status; he recites *slokas* in the morning and performs the *puja* all in Sanskrit; he goes to the university where he is the head of the department of English and teaches romantic poetry and contemporary fiction (both of which he says, in private conversation, are full of immorality) all in English; at home, he uses only Tamil; in the evening, he goes to a local club, where he drinks imported whisky, and talks to his friends in Telugu or Hindi; he learnt these languages at school and uses them in appropriate social situations; he declares that he is a Hindu fundamentalist and he is a member of one such organization; his family-physician is a Christian but when his child is seriously ill, he takes him/her to a Muslim saint in a nearby *dargah* for faith-healing; sometimes he is invited by the local Tamil Association to preside over some function where he gives a talk on the glories of Sangam literature; he has a reading knowledge of French, as part of the requirement as a graduate student in an American university. He operates within the various 'modules' without any sense of conflict or contradiction because he has compartmentalized his life; he lives his 'English-life' in one of those modules, may be out of necessity. The way he lives his many lives, including his linguistic lives, cannot be comprehended in terms of notions like 'restricted' and 'elaborated' codes, or 'deficit' and 'difference' and Western pragmatics has no tools for handling such 'multi-modular' phenomena.

The language data given confirms one aspect of the modular theory — the linguistic aspect. The restricted interaction of English in India and the induced affiliation of Indians to English are, no doubt, related phenomena. Maybe, it is the 'modular use' of English that allows some Indians to use English according to their needs, and yet keep it separate from their local 'identity' which is deeply rooted in their ancient past and in the several layers of a pluralistic pattern. This kind of contemplation can also account for other phenomena such as (a) the absence of pidginization in Indians' English, (b) the existence of a variety that can be called 'un-Indianized English' which is advantageous in several areas like science and technology, diplomacy and international trade, or employment and mobility, (c) the ambivalence towards 'Indian English' to accept it or not to accept it, to use it or not, why use it when there is no status or monetary benefit involved and (d) the admiration for, and the desire to use English with a 'touch of India' in certain domains — with expressions translated from Indian languages or Indian words and phrases with some stylistic features, and with semantic and cultural associations.

5.3 Nomenclature: Indians' English and Inglish

But as part of their everyday practice, Indians, who have to cope with pluralistic situations, have always compartmentalized life and created space in the form of pigeon-holes to accommodate various waves that come to influence their life to keep their feet firmly on the ground. As part of their tactics, they keep the windows open but the walls firm to preserve the identity of their home. These tactics can be considered a form of subversion as is done by a population when subjected to an invader/colonizer. It, in a way, works both ways; power, as part of its strategy, allows some form of outlet for its own survival since absolute power and total control cannot be exercised all the time over all people in all places; it must allow some form of subversion as a token of 'freedom'. At the same time, resistance to power is not all the time in terms of revolutions, rebellions, revolts and mutinies — the noticeable and recorded forms that have been romanticized. As Michael Adas (1991: 297–8) says,

> Serious attention to alternatives to violent confrontational protest has been a rather recent development in studies focused on African and Asian societies. . . . Anthropologists and political scientists working in contemporary societies have explored the forms of 'everyday resistance' — from mockery to sarcasm to pilfering and arson — that subordinate groups employ to combat the hegemonic claims of landholding or political elites and to counter what are viewed as exploitative demands for taxes or a share of the crop.

... For scholars dealing with past situations, for which source materials on everyday forms of resistance are at best meagre, other, less ephemeral, modes of response, which have been characterized as 'avoidance protest', have been the focus of attention.

Resistance to cultural and linguistic invasions has not been studied in terms of everyday resistance and subversive tactics. Subversion in this sense is not a form of active resistance but a helpful tool or tactics for survival. Compartmentalization or restricting the operational domains is one such form of subversion because it 'does something from within'. This applies not only to English and Western influences but also to other forms of 'invasion' like religion, culture, other languages, and all other aspects of life, be it Sanskrit, Persian, Islam, or Christianity. This 'inevitable tendency towards subversion' (Ashcroft et al. 1989: 39) and the 'productive subalterneity' (Parakrama 1995) may give birth to new languages like Urdu or operations like switching in the heteroglossic realms; the 'switching' is not just confined to codes; it happens in all areas — language, accent, culture, religion, music, customs, beliefs, etc. It is mind-boggling for any outside observer but quite natural in a pluralistic context; people live 'several lives' without 'mixing' levels.

Thus, domain restriction and switching have their motivation and, maybe, they enable the common people to preserve their inner-self and the *core* aspects of life 'unaffected' and 'stable', in the case of civilizations that have traditions established through restricting domains.

In keeping with the multi-modular style of Indian life, we have to name the 'Module English' appropriately to make 'a distinction between the received English which speaks from the centre and the local english' (Ashcroft 1989: 39) that bears the burden 'of one's own cultural experience — the process of appropriation'. But, again capitalizing on the capital letter is not very satisfactory since the local variety is not 'small' in any sense of the term. The local variety is a 'Modulect' — a variety that is controlled by the command module but one that is, at the same time, used independently. This 'Modulect' in India has again two sub-modules that operate at two levels of use. The first one functions at the *international* level where English is used by 'Indians' and that variety is identified more by their nationality, colour, name and supra-segmental features; that variety can be called **Indians' English**. The second one is at the *intranational level* where the variety of English used manifests stronger influences of Indian languages and displays a higher ratio of loan-words; this can be called INGLISH — a term that onomatopoeically captures the regional features of the varieties spoken within the country. In both cases, the basic structure of English remains the same; English in India is not a 'dialect', but a 'modulect'.

If English has become a module for Indians, it is an indication that we have to review the concept of language-contact in the context of the modern world. The present study has just made a beginning to examine the areas thrown open by many untrodden paths. The exploration has been limited and focused on English in India. Nevertheless, it has served as a pointer to several research areas which need to be explored in order to develop de-prejudiced perspectives on other language-contact situations. Linguistics, cultural studies, sociology, and historical studies must come together to study how users change or manipulate communicability of languages in the modern world. It is an interesting area for research which ultimately might show that the paradoxes and contradictions that are apparent and supposed to be perpetual are not paradoxes but practices and strategies for coping with changes taking place in the world.

Appendix

Phase I: 1600–1813

Part I: Contingent History (Events contingent to the history of English in India)

AD
Year

1611	East India Company (EIC) opened a factory at Masulipatam.
1623	EIC opens another factory at Surat.
1639	EIC acquired Madras on lease from the native Indian king; the lease authorized EIC to fortify and administer Madras and to coin money on conditions of payment to the king of half the customs revenue of the port. EIC built a factory and Fort St. George and shifted their centre from Masulipatam to Madras.
1651	EIC permitted by the Mughal rulers to trade at Hugli in Bengal.
1668	EIC acquired Bombay from Portugal; Bombay was fortified and became EIC's centre on the West coast of India.
1686	EIC suffered defeat and was driven out of Hugli by the Mughal rulers; their factories at Surat and Masulipatam and their fort at Bombay were besieged. EIC sought pardon; Aurangzeb pardoned and permitted them to resume trade on payment of penalty.
1688	In England, Parliament became supreme as a result of the Revolution which overthrew Stuart King James II and invited William III and his wife Mary to be the joint sovereign of Britain.
1691	EIC resumed its activities at Calcutta, Bombay, and Madras.

1698	Charter Renewal which allowed the missionaries to come to India; till then EIC had prevented missionaries from coming to India.
1600–1700	Till the end of the seventeenth century EIC was trying to get a foothold on the Indian subcontinent; EIC had to face rivals in England, European rivals in India, and Indian rulers; missionaries were allowed to come to India for the benefit of Englishmen stationed in India. EIC was subservient to the Indian rulers whose permission they petitioned to begin and continue trade, and remained 'petitioners' in the native feudal courts.
1691–1740	In 1698, EIC acquired the zamindari of three villages and built Fort William around its factory; the three villages came to be known as Calcutta.
1717	EIC secured permission from Emperor Farrukh Siyar to extend trade to Gujarat and Deccan.
1757	English victory at the Battle of Plassey; with that the Mughal rule became subservient to EIC.
1765	EIC secured the Diwani (right to collect revenue) of Bengal, Bihar, and Orissa from Shah Alam II, the titular head of the Mughal Empire.
1780–95	English newspapers started during this period: *India Gazette, Calcutta Gazette, Bengal Journal, Oriental Magazine of Calcutta Amusement, and Calcutta Chronicle* (from Calcutta); *Madras Courier, Harkaru, Madras Gazette, Indian Herald* (from Madras); *Bombay Herald, Courier, Bombay Gazette* (from Bombay).
1781	Calcutta Madrassah (an educational institution for higher learning) established by Warren Hastings.
1791	Banares Sanskrit College established.
1792	Tipu defeated by the British and signed a treaty; the Srirangapatnam Treaty made EIC politically strong in the south of India.
1794	William Carey, an English missionary, started his first school in Bengal but the medium of instruction was Bengali.
1795	Censorship on newspapers introduced in Madras;

	'Madras Gazette' was required to be submitted to the scrutiny of the Military Secretary.
1797	Charles Grant began to persuade EIC and the Parliament in England to impart English education to Indians.
1798–1805	Wellesley started the policy of Subsidiary Alliance which weakened the Indian rulers. It was a system under which the ruler of the allying Indian State was compelled to accept the permanent stationing of a British force within his territory and to pay a subsidy for its maintenance, to accept the posting of a British Resident at his Court, and several other conditions which restricted the political authority of Indian rulers.
1799	Tipu dies in battle; Mysore conquered by EIC.
	Censorship regularized; newspapers required 'under pain of penalty' to print the names of printer-publisher and the editor and to submit all material for censorship to Secretary, Government of India.
1800	Bengali elementary school opened at Serampore, Bengal.
1813	Charter Act; education was made the responsibility of EIC.

Part II: The Data

Specimen I: Political — Bureaucracy (petitions)

(Source: *Home Dept., Public Proceedings,*
Volumes 10th January, 1771, No. 14)

Year: 1771

To
The Hon'ble John Carter Esq.
President & Governor & cat Council of Fort Williams

The Humble Petition of some of the Principle
Merchants of Calcutta now in Confinement in the Jail of Calcutta

Most Humbly Sheweth

That your Petitioners several of whom from unavoidable losses together with the Badness of the Times have been obliged to remain in Confinement some nearly Two years some a year & some several Months are thereby deprived of every means whatever of satisfying their Creditors, Their Houses, goods, Effects & Merchandises having been sold by the shraff for a quarter part or less of their value so that they are at present destitute of where withal to support themselves, their wifes & children who are as now in the greatest distress & almost starving & must inevitably be ruined for ever unless your Honars will be pleased to take their hard & Lamentable cases into your serious & charitable considerations & thereby Prevail on the different creditors of your Humbly Petitioners to show their **** towards them & grant them letters of science according to the sums they are indebted, that your Petitioners may thereby be enabled to discharge the Debts due to their several creditors which by their being confined in prison it is impossible for them to do & their families and themselves thereby utterly reduced to perish for want

And your Petitioners as in Duty
bound shall Ever Pray

Calcutta
10 January, 1771

Specimen II: Political (conspiracy)

Gulam Qadir Khan's letter to the Governor General
(Source: *Poona Residency Correspondence, Volume I*)

Year: 1788

I have had the happiness to receive your Lordship's friendly letter and overjoyed at hearing of your health. There is no necessity for writing what your Lordship has expressed respecting friendship; that friendship which is of old firm between us will daily increase and there can be no distinction in it. Your Lordship has written for my information that you had stationed troops towards the westward. This is highly proper and advisable. As our affairs are in every respect the same, all these troops that are (mine are) are also your Lordship's. Whatever business for them there may be depending on this quarter, your Lordship without scruple will inform me of it, that it may be accomplished according to your wish. Your Lordship should even write to the officers of these districts, to inform me of whatever may be necessary. Whatever demand they may make of troops they shall be sent from hence. Your Lordship will always write me friendly letters.

Phase II: 1813–57

Part I: Contingent History

1813 Charter Renewal. Education was made the responsibility of EIC and EIC was brought under the control of the British Parliament by the Pitts India Act of 1784;

	this Act made the EIC answerable to the British Parliament although the latter did not directly control the administration of 'Indian Affairs'.
1813–23	Lord Hastings' Governorship; five Indian States — Baroda, Hyderabad, Travancore, Poona and Oudh — brought under British domination.
1815	The Bombay Native Education Society set up under Elphinstone's patronage.
1817	The Hindu College, Calcutta, imparted English education.
1818	British hegemony was established upto Sutlej.
1819	First British House in Simla.
1821	Sanskrit College, Poona.
1823	Agra College, Agra
	The General Committee of Public Instruction appointed; the Committee opined against English as well as education through English.
1824	Sanskrit College, Calcutta.
1829	College at Delhi (All these Colleges were institutions for oriental learning; the Hindu College came up due to individual initiative and the others were the outcome of the patronage of ECI).
1828–35	Lord Bentinck's Governorship; he made the custom of 'Sati' and 'Thugee' illegal by abolishing them; he encouraged the native press, voiced the opinion that Western education be imparted to Indians; he remodelled the judiciary, increased the number, salary and jurisdiction of Indian judges.
1823–40	The Bombay Native Education Society set up District English Schools in Bombay Presidency.
1833	English introduced as a subject in Agra College and Calcutta Madrassah due to the demand of some Indians; District English Schools were set up in Delhi and Banares.
1835	Macaulay's Minute on Education that became the blueprint for English education in India.

1837	By 1837 the missionaries had begun to provide a significant part of the facilities for learning English; English became the language of administration and soon after the language of judiciary (though 'vernaculars' were permitted in the courts).
1841	A high-school called 'The University' was set up in Madras; imparted education in English; turned into a university by a government order in 1853.
1844	Office jobs (subordinate positions in the British bureaucracy) thrown open to Indians by a government resolution.
1846	British acquire control over the Punjab.
1848	Lord Dalhousie's Governorship; he brought in a policy of annexation as the Doctrine of Lapse by which the sovereignty of an Indian State dependent on the British lapsed if the ruler died without a son or a natural heir; through this some Indian States were annexed.
1850s	First major road called 'Grand Trunk Road' from Calcutta to Delhi completed (work began in 1839).
1853	First railway line opened — Bombay to Thana; first telegraph line opened joining Calcutta and Agra; postage stamps were introduced around the same time; Charter Renewal. Civil Services thrown open to competition and Indians were allowed to appear for the Civil Services Examination.
1854	Wood's Despatch: the first education policy of EIC; Charles Wood, Lord Halifax, President of Control of the EIC, was the first British official to voice the need for mass education and to visualize a system: (a) instituting universities at the three Presidency cities, (b) setting up institutions to train teachers, (c) introducing 'Grants-in-aid' system; Education Department formed as a separate administrative unit.
1857	Three universities were established at Bombay, Calcutta and Madras; Mutiny.

Print-media

130 English newspapers and periodicals in Bengal alone and some of them were owned-managed by Indians; some are listed below:

Name	Year of establishment
Times of India, Bombay	1838
Calcutta Review, Calcutta	1844
Examiner, Bombay	1850
Guardian, Madras	1851

Literature

Some of the Indians credited with literary writing in English

Name of the writer	Region/city the writer belongs to
Henry Derozio (a Hindu converted to Christianity)	Calcutta
Kasiprasad Ghose	Calcutta
Michael Madhusudan Dutt	Calcutta
Krishna Mohan Banerji	Calcutta
Bal Shastri Jambhekar	Maharashtra
C.V. Boriah	Madras

Part II: The Data

Specimen I: Bureaucracy (a formal letter)

Raja Rammohan Roy's letter to
Lord Amherst on Western education

(Source: *Indian-English Prose: An Anthology*,
Edited by D. Ramakrishna)

Year: 1823

To
His Excellency the Right Hon'ble William Pitt, Lord Amherst

My Lord,

Humbly reluctant as the natives of India are to obtrude upon the notice of the Government the sentiments they entertain on any public measure, there are circumstances when silence would be carrying this respectful feeling to culpable excess. The present Rulers of India, coming from a distance of many thousand miles to govern a people whose language, literature, manners, customs, and ideas are almost entirely new and strange to them, cannot easily become so intimately acquainted with their real circumstances, as the natives of the country are themselves. We should therefore be guilty of a gross dereliction of duty to ourselves, and afford our Rulers just ground of complaint at our apathy, did we omit on occasions of importance like the present to supply them with such accurate information as might enable them to devise and adopt measures calculated to be beneficial to the country, and thus second by our knowledge and experience their declared benevolent intentions for its improvement.

The establishment of a new Sangscrit School in Calcutta evinces the laudable desire of Government to improve the Natives of India by Education, — a blessing for which they must ever be grateful; and every well wisher of the human race must be desirous that the efforts made to promote it should be guided by the most enlightened principles, so that the stream of intelligence may flow into the most useful channels.

We now find that the Government are establishing a Sangscrit school under Hindoo pundits to impart such knowledge as is already current in India. This seminary (similar in character to those existed in Europe before the time of Lord Bacon) can only be expected to load the minds of youth with grammatical niceties and metaphysical distinctions of little or no practicable use to the masses or to society. The pupils will there acquire what was known two thousand years ago, with the addition of vain and empty subtleties since produced by speculative men, such as is already commonly taught in all parts of India.

In representing the subject to your Lordship I conceive myself discharging a solemn duty which I owe to my countrymen and also to that enlightened Sovereign and Legislature which have extended their benevolent cares to this distant land actuated by a desire to improve its inhabitants and I therefore humbly trust you will excuse the liberty I have taken in thus expressing my sentiments to your Lordship.

I have etc.,
RAMMOHAN ROY

Calcutta,
The 11th December 1823

Specimen II: Print-media communication

An Editorial

(Source: *Selections from English Periodicals of 19th Century Bengal, Volume I: 1815–33*)

Year: 1833

SALAM SABB!

... In the ceremony of Natives Salaming (saluting) the Europeans and East Indians there appears to be a good deal of aristocratical prejudice. We have known Natives insulted for making salam to an European on the plea that there being no acquaintance between the parties the salam was a mark of impudence. On the other hand, strange to say we have also known Europeans offended if a Native, being a perfect stranger, did not salam: the latter being considered proudly and haughty. ... Those who think proper to be a little more reasonable towards the Natives and seem willing to accept the ceremony of salutation, accept it as a matter of fact that the Natives should first make a salam, their business being only the acceptance of it by a return of the compliment and this without reference to the rank or circumstances of the parties.

Many other instances of this kind could be mentioned, all of which would tend to prove, that if the Natives have from religious motives kept at a distance from the Christians, the latter have from much worse motives discarded them from their society. At present there are many Natives who have so far abandoned the prejudices of caste as to have no objection to associate with Christians: but we regret to perceive that even these are shunned ....

The East Indians must look upon the Natives as their countrymen; for circumstances show that ultimately there will be less distinction between than what now exists ....

(From: *The Reformer*, 2 June 1833)

Specimen III: Education

Examples of students' writing

(Source: *The Eighth Annual Report* from the Governor of the Madras University, 1848–9 and the *Ninth Annual Report* from the Governor of the Madras University, 1849–50)

Year: 1848–50

Given below are answers/essays written by students of Fourth Class in the final examination answer papers. These specimens are taken from the Annual Report of the Madras University. The report cites answers written by top-rankers (with details of their marks) and a few essays written by top-rankers for competitions which won prizes; and a few answers written by other students are also cited along with clarifications that these students are not 'achievers'. One example of each is given below:

A

Question I: What is the object of the Poet in this play?

Answer: The leading object which the poet has in view through the play of Hamlet is to teach us the moral necessity of keeping a due balance between our powers of reflection and those of action. This he effects by means of Hamlet, whom he represents by falling a sacrifice to his too philosophic character. There is also another great moral lesson taught us by the poet which may however be considered as subordinate to the first. By what happens to Claudius, we learn 'that honesty is the best policy': that the objects we gain by deviating from the paths of virtue, will eventually be taken away from us, and our guilt with all our secrecy being discovered, we shall be visited with retributive justice; or as the poet himself expresses:

> Four deeds will rise,
> Though all the earth overwhelm them.

C. Rungacharry (IVth class; Ist Rank)

B

(An extract from the essay that won the 'Elphinstone Prize')

Topic: How does an intimate communication between nations, or even a mixture of their races, affect their progress?

Answer: . . . Also the arts and sciences have their rise, growth and development in certain countries in preference to others — not that they cannot be introduced and cultivated in these latter, but that they do not there come and suggest themselves naturally to man, and do not in fact own the countries as their own. In Egypt, India, and China where nature bestows her blessings in spontaneous profusion, the human intellect was first called into play, and employed its power in the invention of arts: while in countries more to the north there being nothing to attract the curiosity and attention of man, he was sunk in a state of lethargic slumber. In the former countries the arts and sciences, after having been carried to a certain degree of perfection, were incapable of further development. the soil which nourished them was exhausted, and it was necessary that they should be transplanted into countries more propitious to their growth. Accordingly they passed away into Greece and Italy, where men were fresh from the hands of nature, and after attaining as before a further degree of growth, they declined, and were transplanted into the more northern countries of England and France. . . .

C. Rungacharry (IVth class; Ist Rank)

C

Paper: Russel's Modern Europe

Question 12:   State the origin and describe the nature of the Institution of Chivalry.

Answer: The origin of Chivalry is generally traced to the disorders and anarchy of the feudal system which about the 11th century, almost degenerated into a system of oppression. The helpless and the weak were put to great distress, and women were degraded in the scale of humanity. In order to remove this state of oppression, the strong and the powerful joined together, and combined their efforts. Thus Chivalry had its origin. It produced consequences, some beneficial and others pernicious to society. It raised on the one hand the female to a suitable rank among men, and characterized a gentleman by honour, courtesy and other amiable virtues. On the other hand it armed half of the species against the other, and precipitated the Europeans upon Asia.

A. Narrain Row (Fourth Class)

Specimen IV: Creative writing

(Source: *The Golden Treasury of Indo-Anglian Poetry: 1828–1965*, Edited by V.K. Gokak, 1970)

Satan

A form of awe he was — and yet it seemed
A sepulcher of beauty — faded, gone,
Mouldering where memory, fond mourner, keeps
Her lonesome vigils sad — to chronicle
The Past — and tell its tale of coming years.
Or like a giant tree in mighty war
With storm on whirlwind car and fierce array

> Blasted and crushed — of all its pride bereft
> Or like a barque which oft had walked the deep
> In queen like majesty — and proudly brave —
> But by the fiery hand of some dread fiend
> Nursed in starless caves of ocean, shorn
> Of all its beauty in the boundless surge
> A phantom of departed splendour lone.
>
> *Michael Madhusudan Dutt*

Phase III: 1857–1904

Part I: Contingent History

1858	The Crown takes over (transfer of power from the EIC to the Crown).
1859	Lord Stanley, the first Chief Secretary of the State under the Crown, confirmed Wood's Despatch as the official education policy.
1861	Indian Councils Act (brought local autonomy).
1882 & 1887	Universities of Punjab and Allahabad established.
1882	Indian Education Commission set up to review progress of education. In its report (1884), it recommended improving primary education and confirmed policy of university education.
1883	Ilbert Bill gave equal status to Indian judges — on par with the British
1884	Lord Ripon's Self-Government Act: as a result, Municipal Corporations, District Boards, Tahsils/Taluka Boards came into being; during Lord Ripon's tenure (1880–84) a series of Acts were passed, framing a scheme of local self-government on the model of English County Councils; the system of local self-government was extended to the taluka level.
1885	Indian National Congress founded.
1892	Indian representation in the legislature; Dadabhai Naoroji was elected to the British Parliament as India's representative.

1899–   Lord Curzon's Governorship; partition of Bengal.
1905
1904   The Indian Universities Act was passed giving the government a tighter control over colleges and universities.

Expansion of the education system:

1901–02

Types of institutions	No. of institutions	No. of students
Arts Colleges		
English	140	17,048
Oriental	5	503
Professional Colleges		
Law	30	2,767
Medicine	4	1,466
Engineering	5	190
Teaching	4	865
Agriculture	3	70
Total	191	23,009

The expansion is the highest in the Arts Colleges which offered subjects like English Literature, History, etc.; professional education forms a negligible part of the educational system.

1882–3   The Indian Education Committee (known as Hunter Committee) stressed the need to pay more attention to primary education but the suggestion was ignored by the government. Lord Ripon's self-government Acts delegated the responsibility of managing primary education to the local bodies.

1883–5   Grants-in-aid system was developed; this along with the Indian Universities Act of 1904 resulted in Indians taking over the agencies of education but the government retained its control over these agencies. During Lord Curzon's Governorship primary education was centralized under the Director General of Education; Lord Curzon also appointed the University Commission

(Raleigh Commission) and on its recommendation made changes in the administrative structure and the functioning of universities. By 1902 Indians were dominating the educational enterprise completely; missionary schools and colleges were still manned by Europeans; the indigenous educational system of the subcontinent almost disappeared by 1902; Sanskrit, Arabic, and Persian were offered as optional subjects by a few colleges. English became the medium of instruction at secondary and college level, and the mother tongue as the medium of instruction was sidelined. Primary education was totally neglected.

Print-media

English newspapers and periodicals on the increase:

Name of newspaper/periodical	Year of establishment
Pioneer, Lucknow	1865
Mail, Madras	1867
Amrit Bazar Patrica, Calcutta	1868
Sathia Varthamani, Madurai (English – Tamil bilingual newspaper)	1870
USI Journal, New Delhi	1870
Indian Witness, Delhi	1871
Subodh Patrika, Bombay (Marathi-English bilingual)	1873
Bihar Herald, Patna	1874

Literature

Some well-known names in the area of creative writing:

Poetry: Michael Madhusudan Dutt, Toru Dutt, B.M. Malabari, Sri Aurobindo, Rabindranath Tagore, Sarojini Naidu, Manmohan Ghose

Prose: Sri Aurobindo, Rabindranath Tagore, Swami Vivekananda, V.S. Srinivasa Sastri, A.K. Coomaraswamy

172 • *Appendix*

Part II: The data

Specimen I: Social

(Source: *Selections from English Periodicals of 19th Century Bengal, Volume IV: 1857*)

Year: 1857

ADDRESS TO CAPT. RICHARDSON
FROM THE STUDENTS

Honoured and Dear Sir,

We have heard with feelings of unmixed sorrow of your intended departure from India and our regret is the greatest as it is ill-health which compels you to quit these shores. . . . You found our elders earnest in the discussion of plans, for the diffusion of knowledge and enlightenment among their sons and posterity, and all your sympathies immediately went forth with them. The result of your hearty co-operation was this noble foundation — the Hindoo Metropolitan College — the only national scholastic Institution in the land. . . . If ever we ought to be able to show that the Hindoo mind is not an arid soil, that it has indeed profited from your noble precepts and example; that your success in awakening its power and enlisting its sympathies on the side of whatever is true, generous and noble, is unequivocal . . . .

From: *Hindu Intelligencer*, 24 April 1857

Specimen II: Print-media communication

A letter written to the editor of the Hindoo Patriot

(Source: *Selections from English Periodicals of 19th Century Bengal, Volume V: 1858–60*)

Year: 1859

The Editor of the Hindoo Patriot

Dear Sir, — I beg to communicate to you some information of a Shuva, which promises a great deal of good if the Almighty adds stability to its basis. This Brahma Shuva of which I am going to speak had been instituted some 10 or 12 years ago by Baboo Debendra Nauth Tagore, but was in a state of consumption till it obtained some revival by the continual and respected endeavours of Baboo Brojo Nauth Mookerjee who has now raised it to attain the highest pitch of excellence. Worthy thanks to the aforesaid Baboo and thousand thanks to some other gentlemen who were pleased enough to take into their hands the sole charge for the enhancement of the Shumaj. It includes a weekly meeting on every Wednesday regularly when the members present themselves; discourses and discussions upto topics of religion, and other subjects too which may be deemed beneficial to the community. On the whole, suffice it to say, that the Shuva is going on well, we are likely to be favoured with an annual meeting in the present month, the proceedings of which I desire to inform you hereafter.

I remain yours obediently
A Resident
Krishnagar, 1st January 1859

6 January 1859

Specimen III: Print-media communication

(Source: *Selection from English Periodicals of 19th Century Bengal, Volume VIII: 1875–80*)

Year: 1875

THE POOR BANIAN

To the Editor of the Indian Statesman

Sir, — When European merchants first came to Calcutta, they, like all strangers in a strange land, had been aliens to its trade. Hence it was necessary to have a body of native gentlemen of intelligence and position to assist them in the sale, and purchase of their goods, and to take the risk of such sale, for which, the merchants allowed a commission. These gentlemen went by the name of Banians. In those days, owing to less competition in commerce, and the absence of railways and telegraphs, the merchants throve remarkably well, and the Banian prospered with them also. The good old days of mercantile prosperity in Calcutta have, however, I regret to observe passed away. In the place of a comparatively few houses there have sprung up in this city many, so that the business which had to be carried on by one has been divided. Under such circumstances it is not unlikely that the merchants' income must be decreased in the same proportion. The consequence would be, as I apprehend, the reduction by the merchant of his expenses. To do so, his first heavy item of expenditure appears to be the allowance to the Banian, the commission which I have above adverted to. Some of the firms here, especially the Greek houses, have actually dispensed with the services of the Banian, and can manage with the aid of a paid Banian. If therefore, the Banian cannot be entertained on the score of expense, the merchant, what, one would naturally inquire, would the native capitalist eventually do? Most of the Banian Babus though possessing immense wealth, are nevertheless men of little or no experience in the Indo-European commerce. Inland trade, to which the Marwaree is brought up and of which he has a monopoly is not his forte. Lending money on Government securities, or other good, sound, and safe securities, would very willingly be taken up prima facie as his principal business, but that would hardly keep him employed all his time. Idle the Baboo cannot be, for —

'Satan always finds some mischief for idle hands to do'

The old Banian might probably retire to some religious shrine, as must moneyed orthodox Bengalees do in ripe age, but what is to be the future work of young hopefuls of our native mercantile capitalists — I mean their children — in these days of less work and more men? I leave the subject to the consideration of our mercantile political economists. — Yours etc.

From: *The Statesman*, 4 July 1875

Specimen IV: Bureaucracy (petition)

(Source: *Selection from English Periodicals of 19th Century Bengal, Volume VIII: 1875–80*)

Year: 1878

MEMORIAL OF THE BRITISH INDIAN ASSOCIATION AGAINST THE VERNACULAR PRESS ACT

To His Excellency the Viceroy and Governor-General in Council

The humble memorial of the British Indian Association

Respectfully Sheweth, — That your memorialists desire to avail themselves of the opportunity, which has been afforded to the public by the introduction into Your Excellency's Council for making laws and regulations of the Bill entitled a Bill to amend Act IX of 1878, to submit a few remarks and suggestions regarding the Vernacular Press Act for the consideration of your Excellency in Council.

Your memorialists in common with the public at large were not a little taken by surprise, when at a single sitting in March last, a Bill was passed into law, imposing serious restrictions upon the liberty of the Vernacular Press of this country. The Bill was of the highest moment to the cause of Indian literature and progress, and when it was hurried through with such inordinate precipitancy, your memorialists were led to fear that the empire was perhaps threatened with a danger, of which they had no knowledge and of which the calmness of the political atmosphere had afforded no indication . . . .

In conclusion your memorialists pray that your Excellency in Council will be pleased to repeal Act IX of 1879, but in case your

Excellency in Council in considerations of State policy should decline to repeal the Act, your Excellency in Council, may be pleased, astly to modify it by restricting its scope only to the offence of sedition, by leaving the criminal intimidation of private individual's and public officers for extortion or evil purposes to the operation of the ordinary law of the land, 2ndly, to omit the restrictive clauses relating to oriental literature, and 3rdly, to provide a fair judicial trial for all offences under the Act.

And your memorialists as in duty bound shall every pray,

JOTENDRO MOHUN TAGORE
Honorary Secretary

From: *The Statesman*, 23 September 1878

Phase IV: 1904–47

Part I: Contingent History

Political

1906	Muslim League founded.
1911	Capital moved from Calcutta to Delhi; Bengal partitioned by Lord Curzon reunited.
1917	Declaration of self-government.
1919	Government of India Act; Diarchy started. Central legislature made bicameral.

Executive Council	Provincial Legislature	(Indians as ministers given the education portfolio)

(Indians could become ministers but the executive level positions were held by the British.)

1920–2	Non-cooperation movement; Khilafat movement.
1930	Dandi March.
1935	Government of India Act: more powers to Provincial Legislatures.
1937	Provincial Autonomy: Congress ministers assume power.
1939	World War II; resignation of Congress ministers.

1940	Demand for Pakistan by the Muslim League.
1942	'Quit India' Movement.
1947	India's political independence.

Industry

1940	By 1940s India had indigenous industries in three major areas — steel, cotton and sugar.

There was a class emerging (entrepreneurs, industrialists, scientists, technologists, and engineers) which had become aware of English as the language of modernization, of progress, and of commerce and industry.

Education

1913	Resolution of Educational Policy; recommends need for establishing new universities and six more were established during 1913–20.
1915	The Bill seeking to encourage Indian languages as media of instruction was turned down.
1917	University Commission (Sadler Commission); universities were made teaching institutions (earlier they were only examining bodies).
1919	Montagu-Chelmsford Reforms; recommends far-reaching constitutional changes; education comes under the respective ministries for education in the provinces.
1921	Department of Education transferred to the control of Indian ministers.
1925	Inter-university Board established.
1936–7	Education Department (including the bureaucratic network that controlled education taken over by Indians).
1944	The Central Advisory Board of Education submitted its plan for education; recommended that English be made a second language, and that the mother tongue be the medium of instruction upto the high school level.
1946–7	Expansion of education.

Type of Institution		1946–7 figures
Primary schools	93,604 (in 1901–2)	134,866
Degree colleges	231 (in 1921)	385 (in 1939)
Universities	5 (in 1916)	19

Print-Media

1937–47 Rapid increase in newspapers and periodicals.

Year	No. of English Dailies	No. of English Weeklies
1937	32	32
1947	51	258

1908   K.C. Roy, an Indian, established India's first news agency: the Associated Press of India (API); it was taken over by the Government of India in 1947.

1919   Reuters (an international agency) formed the Eastern News Agency with K.C. Roy as the Director.

1927   S. Sadanand established a news agency called the Free Press of India (But it ceased to be in 1933); the first teleprinter link connecting the Provincial towns was set up by the API); the Indian Broadcasting Company, a commercial undertaking, started functioning from Bombay and Calcutta, but by 1930 it went into liquidation.

1936   The Govt. of India took over broadcasting; separate office set up and funds allocated; one more radio station set up in Delhi; the nomenclature 'All India Radio' (AIR) was given on 8th June 1936; the first Controller of Broadcasting appointed was Lionel Fielding.

1937   Provincial important centres (urban and semi-urban areas) were linked by teleprinter system of the API; this was India's first teleprinter link.

Literature and intellectual writing

Political prose: Gandhi and his associates; M.N. Roy, Lohia, Ambedkar, Tilak and others

Philosophical prose: Radhakrishnan, Aurobindo, Tagore, Vivekananda, and others

Intellectual prose: Ansari, Rajni Patel, Gokhale, Sapru, Frank Moraes, and others

Literary writing: Mulk Raj Anand, Raja Rao, R.K. Narayan

Part II: The data

Specimen I: Bureaucracy

An Indian bureaucrat's letter about the acquisition of the site of a 'Samadhi'
(Source: *Gandhiji's correspondence with the government 1942–4*)

From
The Secretary to the Government of Bombay, H.D.
No. S.D. VI /–75
Home Department (Political)
Poona, 7th July, 1944

To
M.K. Gandhi, Esquire

Sir,

I am directed to refer to your letter dated the 6th May, 1944, in which you request that the Government should acquire the plot on which the bodies of Mrs Gandhi and Mr Mahadev Desai were cremated, together with the right of way to it through His Highness the Aga Khan's grounds so as to enable relatives and friends to visit the cremation ground whenever they liked. In reply I am to inform you that it is legally impossible for Government to acquire the site compulsorily under the Land Acquisition Act. Government considers that the matter is one for private negotiations between you and His Highness the Aga Khan. I am to add, however, that your request has been communicated to His Highness the Aga Khan and is now understood to be under his consideration. Government understands that he has no objection, in the meanwhile, to the relatives of Mrs Gandhi and Mr Mahadev Desai and any other persons suggested by you going through the palace grounds to the place of cremation on the understanding that this is by his leave and licence.

Your obedient servant,
H. Iyangar,
Secretary to the Government of Bombay, H.D.

Specimen II: Bureaucracy

An extract from 'Minute of Dissent' by C. Sankaran Nair, a Member of the Committee appointed to look into constitutional reforms.

(Source: *Tenth Despatch on Indian Constitutional Reforms — Champaran and Kaira Cases, 1919*)

Year: 1919

In consideration of the facts set out above, I am unable to agree with the view accepted by my colleagues which no doubt is in accordance with the view put forward by the Local Government in their resolution appointing the Committee. It is impossible to deny, in these circumstances, that the ryots and those who supported them had some grounds for believing that the refusal to publish Mr Gourlay's report was due to the disinclination to disclose the legitimate grievances of the ryots and the remedies proposed therein. Except two or three of them, the grievances are old-standing. Most if not all of them were noticed in Gourlay's report. Some of them were declared illegal by the Advocate General. But the Government, giving some relief by increasing the price of indigo, refused to interfere in all other matters, not on the ground that the settlement operations must be carried out or concluded, but that any redress afforded to the ryots will heavily hit the planter. See the letter to the Government of India, 4th June 1910. I cannot agree therefore that the Local Government had any legitimate excuse for delay.

The correspondence between the Government of India and the Local Government also bears out what I have stated. The Despatch bears testimony to the unwillingness of the Local Government to start the enquiry to which they after all agreed only on the pressure by the Government of India.

Specimen III: Social

A handwritten letter received by Shanta Bhalerao
(Source: *All India Trade Union Congress Papers, Sub-file: Letters revived by Shanta Bhalerao*)

10 B Morarji Building
Bombay
29-7-1942

My dear Shanta,

Thanks very much for your letter. I have been thinking quite a lot about you & your family from the time my father started sinking slowly but steadily to meet his end. We too have lost three dearest members of our family one after the other during the last two years. My father's death is altogether unexpected. I find myself unprepared for the consequences of such a tragedy.

I suppose you know that my father's death is only a part of the sad story.

—— is down with Typhoid and that is why I had to rush to Poona & stay there so long. He seems to be coming out of danger now & we hope for his speedy recovery.

I should to see you too & have a long chat if you can find time for the same. I tried to ring you up at 42810 yesterday, but could not get a ring. Something must be wrong with your phone.

I go back at about 6 P.M. everyday & if you can go to Chihhal . . . & see me there, please do so, on any evening you get free. I know how difficult for you to find time in the evening, but I am busy all through the day.

I wonder if you go to the Fortside during the day. I can manage to be free for sometime anytime in the afternoon after 2 P.M. if you care to come to the Institute. You may even get me on the Institute phone after 2 P.M. I have to lecture only during the morning periods. Hoping to see you,

Yours aff'ly
Maina

Specimen IV: Print-media communication and commercial

An advertisement

(Source: *Karmayogin.* An English newspaper published from Calcutta)

Date: 24-7-1909

WONDERFUL
CURRY POWDER

Indispensable in Kitchen. Best Companions to Cooks.

Prepared Scientifically with due antiseptic precautions from various Indian spices of every day use untouched by hand. Can be used successfully with all preparations from fish, flesh, vegetables, in fact with all known foods.

The ingredients from which it is prepared are rare and strongly conductive to health. It has been put to the test of many eminents physicians and respectable persons. It is specially beneficial for those who are suffering from indigestion, dyspepsia and other similar disorders and bowel complaints. It helps digestion and speedily gives health, strength and cheerfulness. It is not conducive to corpulence or superfluous fat.

Quantity to be used may be fixed according to the taste. It may be regulated after using two or three times generally with one seer of vegetable one spoonful, one seer of fish two spoonfuls (each tin contains a spoon measure) and nothing but salt to be mixed.

PRICE AS RS SIX PER TIN ONLY
THE EAST BENGAL MANUFACTURING CO.,
46, Grey Street, Calcutta.

Specimen V: Print-media communication and commercial

An advertisement

(Source: *The Star.* An English Journal published from Bombay)

Date: 21st April 1946

AFGHAN SNOW
SOLE AGENTS:
PATANWALA LTD ESP BOMBAY-3

Through the ages. . . .
Three centuries back the Famous Mogal EMPRESS was the most beautiful woman of her time and she owed the delicate bloom of her skin from the fountain of real orient Attars derived from the various kinds of selected flowers rarely available.

Miladies of twentieth century owe the Dazzling beauty of their smooth velvety skin to AFGHAN SNOW.

AT ALL CHEMISTS & STORES

Specimen VI: Creative writing

(Source: *Onions & Opinions,* A Collection of Essays by N.G. Jog, 1944)

Year: 1940

THE PERFECT WIFE

The quest for the Perfect Wife has continued from the time of Adam. But I must correct myself, for poor old Adam had obviously no choice in this matter. He had to take Eve or leave her and being rather a good fellow, he could not have possibly done the latter.

Having taken her, he was shrewd enough not to grouse or grumble. Adam knew how to put a good face on things — he did. With what astute foresight did he compose that bitter quarrel after Eve had eaten the forbidden fruit, and he, too, had followed suit in the vehemence of his passion.

One would have given a lot for a verbatim report of the first quarrel between the first husband and wife. With what quiet serenity, even dignity, did Adam make his exit from Paradise hand in hand with the errant Eve — the cause of it all! That by itself proves what a Perfect Husband he was, — one may even say, the Most Perfect Husband of all time.

It is strange indeed that while man is always trying to find that will-o'-the-wisp — the Perfect Wife — woman is content to seek just a husband. Now and then a much married Hollywood star may air her views on the Perfect Husband, but it is merely a theoretical discourse. Woman being more practical knows intuitively that there is no such thing as a Perfect Husband.

Old Bard Shakespeare, too, was wise in his day when he made his Rosalind say: Men are April when they woo, December when they wed; Maids are May when they are maids, but the sky changes when they are wives. All this points to the fact that the Perfect Wife, like the Hare's Horns, simply does not exist!

But great is the vanity of humanity and immense its optimism. If the Perfect Wife cannot be born, they are out to manufacture one. There have lately sprung up in the United States a number of schools whose job it is to turn out Perfect Wives as fast as they can make them.

Specimen VII: Creative writing (Poetry)
(Source: *The Golden Treasury of Indo-Anglian Poetry: 1828–1965*, Edited by V.K. Gokak, 1970)

Year: 1904–47

SITA-RAMA

While the infant hours of morning
Glide so playful by the door,
And the village-women hasten
To the Ganga's holy shore;
While the maidens gather flowers
Under fragrant jasmine-bowers
For the temple-god and go:
Suddenly a voice there towers
Over all below:

> Sita-Rama, Sita-Rama,
> Sita-Rama, Ho!

. . .
. . .
. . .

While the temple bells are ringing

> At the slow-departing day,
> And the closing lips o' the lotus
> Kiss the last lingering ray;
> While the village-wives are burning
> Purest incense with a yearning
> For their joy and peace below;
> Oh! the echoes there returning
> With the breezes blow:

Sita-Rama, Sita-Rama,
Sita-Rama, Ho!

A.F. Khabardar

Phase V: 1947–90

Part I: Contingent History

Political

1947   India became politically independent.
1949   India's relationship with the British Commonwealth of Nations was defined at the London Conference of

Prime Ministers on 27th April; the Constituent Assembly of India ratified the agreement regarding the membership of the Commonwealth on 17th May; the Constitution of India was adopted by the Constituent Assembly on 20th November.

The Reserve Bank of India nationalized and it became the government's banker and adviser; it was given the sole right to print currency and regulate commercial banks.

1950	India became a sovereign democratic republic on 26th January.
1951	The first general election.
1956	States Reorganization Act (States formed on the basis of regional languages).
1957	The second general election.
1958	Metric system of weights and measures introduced.
1961	India occupies the Portuguese enclaves of Goa, Daman and Diu (which became Union Territories).
1962	China attacks India; a war follows.
1963	Nagaland became a State of the Indian Union.
1965	Indo-Pakistan war.
1969	Nationalization of banks.
1970	State of Meghalaya came into being.
1971	Himachal Pradesh became a State.
1972	Manipur and Tripura became States; Arunachal Pradesh and Mizoram became Union Territories.
1987	Arunachal and Goa granted Statehood.

Science and Technology

1975	Indian satellite 'Aryabhatta' launched from a cosmodrome in U.S.S.R.
1979	Rohini 200, first monsoon experimental rocket, launched from Thumba on Jan. 6; Soviets launched India's second satellite.
1981	APPLE, India's first geostationary experimental

	telecommunications satellite launched from Kouru, French Guyana.
1982	21 member Indian team lands on Antarctica (Jan. 14); INSTAT-IA placed in orbit.
1983	First nuclear power station at Kalpakkam goes critical; INS Godavari, first frigate fully designed by the Indian Navy and built at Mazgaon, commissioned.
1984	Squadron Leader Rakesh Sharma becomes India's first spaceman when he was sent abroad Soyuz T-II of the erstwhile Soviet Union.
1988	India's first remote-sensing satellite, IRS-IA launched; India's first nuclear-powered submarine INS Chakra launched.
1989	IRBM (intermediate range ballistic missiles) 'Agni', India's first missile launched.

(Notice that Indian scientists use Sanskrit names for missiles and satellites though English is used as the language of science, technology, and commerce; the use of the names should not be mistaken for 'Indianization' of English; for example, the Reserve Bank of India is called 'Bharatiya Reserve Bank' — only 'Bharatiya' is Sanskrit based Hindi.)

Education

1947	The Ministry of Education was constituted in Delhi.
1948	University Education Commission with Dr Radhakrishnan as its Chairman (The Commission included three foreigners: Sir James Duff from Durham and Directors Morgan and Tigret from the USA); the Commission recommended (report submitted in 1951) that Hindi be made the medium of instruction; English to continue.
1950	Constitution grants English the status of associate official language (English to be used in this capacity till January 26, 1965); Article 351 of the Constitution enjoins the Indian Union to promote and spread Hindi.
1951	Indian Institute of Technology, Kharagpur, established.

1952–3 Secondary Education Commission (Chairman: Dr Mudaliar); recommended that English and Hindi be introduced at the middle school level but not simultaneously. However, the medium of instruction be the regional language/mother tongue till secondary school level.

1953 University Grants Commission (UGC) formed; autonomous status granted by the Parliament in 1956.

1955 Indian Council for Secondary Education formed.

1956 Report of Official Language Commission; notes that literacy in English constitutes 6.41 per cent of total literacy, and 1.06 per cent of that of total population; recognizes the value of English as 'pipeline' within the country and 'window' to the rest of the world; recommends its continuation without any restrictions for all or any official purpose of the Union.

1957 Kunzru Committee Report; set up by the newly formed UGC; recommends the following: (i) the change from English to an Indian language as the medium of instruction at the university level should not be hastened; (ii) even when a change in the medium of instruction is made, English should continue to be studied by all university students; (iii) the teaching of English should be given special attention in the pre-university class (a three-year degree course was proposed in place of the four-year undergraduate course); (iv) the teaching of English literature should be related to the study of Indian literatures in order to promote critical thinking and writing in Indian languages; and (v) English be retained as a properly studied second language at the university level.

1958 Central Institute of English, Hyderabad, established with the co-operation of the British Council and the Ford Foundation.

1960 Committee of Experts (Chairman: G.C. Banarjee) set up by UGC to examine issues involved in the teaching of English; a Central Hindi Directorate set up for evolving Hindi terminology, preparing dictionaries, etc.

1961 National Council of Educational Research and Training (NCERT) formed; Report of Working Group set up by UGC regarding the switch-over from English to an Indian language as the medium of instruction; recommends that the switch-over should not be hastened and that English should be retained as the alternative medium; Conference of Chief Ministers recommended the three language formula at school level: (a) Regional language, or mother tongue if different from regional language; (b) Hindi, or any other Indian language in Hindi speaking areas; (c) English, or any other European language.

1961–2 Emotional Integration Committee (Chairman: Dr Sampurnand); recommended that 'the two link languages — English and Hindi — should be effectively taught at university level so that conditions of emotional and intellectual isolation are not created'.

1963 Official Languages Act. English to continue as associate-official language even after 1965 without any time limit.

1964–6 Indian Education Commission (Chairman: Dr Kothari); confirms the three language formula; a choice between Hindi and English allowed and whichever was not chosen had to be taken at the higher secondary level; recommends the use of regional languages as the media of instruction; use of English to continue as 'library language; recommends special units to be set up for teaching English as a language skill as distinct from teaching it as literature; English to be continued as the medium of instruction at university level'.

1967 Official Languages Amendment Bill gives statutory recognition to the continued use of English as long as the non-Hindi speaking people do not want a change; compulsory knowledge of Hindi not required for the selection of candidates for Union services and posts; non- Hindi-speaking persons would be required to know English; English translations of all official communications in Hindi to be attached. Report on Study of English in India by the Study Group set up by the Ministry of Education (Chairman: V.K. Gokak); endorses three language formula; English to be studied at the college level.

1968   National Policy on Education; embodies recommendations of Kothari Commission Report; the study of regional languages to be encouraged and provision made for textbooks; the study of English to continue as alternative language and as the medium of instruction at higher levels.

1976   Constitutional amendment places education on Concurrent List.

1979   Draft National Policy on Education; the three language formula to be implemented at the secondary stage in the entire country; it includes the study of a modern Indian language, preferably a South Indian language, in addition to Hindi in Hindi speaking States, and of Hindi in addition to the regional language and English in non-Hindi speaking States; the target set for implementing the new education policy envisaged in the 1979 draft was 1986–87.

1986   National Policy on Education and Plan of Action (NEP & POE); it reviewed the 1968 National Policy and recommended a 'dynamic' approach; recommended the following: consolidation and expansion of institutions; the development of autonomous colleges and departments; the redesigning of courses; the training of teachers through Academic Staff Colleges; delinking degree requirement for employment; development of English Language Training institutions; establishment of Navodaya Vidyalayas in rural areas for promoting excellence; no mention of medium of instruction in the chapter on higher education; suggests more co-ordination among agencies, mobility and vocationalization.

1989   According to the University Handbook of 1989, there were 120 universities, 23 Deemed universities and 26 agricultural universities; these 169 universities employed 234 thousand teachers for teaching and research; the enrolment of students for degrees and diplomas is 3.58 million.

1990   Acharya Ramamurti Commission Report; the Commission was set up to review NPE & POA; endorses the recommendations of 1986 report and the three language formula; recommends a further use of technology for language development; suggests the development of Hindi, Sanskrit, foreign languages, and English, and merging of institutions concerned with the planning and implementation of language teaching.

Print-media, Radio and Television

Publication of newspapers at the end of 1988

	Total output	Output in Hindi	Output in English
Dailies	2,281	888	190
Tri/Bi Weeklies	134	39	17
Weeklies	7,813	3,756	509
Fortnightlies	3,485	1,451	407
Monthlies	8,369	1,773	1,832
Quarterlies	2,227	301	904
Annuals	264	18	109
Others	963	96	409
Total	25,536	8,222	4,458

(About one third of published books and one fifth of all periodicals are in English.)
— Most of the English newspapers are published from urban centres and their sale is in urban centres and semi-urban places.
— According to 1981 Census the proportion of the urban population to the total is 23.31 per cent and the rural population constitutes 76.69 per cent of the total.

News Agencies

Press Trust of India (PTI) — established on August 27, 1947.

United News of India (UNI) — established on November 10, 1959; its Indian language news service was started in May 1982.

190 • *Appendix*

Two other agencies are also mentioned in the records — Samachar Bharati and Hindustan Samachar; the focus of factual information is on PTI and UNI.

Radio: Started in 1927 and named AIR in 1936; called 'Akashvani' in 1957.

Television: Started from Delhi in 1959 and acquired the name 'Doordarshan'.

(The language of radio and TV is not predominantly English; Hindi and other Indian languages are more prominently used by the electronic media.)

Literacy and proficiency in English: Some statistics

Overall literacy rate:	36.23 per cent of the population (1981 Census Report)
Literacy rate in English:	6.41 per cent
Literacy in English of total population:	1.06 per cent (Report of Official Language Commission 1956)
Student enrolment	
Higher education:	3.1 million in 1987–8
Number of universities:	157; deemed 19
Number of colleges:	8856 in 1986–7

Part II: The data

Specimen I: Bureaucracy (semi-official)

A member of the Punjab Legislative Council writes to Smt Rameshwari Nehru

(Source: *Smt Rameshwari Nehru Papers, Sub-file — Personal Correspondence*)

> Mul Raj Sharma
> Member
> Punjab Legislative Council
> JULLUNDER CITY
> Dated 21st October, 1953

Smt Rameshwari Nehru,
Hony. Adviser, Women Section,
Ministry of Rehabilitation,
Govt., of India, NEW DELHI.

Dear Bhain Ji,

Jai Hind — I hope this letter will find you hale, hearty and in the best of spirits.

I have been approached by an unfortunate father of an unfortunate young and beautiful girl of 18 years of age with the request to help them. I am perplexed and am unable to take a decision in the matter as this case of victimisation is of its own type and I wonder if you have ever heard of the social evil of the nature. I am sending a copy of the letter received by me and shall be grateful if you will kindly do needful as I feel that you are the right person with matured experience. I shall, of course be at your command and carry out your instructions. This may kindly be treated as immediate.

With best wishes and regards,

> Yours truly,
> (Signature)
> (Mul Raj Sharma)
> President
> Vidhwa Vivah Sahayak Sabha,
> Jullunder,
> Punjab

192 • *Appendix*

Specimen II: Social (personal communication)

Year: 1991

Dear R . . . .

Am getting married this summer — June 26 to be precise. Please come. The invites aren't ready but am wtg ahead so that you can book your ticket & make alternate arrangements if necessary. Its going to be here in Bombay 'cause of various reasons so it'll be easier for you. Please come R . . .

Am going home on April 5 so you can write & tell me about your coming at my home add. I'll be back here for the wedding only in the first week of June.

I didn't know getting married is going to be such an ordeal. The worse part of it is that I have to do everything alone. My parents 'approve' but don't 'really approve' so you see its quite difficult!

Please don't let me down R . . . Am looking forward to seeing you again. It'll be great if you can come earlier even! Let me know.

Love lots,

E . . .

Specimen III: Print-media communication and commercial

Instructions printed on the cartons of two very common products

Year: 1986

1

1. Prepare a dough without lumps by mixing one volume of the powder with 1/4 volume of water. 2. let the dough to stay for about 5 minutes. 3. After preparing the dough to required shape and size. It should be fried in ghee or refined oil with low heat.

IMPORTANT: Ghee or oil should not be heated to give fumes.

SUGAR SYRUP: One volume of sugar to be dissolved in one volume of water. Boil for 5 minutes. Saffron, Cardamom and Essence may be added to Syrup to taste. 600 gms sugar needed.

2

KING LAUNDRY STARCH
Directions

Mix 25 gm (or one Heaped table spoonful) of KING LAUNDRY STARCH with just enough cold water to make the solution Milky and see that no starch globes remain unmixed. Now add some more water BOIL the solution still it well all while till the solution become Transparent. Dip garments squeeze thoroughly and iron both ways till dry.

NOTE:- For thin garments thick solution for thick garments a thin solution.

Smooth Raishing	Max Price Rs
Optical Whiteness	Plus Tax extra
Preserves Fabrice	Date

Specimen IV: Print-media communication

A letter published in *The Times of India*

July 25, 1969

READER'S VIEWS
Nationalised Banks

To
The Editor,
The Times of India

Sir, — I support Mrs Indira Gandhi's bold and historic step in nationalising 14 commercial banks.

These banks with a small aggregate paid-up capital were controlling a huge amount of public deposits and thus encouraging the concentration of power and wealth as well as the growth of monopolies. The Monopolies Enquiry Commission observed in its report in December 1965 that management control was more concentrated than ownership control. Nationalisation will remedy this social evil to a great extent.

The commercial banks were dominated by industrialists. In many cases, these business houses used bank funds for speculative purposes. They allowed large advances to directors.

The commercial banks have grossly neglected the credit needs of agriculture and small-scale industry. Nationalisation will enable banks to open new branches in the rural and semi-urban areas and thus accelerate the rate of savings there.

Nationalisation will provide 100 per cent security to depositors and partially remedy the evil of unaccounted money and concealed income and wealth.

GOVIND PRASAD SHARMA
(Rajasthan)

Specimen V: Creative writing (poetry)

(Source: *The Golden Treasury of Indo-Anglian Poetry: 1828–1965*, Edited by V.K. Gokak, 1970)

Slum Silhouette

Towards the car the little ones come running
Their bare skinny bodies are dust-stained.
Their hair is tousled, their pants
Held up by a piece of string

They giggle, make comic gestures,
And laugh aloud to see
Their convex reflections on the polished
Surface of the car, as curious caricatures.

They talk together, and make a clatter
Of toys in coming for their milk.
Some are indifferent, and continue
To play in the muddy gutter.

Some mothers raise loud cries
And demand the milk. Others
With babies at their breasts, too listless
To move, beg with their eyes.

Leela Dharmaraj

Bibliography

Abbas, Shameem (1993), 'The Power of English in Pakistan', *World Englishes*, vol. 12, no. 2, pp. 147–56.
Abbot, Gerry (1991), 'English Across Cultures: The Kachru Catch', *English Today*, 7 (4), 55.
Adas, Michael (1996), 'South Asian Resistance in Comparative Perspective', in Haynes, Douglas and Gyan Prakash (eds), *Contesting Power: Resistance and Everyday Social Relations in South Asia* (Berkeley and Los Angeles: University of California Press), pp. 290–302.
Agnihotri, Rama Kant, Amrit Lal Khanna and Mukherjee (1988), *Tense in Indian English* (New Delhi: Bahri Publications).
Agnihotri, R.K. and A.L. Khanna (eds) (1994), *Second Language Acquisition: Socio-Cultural and Linguistic Aspects of English in India* (New Delhi: Sage Publications).
Ahmad, Aijaz (1992), *In Theory: Classes, Nations, Literatures* (London/New York: Verso).
—— (1995), 'The Politics of Literary Postcoloniality', *Race & Class*, 36, 3: 4.
Anderson, Benedict (1983/1986), *Imagined Communities: Reflections on the Origin and Spread of Nationalism* (London: Verso).
Annamalai, E. (ed.) (1979), *Language Movements in India* (Mysore: Central Institute of Indian Languages).
Appadurai, Arjun (1993), 'Number in the Colonial Imagination', in Breckenridge, Carol A. and Peter van der Veer (eds), *Orientalism and the Postcolonial Predicament: Perspectives on South Asia* (Philadelphia: University of Pennsylvania Press).
Ashcroft, Bill et al. (1989), *The Empire Writes Back: Theory and Practice in Post-Colonial Literatures* (New York: Routledge).
Bakhtin, M.M. (1981), *The Dialogic Imagination*, Michael Holquist (ed.) (Trans. Caryl Emerson and Michael Holquist.) (Austin: University of Texas Press).
Bansal, Ram Krishna (1969), *The Intelligibility of Indian English* (Hyderabad: Central Institute of English and Foreign Languages, Monograph No. 4).
Basham, A.L. (1975), *A Cultural History of India* (Oxford: Clarendon Press).

Baumgardner, Robert J. (ed.) (1993), *The English Language in Pakistan* (Karachi: Oxford University Press).

Bhabha, K. Homi (ed.) (1990), *Nation and Narration* (London: Routledge).

Bhalla, Alok and Sudhir Chandra (eds) (1993), *Indian Responses to Colonialism in the 19th Century* (New Delhi: Sterling Publishers).

Binyon, Michael (1989), 'Europe Takes a Tongue-Lashing', *The Times* (London), Oct. 23.

Borges, Jorge Luis (1972), 'Of Exactitude in Science', in *The Universal History of Infamy* (Trans. N. di Giovanni), (New York: Dutton), p. 141.

Borden, M. Carla (1989), 'Prologue: Designs', in Borden, Carla M. (ed.) *Contemporary Indian Tradition* (Washington and London: Smithsonian Institution Press), p. 20 (Writer 1).

Burchfield, Robert (1989), *Unlocking the English Language* (London, Boston: Faber and Faber).

Burde, Archana S. (1992), *A Sociolinguistic History of English in India: A Profile of the Written Mode*, unpublished, Ph.D. thesis (Hyderabad: Central Institute of English and Foreign Languages).

Calhoun, Craig, Edward LiPuma and Moishe Postone (eds) (1993), *Bourdieu: Critical Perspectives* (Chicago: The University of Chicago Press).

Campbell, Joseph with Bill Moyers (1988), *The Power of Myth* (New York: Doubleday).

Certeau, Michel de (1984), *The Practice of Everyday Life* (Trans. Steven F. Rendall) (Berkeley: University of California Press).

Chandra, Bipan (1979), *Nationalism and Colonialism in Modern India* (Hyderabad: Orient Longman).

Chatterjee, Partha (1983/1986), *Nationalist Thought and the Colonial World* (Minneapolis: University of Minnesota Press).

—— (1986), *Nationalist Thought and the Colonial World: A Derivative Discourse* (Minneapolis: University of Minnesota Press) (Writer 4).

Chatterji, Reena (1983), *Impact of Raja Rammohan Roy on Education in India* (New Delhi: S. Chand and Co.).

Chatterji, Suniti Kumar (1963), *Language and Literatures of Modern India* (Calcutta: Bengal Publishers).

Chaudhary, Shreesh Chandra (1984), *Some Aspects of the Phonology of Indian English*, unpublished, Ph.D. thesis (Hyderabad: Central Institute of English and Foreign Languages).

Christensen, Torkil (1992), 'Standard English and the EFL Classroom', *English Today*, 31 July.

Collingwood, R.G. (1945/1970), *The Idea of History* (London: Oxford University Press).
Connolly, William E. (1984), 'The Politics of Discourse', in Shapiro, Michael (ed.) *Language and Politics* (Oxford: Basil Blackwell), pp. 115–31.
Coulmas, Florian (1989), *The Writing Systems of the World* (Oxford: Basil Blackwell).
Dasgupta, Probal (1993), *The Otherness of English: India's Auntie Tongue Syndrome* (New Delhi: Sage Publications).
Das, Sisir Kumar (1982), 'Indian English', in Pride, John (ed.), *New Englishes* (Rowley, Massachusetts: Newbury House Publishers).
Devy, G.N. (1992), *After Amnesia* (Hyderabad: Orient Longman).
Dhamija, P.V. (1976), *A Phonological Analysis of Rajasthani English*, unpublished M. Litt. dissertation (Hyderabad: Central Institute of English and Foreign Languages).
Dharampal (1983), *The Beautiful Tree: Indigenous Education in the Eighteenth Century* (New Delhi: Biblia Impex).
Dustoor, P.E. (1968), *The World of Words* (Bombay: Asia Publishing House).
Foucault, Michel (1976), 'Disciplinary Power and Subjection', in Lukes, Steven (ed.), *Power*, 1986.
—— (1981), 'The Order of Discourse', in Shapiro, Michael (ed.), *Language and Politics*, 1984.
Galbraith, John K. (1984), 'Power and Organization', in Lukes, Steven (ed.), *Power*, 1986.
Galtung, J. (1980), *The True Worlds: A Transnational Perspective* (New York: The Free Press).
Gellner, Ernest (1983), *Nations and Nationalism* (Oxford: Basil Blackwell).
Gokak, Vinayak Krishna (1964), *English in India: Its Present and Future* (Bombay: Asia Publishing House).
Gokhale, S.B. (1978), *A Study of Intonation Patterns in Marathi and Marathi English*, unpublished M. Litt. dissertation (Hyderabad: Central Institute of English and Foreign Languages).
Goody, Jack (1986), *The Logic of Writing and the Organization of Society* (Cambridge: Cambridge University Press).
—— (1987), *The Interface Between the Written and the Oral* (Cambridge: Cambridge University Press).
Gramsci, Antionio (1985), *Selections from Cultural Writings* (London: Lawrence and Wishart), pp. 256–7.
Haynes, Douglas and Gyan Prakash (eds) (1991), *Contesting Power:*

Resistance and Everyday Social Relations in South Asia (London: Oxford University Press).

Herman, S. Edward and Noam Chomsky (1988), *Manufacturing Consent* (New York: Pantheon Books).

Hosali, Priya (1982), *Butler English: Form and Function*, unpublished, Ph.D. thesis (Hyderabad: Central Institute of English and Foreign Languages).

Joseph, John E. and J. Talbot Taylor (eds) (1990), *Ideologies of Language* (London/New York: Routledge).

Kachru, B. Braj (ed.) (1982), *The Other Tongue: English Across Cultures* (Oxford: Pergamon Press; Urbana, IL: University of Illinois Press), Second Edition 1992.

—— (1983), *The Indianization of English: The English Language in India* (New Delhi: Oxford University Press).

—— (1986), *The Alchemy of English: The Spread, Functions, and Models of Nonnative Englishes* (Oxford: Pergamon Press, Rpt. 1990; Urbana, IL: University of Illinois Press).

—— (1986), 'The Power and Politics of English', *World Englishes*, 5, pp. 121–40.

—— (1991), 'Liberation Linguistics and the Quirk Concern', *English Today*, 7 (1), pp. 3–13.

—— (1994), 'English in South Asia', in *The Cambridge History of the English Language*, Robert Burchfield (ed.), vol. V. *English in Britain and Overseas: Origins and Development* (Cambridge: Cambridge University Press).

—— (1995), 'World Englishes: Approaches, Issues, and Resources', in H. Douglas Brown and Susan T. Gonzo (eds), *Readings on Second Language Acquisition* (Englewood Cliffs, NJ: Prentice Hall Regents).

Kaul, Suvir (1992), 'The Indian Academic and Resistance to Theory', in Sunder Rajan, Rajeswari (ed.), *The Lie of the Land: English Literary Studies in India* (Delhi: Oxford University Press), p. 210 (Writer 2).

Kaviraj, Sudipta (1992), 'The Imaginary Institution of India', in Chatterjee, Partha and Gyanendra Pandey (eds), *Subaltern Studies VII: Writings on South Asian History and Society*, Paperback 1993 (Delhi: Oxford University Press).

Kesavan, B.S. vol. I (1985), vol. II (1988), *History of Printing and Publishing in India* (Delhi: National Book Trust).

Kissinger, H. (1985), *India Today*, Feb. 28.

Kluck, P.A. (1985), 'Linguistic Relations and Ethnic Minorities', in Nyrop, Richard F. (ed.), *India: A Country Study* (Washington D.C.: Foreign Area Studies).

Krishnaswamy, N. (1985), 'The Growth of "INGLISH" in India', *The Hindu*, Nov. 12.
Lal, P. (1951/1987), *The Alien Insiders* (Calcutta: Writers' Workshop).
Lukes, Steven (1974), *Power: A Radical View* (London: Macmillan).
―――― (ed.) (1986), *Power* (Oxford: Basil Blackwell).
Mattelart, Armand (1979), *Multinational Corporations and the Control of Culture: The Ideological Apparatuses of Imperialism* (Translated from the French by Michael Chanan) (Brighton, Sussex: The Harvester Press).
McArthur, Tom (1992), 'Models of English', *English Today* 32, October.
McCrum, Robert, William Cran and Robert MacNeil (1986), *The Story of English* (Viking: Viking Penguin).
Medgyes, Peter (1994), *The Non-native Teacher* (London: Macmillan).
Mehrotra, R.R. (1993), 'Review of Braj B. Kachru's *The Alchemy of English*', in *Language in Society*, vol. 22, no. 2, June (Cambridge: Cambridge University Press).
Nagarajan, S. (1978), 'The Decline of English in India: Some Historical Notes', in Manuel, M. and K. Ayyappa Paniker (eds), *English in India* (Madras: Macmillan).
Nandy, Ashis (1980), *At the Edge of Psychology: Essays in Politics and Culture* (Delhi: Oxford University Press), p. 47 (Writer 3).
―――― (1983/1988), *The Intimate Enemy: Loss and Discovery of Self Under Colonialism* (Delhi: Oxford University Press).
Nehru, Jawaharlal (1936), *An Autobiography* (London: Bodley Head).
―――― (1946), *The Discovery of India* (New York: John Day).
Nihalani, Paroo, R.K. Tongue and Priya Hosali (1979/1987), *Indian and British English: A Handbook of Usage and Pronunciation* (Delhi: Oxford University Press).
Parakrama, Arjuna (1995), *De-Hegemonizing Language Standards-Learning from (Post) Colonial Englishes, about English* (New York: St. Martin's Press).
Pennycook, A. (1989), 'The Concept of Method, Interested Knowledge, and the Politics of Language Teaching', *TESOL Quarterly*, 24 (1), pp. 589–618.
Phillipson, Robert (1992), *Linguistic Imperialism* (Oxford: Oxford University Press), p. 46 (Writer 5).
―――― (1995), 'Review of Probal Dasgupta: *The Otherness of English: India's Auntie Tongue Syndrome*', in *Applied Linguistics*, vol. 16, no. 2 (Oxford University Press).
Prator, H. Clifford (1968), 'The British Heresy in TESL', in Fishman,

J.A., C.A. Ferguson and J.T. Das Gupta (eds), *Language Problems of Developing Nations* (New York: John Wiley and Sons).

Premalatha, M. (1978), *The Vowels of Malayalee English: A Generative Phonological Study*, unpublished M. Litt. dissertation (Hyderabad: Central Institute of English and Foreign Languages).

Quirk, R. and H.G. Widdowson (eds) (1985), *English in the World: Teaching and Learning the Language and Literatures* (Cambridge: Cambridge University Press, for the British Council).

Ramiah, L.S. (1988), *Indian English: A Bibliographical Guide to Resources* (Delhi: Gian Publishing House).

Rubdy, Rani (1981), *A Study of Some Written Varieties of Indian English*, unpublished, Ph.D. thesis (Hyderabad: Central Institute of English and Foreign Languages).

Said, Edward (1978), *Orientalism* (New York: Vintage Press).

Selinker, L. (1974), 'Interlanguage', in Richards, J.C. (ed.), *Error Analysis: Perspectives on Second Language Acquisition* (London: Longman), pp. 31–54.

Shastri, S.V. (1983), 'Towards a Definition of Indian English', *CIEFL News Letter*, vol. XVIII, nos 3 & 4, July/Oct., pp. 1–8.

Sheik, Gulam Mohammed (1989), 'Among Several Cultures and Times', in Borden, Carla M. (ed.), *Contemporary India* (Delhi: Oxford University Press).

Smith–Pearse's *The English Errors of Indian Students* (1968) was published as *The English Errors of Pakistani English* (1975) and both are out of print now. It is the same book.

Sonntag, K. Selma (1995), in *Power and Inequality in Language Education*, James W. Tollefson (ed.).

Stokes, Eric (1959), *The English Utilitarians and India* (Oxford: Oxford University Press), pp. 1–2 (Writer 6).

Sunder Rajan, Rajeswari (ed.) (1992), *The Lie of the Land: English Literary Studies in India* (Delhi: Oxford University Press).

Thapar, Romila (1984), *From Lineage to State* (Bombay: Oxford University Press).

—— (1989), 'Imagined Religious Communities? Ancient History and the Modern Search for a Hindu Identity', *Modern Asian Studies*, vol. 23, pp. 209–31.

—— (1991), 'Religion, Culture and Nation', *Seminar*, 377, January, pp. 38–40.

Thiong'o wa Ngugi (1986), *Decolonising the Mind* (London: Currey).

Tirumalesh, K.V. (1990), 'In a Manner of Speaking', in Tirumalesh, K.V., *Derrida's Heel of Achilles and Other Essays* (Delhi: Bahri

Publications) (First Published in *Weekend Newstime*, Hyderabad, Sunday, Aug. 31, 1986, p. 11).

Tirumalesh, K.V. (1990), 'Indian English', in Tirumalesh, K.V., *Derrida's Heel of Achilles and Other Essays* (Delhi: Bahri Publications) (First Published in *The Hindu*, Madras, Tuesday, Jan. 7, 1986, p. 19. Under the Title 'Indian English: An Interlanguage Phenomenon').

Tollefson, J.W. (1991), *Planning Language, Planning Inequality: Language Policy in the Community* (London: Longman).

Tomlinson, John (1991), *Cultural Imperialism* (Baltimore: The Johns Hopkins University Press).

Tripathi, P.D. (1992), English: 'The Chosen Tongue', *English Today*, 32.

Turner, Fredrick (1995), *The Culture of Hope: A New Birth of the Classical Spirit* (New York: The Free Press).

US News & World Report, Feb. 18, 1985.

Wilson, Horace (1836), 'Education for the Natives of India', *Asiatic Journal*, 29, p. 14.

Index

Adas, Michael 155–6
Agnihotri and Khanna 33, 38, 44
Aijaz, Ahmad 13–14, 70–1, 77
Anderson, Benedict 62, 63, 64
Annamalai, E. 71
Appadurai, Arjun 10

Baumgardner, Robert J. 8, 11, 12
Bhaktin, M.M. 78
Bhabha, Homi 63
Bhalla and Chandra 35, 36
Binyon, Michael 53
Campbell, Joseph 19

Certeau, Michel de 58–60, 68–70, 73
Chandra, Bipin 20
Coulmas, Florian 64, 65
Crystal, David 9
culture-bound content 151
culture of complaint 57
cultural osmosis 153
cultural translation 151

Dasgupta, Probal 26–7, 28, 33, 38–43
Derrida, Jacques 73
Devy, G.N. 42
Dharampal 67
Douglas, H. and Gyan Prakash 43
Dustoor, P.E. 27–8

education policy 82, 88
education in India (statistics) 8
English as International language 19–20
English education in India 13, 14, 15, 67, 68, 70, 71, 72, 82, 88, 89, 99, 125, 152
English in world (statistics) 6
English in India
   a case study 11–13, 57
   functions of 150–1
   Prakritisation of 24
   users of 12–13
   and Indian language 15–16

Gandhi, Mahatma 67
Gellner, Ernest 60
global users of English 9–10
Goody, Jack 64, 66
Gramsci, Antonio 11, 62

Hobson-Jobson 2, 77

Indian cultural context 24, 34, 77
Indian English
   as a term 25, 28
   as a creole 3
   definition of 29, 63
   identity/problem of 5, 14, 26, 28, 43–4, 46, 127, 150, 153
   literature 2, 26, 27, 40
   cultural context 27

vs. English in India 4–5, 25
Indian loan words in English 2
Indian nationalism 13, 62, 63
Indian Writing in English 26, 27, 112, 126–7, 135
Indianisation 2, 25, 150
Indianisms 27, 29
Indianness of English 4, 17, 18
Indians English
  as a label 155, 157
  bilingual creativity 110, 125, 135, 151
  comprehensibility/cline 88, 99, 124, 127, 151
  domain restriction & heteroglossia 110–11, 154, 156
  features of 82, 85–7, 96–8, 107–10, 122–7, 133–5
indigenous education 67, 71, 81, 96, 97, 111
Inglish 155, 157
interlanguage 36, 37

Jamaican Creole 3–4
Joseph and Taylor 7, 11

Kachru, Braj 5, 8, 9, 14, 19, 26, 28, 30, 44, 70
Kachru, Yamuna 33–4, 45
Kaviraj, Sudipta 61–2, 62–3
Kesavan, B.S. 66
Kissinger, Henry 13

Lal, P. 3, 26, 27
language trade 10–11
linguistic hegemony/ imperialism 8, 11, 65–6
Lyotard, Jean-Francois 73

Macaulay 14, 15, 38, 72

Mattelart, Armand 53, 57
Mayhew, Arthur 153
McArthur, Tom 6,8
McCrum, Robert et al 1–4
Medgyes, Peter 74
models of English 14, 28–9, 47
module
  English as a module 152
  modular Indianness 153–4
  module English 156
  modulect 156, 157
Mukherjee, Meenakshi 32

Nagarajan, S. 1
Nandy, Ashis 153
nation-India 13, 62, 63, 67, 68, 136, 152
native speaker 6, 74, 75, 76, 77
Nehru, Jawaharlal, 68
New Englishes/ World Englishes 2, 4, 8, 11, 152
Nihalalni et al. 28
non-native
  users of English 9, 77
  users' attitude to English 14
  varieties of English 20

Pakistani English 16–7, 18–9
Pennycook, a 20
Phillipson, Robert 8, 42
politics of English 8, 11, 15, 21
power, concept of
  Bourdieu, Pierre 51
  Burke, Edmund 49
  Chomsky, Noam 50
  Connolly, Williams E. 51–2
  Foucault, Michel 50
  Galbraith, John K. 50
  Lukes, Stevens 49
Prator, Clifford 41–7
Prakrit 22

printing 64, 73
printing in India 66–7
print capitalism 60, 64, 74
print market 66
print-publishing trade 71, 72

Quirk, Randolph 9, 35

Raja Rammohan Roy 15
Rajagopalachari, C. 13
Renan 63
roles of English 15, 16, 19, 110
Roshomon effect 46
Rubdy, Rani 29

Sanskrit and English comparison 40
Sankritisation 21–2, 35, 42
Sanskrit fixation 43
Sanskrit influence 22
Selinker, Larry 36, 37
Shastri, S.V. 36
Singh, Rajendra 33, 45
Sonntag, K Selma 71
South Asian English 19
studies on
    World Englishes 8, 55, 152
    aspects of English in India 43

Thapar, Romila 66, 153

Thiong'o wa Ngugi 8
Third World Englishes 11
Tirumalesh, K.V. 36, 37
Tollefson, J.W. 11, 71
Tomlinson, John 8
Tripathi 30
Turner, Fredrich 54–6

un-Indianised English 155
Urdu 12, 23–4, 35, 156
use of English in India
    restricted/ domain restricted 77, 82, 89, 98, 136, 137
    induced needs for 89, 99, 127
    minority use 88, 151
    modular use 99–100, 110, 112, 153, 154, 156, 157

varieties of English 10–11, 20, 152
victim mythology 53

writing
    concept of 73, 75
    functional diglossia in India 65
    history of writing in India 65
written mode 64, 65, 66, 77
written functions 65